TOTALITARIANISM

Temporary Madness or Permanent Danger?

PROBLEMS IN EUROPEAN CIVILIZATION

TOTALITARIANISM

*Temporary Madness or
Permanent Danger?*

Edited with an introduction by

Paul T. Mason, Duquesne University

D. C. HEATH AND COMPANY · BOSTON

Library of Congress Catalog Card Number 67–23305

COPYRIGHT © 1967 BY D. C. HEATH AND COMPANY

Printed May 1967

Table of Contents

Introduction

I T IS A FACT of considerable importance that the interests of twentieth century historians have been significantly broadened. This development, however, must be seen from various points of view. In one sense, the old concept of history as simply the history of politics has disappeared. Thus many historians have turned away from the history of politics to subjects like the history of economics, the history of science, or the history of ideas. But to note only this is to see the matter in a too simple fashion. That the historian has broadened his interests does not so much mean that he has neglected the history of politics; rather it means that he has enriched the history of politics by the realization that politics is the work of man and can therefore be understood only within the total context of all that man is and all to which he is subject.

In another sense, some historians have come to utilize a different method of presentation. All historiography demands the endless search for new documentary material, but there are various ways that this material can be handled. Some historians will wish to weave it into a dramatic narrative. Others, however, will find it necessary to analyse the material, to pose important questions for which the material that has been discovered will hopefully provide an answer. Thus even if the historian concentrates mainly on the unique and even if his primary purpose is not the construction of generalizations, he nevertheless finds generalizations of some sort indispensable. Moreover, whether or not the historian is a social scientist, he cannot neglect the work of the social scientist. The social scientist hopes to discover certain regularities in social phenomena. He attempts to suggest fruitful hypotheses and concepts which will make it possible to deal more effectively with the phenomena under consideration. The historian clearly has need of such hypotheses and concepts as a way of organizing his own material.

The term "totalitarianism" is an interesting case in point. "Totalitarianism" is one of those concepts around which the works of the historian and the social scientist converge. For the historian, the concept of totalitarianism is a way of organizing material, which at first sight appears rather diverse, into manageable relationships. Because of this, "totalitarianism" has become a basic word in the vocabulary of the twentieth century historian. It is not at all unusual, therefore, for historians to discuss totalitarianism as, for example, they have long discussed conservatism, liberalism, nationalism, imperialism, and the like. Certainly, even the most scrupulous and distrustful of historians would feel little hesitation in occasionally applying "totalitarian" as a descriptive adjective to certain regimes with which he deals. Yet, it is also true that many historians feel a bit uneasy in using the term. There are, indeed, certain difficulties with it.

As has already been mentioned the historian tends to stress the unique and he is therefore likely to be suspicious of any term which has been used to cover both the Soviet Union and Nazi Germany. Clearly these regimes were, or professed to be, direct opposites. Other historians are somewhat dubious about the claim, made by many interpreters of totalitarianism, that the phenomenon is peculiar to our century.

They would urge that twentieth century men are noted for nothing so much as taking themselves too seriously and would argue that if totalitarianism is a new term, it certainly does not refer to a new reality. (That it is a new term is indisputable: the *Encyclopedia of the Social Sciences,* published in 1934, did not see fit to discuss it.) And, if there has been no new reality, then (say these historians) there would seem to be some doubt about the need for a new term.

The real test of a concept for the historian or the social scientist lies in its degree of usefulness and, in order to be useful, a concept ought to be simple and yet generalize as wide a range of data as possible. It is on these grounds that the concept of totalitarianism might be attacked. Some would doubt both its simplicity and its generalizing ability. On the one hand, it is difficult to secure general agreement on any single definition. On the other hand, if one holds to the belief that the term is needed as the result of a new reality peculiar to our century, it is difficult to produce many examples of it. Fascist Italy is sometimes called totalitarian but a significant number of authorities would deny that it meets the necessary criteria, the boasting of Mussolini to the contrary. Such cases as pre-World War II Japan, Franco's Spain, and Salazar's Portugal would be even more questionable. Most would agree that Communist China, Nazi Germany, and Soviet Russia (perhaps along with her satellites in Eastern Europe) are the best examples of totalitarian regimes. But even here, many experts would want to speak about full totalitarianism only in certain restricted periods of those regimes' histories: in the case of Soviet Russia, for example, many would see only the Stalinist period as fully totalitarian. The sceptic might therefore inquire concerning the usefulness of a term which can be applied only to three regimes and then only to certain restricted time periods. He might want to argue that it would be better simply to look upon these cases as examples of autocracy,

despotism, or dictatorship of which history is full of examples. Or he might want to argue that no single case completely matches any given definition of totalitarianism and that on this ground the concept is of no real usefulness.

However, these considerations, even if true, need not thoroughly destroy the usefulness of the term. For a concept need not be considered useless merely because concrete cases of it do not exactly match up at every point. If that were required few scientific laws could survive the test and it would in principle be necessary to construct a different generalization or concept for each unique case of anything — clearly an absurdity — or, what comes to the same thing, to adopt a position of total nominalism. Moreover, it might be suggested that the generalizing function of the concept of totalitarianism is indeed greater than merely that of tying together three regimes: it might be argued that it is a way of dealing with a rather far-flung range of material quite basic to the condition of modern man.

It is with these kinds of problems that this volume proposes to deal. It hopes to pose certain important questions about the nature of totalitarianism. How should it be defined? Is it peculiar to the twentieth century? What are the major characteristics of totalitarian rule and are they really unique and distinctive? What sort of man is the totalitarian? How should one attempt to account for its appearance in the twentieth century? And how persistent is it likely to be? The reader must appreciate that these questions are all closely related and that an answer to one will seriously affect answers to the others.

In order to make it possible for the reader to decide about these questions the readings have been drawn from a wide range of material. Some of the selections are from the works of historians. But many are taken from the writings of political scientists, sociologists, and psychologists. And, since the debate over totalitarianism involves certain basic questions about the nature of man, it is impossible to neglect literary and philosophic works. Perhaps even more significant is the fact that many of the selections are drawn from the writings of men whose interests are very broad and whose precise field of study would be difficult to narrowly define. Here are the views of men who are well qualified, therefore, not only to comment on totalitarianism, but on its meaning for our age as well.

George Kennan has remarked that it is frequently easier to gain an understanding of totalitarianism in the novels of Kafka or Orwell than in a learned study. This leads to an important point: totalitarianism has reintroduced mystery into politics and human affairs. It has brought into the open ideas and practices which hitherto existed only in the hidden recesses of reality. Totalitarian beliefs are a continual reminder of the mysterious: the Nazi emphasis on race and the continual pseudo-religious appeal of its propaganda is one evidence of this; the marvelous tricks performed by the Marxist dialectic is another. This is the reason for the inclusion of the selection from Konrad Heiden's *Der Fuehrer* in the Prologue. It relates the strange course and influence of the famous Protocols of the Wise Men of Zion. At least implicitly, it stresses aspects of totalitarianism to which many commentators have called attention as, for example, that a totalitarian movement operates as a secret society in the open, announcing that its enemies have formed a conspiracy which can be met only by the organization of a counter-conspiracy; a counter-conspiracy which adopts the same methods as the conspiracy which it proposes to fight. Thus, as Heiden points out, the Protocols were important not so much because they claimed to have uncovered a plot to dominate the world, but rather because the alleged plot itself provided the model for the belief that world domination is possible, and that achieving it is largely a matter of simple engineering.

Part I of the volume — Toward a Definition — deals with the central question of the debate about totalitarianism: how should it be defined and does the definition refer to a political reality unknown prior to the twentieth century? The selection from Friedrich and Brzezinski presents a widely accepted view. It argues that totalitarianism is a unique type of society peculiar to the very recent past. On the other hand, in the succeeding selection Timasheff suggests that it might be more fruitful to consider totalitarianism not so much as a type of society, but rather as one possible trait of any society — namely, the extension of the auxiliary functions of the state to such a degree that almost all human activities are regulated by it. Since the analysis of Timasheff suggests the possibility of totalitarianism previous to the twentieth century, the next two selections deal with likely examples. It is quite obvious that Plato did not establish a totalitarian regime. But against the numerous defenders of Plato, Karl Popper argues that Plato was one of the earliest totalitarian ideologists in his advocacy of what Popper has called the "Closed Society." If Popper calls attention to the ideological aspect of totalitarianism, Karl Wittfogel, who finds evidence of totalitarianism in various ancient and oriental despotisms, suggests another viewpoint. His argument stresses the managerial aspects of totalitarianism: totalitarianism being used here in the sense in which Timasheff defines it. Thus totalitarianism appears as a political system in which the bureaucracy has run wild to produce a state which, in Wittfogel's words, is "over-organized, over-defended, over-protected." If the selections from Popper and Wittfogel challenge the view that totalitarianism is peculiar to the recent past, the last selection in Part I attacks the concept itself. Stanislav Andreski, writing in *A Dictionary of the Social Sciences*, expresses strong doubts about its usefulness on the grounds that present definitions of totalitarianism are imprecise and thus fail either to simplify or generalize in a satisfactory manner.

In order to provide some basis from which to judge both the uniqueness and the modernity of totalitarianism, it is necessary to examine more closely some of the characteristics of totalitarian rule. This examination forms the subject matter of Part II. It is clear that the adherence of many people to a totalitarian system is not simply the result of coercion; there is quite obviously a voluntaristic aspect involved. What leads men to subject themselves to a totalitarian system? Numerous authorities have called attention to the roles played by alienation and anxiety in preparing a population to accept totalitarian rule. Franz Neumann explains what is meant by alienation and then shows that the anxiety which accompanies it is not only a preparation for totalitarianism, but that the "institutionalization of anxiety" is itself a technique of totalitarian rule after it is in power. The analysis of Neumann makes it clear that totalitarianism not only operates on the surface of human life, but that it also invades the mind. The selection on propaganda — which is taken from George Orwell's famous novel, 1984 — reinforces this point. Winston, the main figure in the novel, cannot escape the impact of the propaganda despite the fact that he is secretly opposed to the regime. Completely isolated, he can trust no one and is thus unable to compare the propaganda — which is always present on the telescreen — with any other standard of reality. Adherence to a totalitarian regime is not solely dependent, however, on propaganda. The role of ideology must also be considered. Hannah Arendt's examination of totalitarian ideologies leads to a somewhat different understanding of its nature than is contained in many studies of the subject. Arendt does not believe that the essence of a totalitarian ideology lies in its commitment to any definite set of conclusions or beliefs. Rather, in her view, the ideology becomes purely a logic which works itself out with murderous consistency irrespective of reality, and which demands of its adherents absolute obedience and submission to the will of the leadership.

Despite the importance of persuasion for a totalitarian system, it does nonetheless make tremendous use of coercion. And in a totalitarian society coercion ultimately takes the form of terror. The selection from Friedrich and Brzezinski provides a standard description of the nature of totalitarian terror. The final selection in Part II is again drawn from the work of Hannah Arendt. She points to the tremendous degree of confusion which marks the totalitarian administrative structure. Here it appears that the totalitarian system is anything but monolithic. Thus the most serious problem of the subject of such a system is not that he is forced to do this or that, but rather that the sources of authority are so confused and hidden that it is impossible to find out what is expected of him.

What do these views imply with regard to the debate over the uniqueness and modernity of totalitarianism? Neumann's article tends to suggest that the ingredients of totalitarian domination have always been ready at hand, whereas the picture drawn by Orwell, while in a sense confirming this, also seems to indicate that the instruments of modern technology are essential. It must also be noted that the views of Arendt, who believes that totalitarianism is a modern phenomena, sharply contrast with those of Popper and Wittfogel. Whereas Popper stresses the role of the ideology in maintaining stability within society, Arendt takes an opposite view: namely, that the ideology destroys every shred of stability and thus makes possible the achievement of permanent revolution. For Wittfogel, punishment and terror serve some utilitarian purpose in that presumably they force the population to carry out its duties. For Arendt, on the other hand, the shapelessness of the system, although it allows for total domination, is, from a technological point of view, utterly chaotic and ultimately self-defeating. What conclusion is to be reached? Is the terror described by

Friedrich and Brzezinski different in substance or only in degree from that described by Wittfogel? Has Arendt simply overstressed certain accidental characteristics of the Nazi and Soviet regimes or does she point to essential characteristics of the system? On the other hand, are Popper and Wittfogel correct in noting ancient examples of totalitarianism, or have they simply made an unfortunate choice of terms in describing more traditional, authoritarian systems?

It is perhaps possible to gain further insight into the nature of totalitarianism by asking, "What sort of man is the totalitarian?" This is the question which is posed in Part III. The first selection is taken from Arthur Koestler's famous novel, *Darkness at Noon,* based on the Moscow purge trials of the 1930s. Here we see the confrontation between Rubashov, the old revolutionary, and Gletkin, the Neanderthaler, the technician of power. Both men are caught: the one is the victim, the other the executioner of the will of history; both reside in a universe in which men and their subjective intentions do not count at all. Eugen Kogon presents another view. Two passages are taken from his *Theory and Practice of Hell.* In the first, we read the rather idealistic words of an SS officer dreaming of a revived Greek aristocracy. In the second, Kogon describes the activities of Master Sergeant Sommer at Buchenwald. Here the totalitarian appears as the psycho-sociopath placed in such an environment that he is able to impose his distortions as reality. In the concentration camp, terror becomes total. The approach taken by Zevedie Barbu is somewhat different. His analysis is a sociological one which leads, however, not to the conclusion that the totalitarian springs from a certain class, but rather that he is a man who no longer belongs to any class. Finally, is it possible to see the totalitarian as a certain psychological type? If so, the last two readings in this section attempt to identify this type, under the name of the "Authoritarian Personality." The main characteristics of this personality type are listed in the first reading. In the second, Edward A. Shils argues that whereas these characteristics were at first applied only to followers of fascist ideologies they in fact have a broader application. He notes that the nineteenth century distinction between a political Left and Right has largely broken down, and that the characteristics common to the fascist may also be attributed to the followers of communism.

Those who argue that totalitarianism is peculiar to the modern world face the obligation of explaining how it arose in our times. Thus the contention that totalitarianism is solely modern may be partially tested by assessing the validity of such explanations. In an earlier section, Friedrich and Brzezinski argue that totalitarianism can arise only in a context of "mass democracy and modern technology." The selections in Part IV deal more specifically with this question. In the first selection, J. L. Talmon maintains that some forms of totalitarianism are based on a perversion of liberal democracy. The discussion is centered on Rousseau in whom the conflict between freedom and order was particularly acute. Alfred Cobban calls attention to the various ways in which formerly existing checks on the extreme growth of power have been destroyed. Moreover, he notes the peculiar effect which the development of modern education has had in encouraging dictatorship. Erich Fromm, like many other interpreters of totalitarianism, suggests a psychological explanation based on the concept of alienation for which he provides an historical account. In his view, modern liberty has been an ambiguous gift. Despite its benefits, it places a great burden on the individual so that in periods of stress he is likely to collapse and attempt to "escape from freedom." Finally, many observers of totalitarianism have pointed out that totalitarian movements were successful because they enlisted the loyalty of people who previously had not politically counted. José Ortega y Gasset, who wrote on the eve of the full outbreak of totalitarianism, calls attention to the rise of this "mass man," the ordinary man who asserts the rights of the commonplace, and who crushes those who attempt to transcend him and his commonplace beliefs.

The subject matter of the final section of readings — The Future of Totalitarianism — may at first appear somewhat strange to the reader. He may object that speculation about the future is not the business of the historian (who is not, after all, a prophet) and that, at best, the views presented are only a series of personal reflections. (At the worst, they may be no better than misdirected guesses.) The criticism is doubtless well made, but it is hardly possible to avoid the question. For the issue of the future of totalitarianism cuts two ways. On the one hand, without some idea as to the possible future of totalitarianism it is virtually impossible to assess the significance of the eruptions that have already taken place. And, on the other hand, the study of these eruptions should enable us to make at least an educated guess about the possible course of the future. Such guesses can hardly attain certainty, but they are valid within a certain range of probability and, consequently, they might be compared to the work of the weather forecaster. He is not always right, but the purpose of his work is to enable us, whenever possible, to prepare for the worst so that we may not be caught unawares, and so that we may act to mitigate the consequences of a coming storm.

But there is another advantage to speculation about the future of totalitarianism. It is, after all, a way of generalizing the problem, a way of calling our attention to certain fundamental issues of our time which are raised by the spectre of totalitarianism. For that reason, it might be well to focus attention on some of the possible implications of the views presented in the last section.

The view of Teilhard de Chardin is at once the most hopeful and the most troubling. Unwilling to render a completely unfavorable judgment on recent totalitarian experiments, Teilhard organizes his evaluation around a personal vision of the meaning of human evolution. He thus suggests the possibility that recent totalitarian experiments can be seen as expressions (even if clumsy ones) of a far more significant advancement of the human spirit. But despite Teilhard's personal dedication to the values of human freedom, many would have difficulty reconciling his vision with the values of Western society and would question whether the sort of individualism which the West prizes can be preserved in the course of "planetisation" or "totalisation." Teilhard sees the march of the temporal in quest of the eternal. But the world being what it is, can any attempt to collectively assure, in the here and now, the existence of eternal values escape the sort of "spiritualization" which the Nazis represented?

The position of Raymond Aron — the second selection in Part V — leads to a somewhat different conclusion. He argues that the hold of ideology is declining and it would seem to follow that, insofar as totalitarianism is ideologically motivated, its prevalence in the future must also decline. Yet mere absence of ideological fanaticism will not necessarily spell the doom of totalitarianism. It is possible, in fact, to argue the opposite case. If ideology is dead does that not produce the desperation which arises when men no longer have anything in which to believe? Is it not precisely in the times of such desperation that the psycho-sociopaths, such as Master Sergeant Sommer, are able to assert themselves? And who has lost faith in ideology anyway? The totalitarians or the men who previously opposed them? If the latter is the case, especially in the light of Rubashov's admission that he was lost because he no longer believed in his own infallibility, what chance do Aron's sceptics have of resisting the Gletkins of the world?

The last two selections in Part V are concerned with a somewhat different question from those taken up by Teilhard de Chardin and Aron. They do not so much deal with the problem of whether new totalitarian regimes will emerge, as with the "staying power" of those already in existence. Here, too, important issues are raised, especially with respect to the relationship of totalitarianism to rationality and technology. The prognosis of Brzezinski is not encouraging. Disputing the views of those who believe that totalitarian regimes will be eventually transformed from the inside, he denies that the essence of totalitarianism is the irrationality to which Arendt has pointed and warns of the prospect of a continuing "rationalist totalitarianism." If Brzezinski is correct there appears no likelihood that totalitarian regimes can be overthrown short of war. But here it must be remembered that many commentators would argue that war — and the state of tension which arises from the continual danger of war — is one of the things which may force even the democratic West to severely limit personal freedom. Could it not even be argued that the demands of an increasingly growing technological and industrial complex are the same for both West and East, that they are moving to a point of convergence from opposite sides, and that this point of convergence is, indeed, a "rationalist totalitarianism"?

Karl Deutsch takes a stand directly opposite that of Brzezinski. Although he holds out no hopes for the imminent collapse of totalitarian regimes, he does believe that no totalitarian system can withstand the strains that are placed upon its leadership, which must either accept a gradual pluralization of power or face a situation of total chaos. But even here there are difficulties. Deutsch's view might be related to those who argue that totalitarianism is a sort of temporary expedient which occurs in the period of transition from a pre-industrial to an industrial society, but that once this transition is achieved the hard facts of technology will catch up with the regime and force its gradual

transformation into a more traditional or democratic system. If this view is correct then it is necessary only to check the more aggressive tendencies of totalitarianism and allow time to work its transformation. But is this view correct? Is not the process of industrialism so dynamic that it requires not one, but rather a never-ending series of adjustments? And does not this lead to the continual recreation of Barbu's "*déclassés*," the most ardent of the followers of a totalitarian movement? From another point of view, as was suggested above, is not Brzezinski's "rationalist totalitarianism" an alternative in view of the possibility that the demands of technology exact their inevitable price in the restriction of human liberty? Finally, does not man's continual attempt to transform his world, of which industrialism is only the most obvious example, represent, in a larger form, the desire of the totalitarian to endlessly manipulate reality in the name of his ideology? And — to be completely perverse — if all this is so was not Plato right after all: that it is necessary to resist change at all costs? But in this connection it should be remembered that some authorities would insist that the Nazi version of totalitarianism sprang not from the dynamism of industrialism but rather from the attempt to resist that dynamism.

In any case it is difficult to come to a judgment about the future of totalitarianism without making some sort of answer to the major issues raised in this volume. Is totalitarianism an old phenomenon which has occurred with some regularity in the course of man's history? If so, then there is little hope that its claims can always be denied in the future, and our own age may then be seen not so much as too revolutionary, but rather as not revolutionary enough. If, on the other hand, totalitarianism is indeed unique and modern, does its arrival reveal the ultimate meaning of what the modern world is about or does it signify only the last, desperate resistance of those who refuse to accept modernity?

The reader will perhaps recoil from all these questions about a concept the usefulness of which is disputed by more than one historian. He may even feel — as do some contemporary thinkers — that the form which the debate on totalitarianism has taken has become irrelevant and something of a bore, serving more to obscure than to illuminate the central issues of our age. But he dares not reach such a conclusion with respect to those central issues. Surely he will not wish to accept some of the pessimistic conclusions which can be drawn from the concept of totalitarianism. Hopefully, he will insist that there is an alternative to the totalitarian, whether he is seen as the man who wishes to remove every stabilizing factor or rather as the man who wishes to superimpose a rigid framework on society; and that this alternative is the sensible man who — distrustful of all romantic visions of either past or future — constantly seeks to break through the limits of human existence while, at the same time, rejecting the belief that "everything is possible." The reader will hopefully conclude that industrialism and human dignity, that freedom and authority are not incompatible, that, in short, the contradictions from which totalitarianism takes its rise are not contradictions at all, but rather a series of alternate values which the man of good judgment will fit together into a coherent pattern.

It is not necessary for the reader to interpret each selection in this volume as the direct opposite of another. Indeed, he may come to appreciate that many of these views can be meshed together into a common, coherent explanation. But the above considerations should make it clear that it does make a difference how one decides on the central issues raised by the debate on totalitarianism. For only by deciding, and deciding rightly, can one hope to preserve the values which Western society has represented, and does still represent today.

The Conflict of Opinion

What is totalitarianism?

". . . it is our conclusion . . . that totalitarian dictatorship is historically unique and *sui generis*. It is also our conclusion from all the facts available to us that fascist and communist totalitarian dictatorships are basically alike, or at any rate more nearly like each other than like any other system of government. . . ."

— CARL FRIEDRICH AND ZBIGNIEW BRZEZINSKI

"Totalitarianism is the extension of permanent governmental control over the totality of social life. . . . Totalitarianism in this sense is, of course, an ideal type to which concrete cases can only approximate, since no government can control every instance of social interaction."

— STANISLAV ANDRESKI

Is totalitarianism modern?

". . . totalitarian societies appear to be exaggerations, but nonetheless logical exaggerations, of the technological state of modern society. . . . [T]he party, its leader(s), and the ideology link the totalitarian dictatorship to modern democracy."

— CARL FRIEDRICH AND ZBIGNIEW BRZEZINSKI

"The victim of a crude form of despotism does not consider his persecutors less powerful because, under more advanced technical conditions, they may catch and destroy him by different methods or with greater speed."

— KARL WITTFOGEL

"I believe that Plato's political program, far from being morally superior to totalitarianism, is fundamentally identical with it."

— KARL POPPER

What is the meaning and the future of totalitarianism?

"I do not think that we are yet in a position to judge recent totalitarian experiments fairly: that is to say, to decide whether, all things considered, they have produced a greater degree of enslavement or a higher level of spiritual energy. It is too early to say."

— PIERRE TEILHARD DE CHARDIN

". . . the era of revolutionary totalitarianism may not yet be over."

— ZBIGNIEW BRZEZINSKI

"Totalitarianism is by no means immune from processes of disintegration; on the contrary, many of the dictatorial techniques which are intended to combat schism or disintegration may in fact tend to accelerate and intensify these very processes."

— KARL DEUTSCH

PROLOGUE

The Possibility of World Domination

KONRAD HEIDEN

Konrad Heiden, a native of Germany who came to the United States after the victory of Nazism, was one of the earliest opponents of Hitler. As the leader of a small democratic group at the University of Munich he was involved in the often violent struggles which occurred in that chaotic period when Hitler's movement first appeared. Later, Heiden served as a staff member of the *Frankfurter Zeitung*, a highly influential, liberal German newspaper. His book, *Der Fuehrer*, is a summing-up of several earlier works on Hitler and National Socialism. Like many other authors whose works appear in this volume, Heiden was particularly concerned with the psychology which motivated both the leaders and the followers of a movement like Nazism.

The "Protocols of the Wise Men of Zion," with which this selection is concerned, was a famous forgery which purported to reveal a Jewish plot to dominate the world. It is likely that the forgery had its origin in certain satirical attacks directed at Napoleon III. These were later expanded by such Russian propagandists as Nilus and Soloviev and were circulated by the Russian secret police at the end of the nineteenth century. The Protocols found their way into Germany and were widely known there in the 1920s, although they were most often referred to in works of fiction and in crack-pot political literature. The Nazis themselves made extensive use of the Protocols as a propaganda weapon against the Jews.

O NE DAY in the summer of 1917 a student was reading in his room in Moscow. A stranger entered, laid a book on the table, and silently vanished. The cover of the book bore in Russian the words from the twenty-fourth chapter of Matthew: "He is near, he is hard by the door."

The student sensed the masterful irony of higher powers in this strange happening. They had sent him a silent message. He opened the book, and the voice of a demon spoke to him.

It was a message concerning the Antichrist, who would come at the end of days. The Antichrist is no mythical being, no monkish medieval fantasy. It is the portrait of a type of man who comes to the fore when an epoch is dying. He is a man with a white skin, in everyday clothes, dangerously contemporary, and a mighty demagogue. He will talk with the masses, and at his word the masses will rise up and turn a culture to ashes, a culture which has deserved no better, since it has borne the Antichrist in its own image and for its own destruction. The great Russian philosopher Soloviev described him. The Antichrist "does not look like what he is," and therein precisely lies the danger. He is a young man with a strong personality and seductive power of speech and writing. He is an ascetic and a vegetarian. He will win fame

From Konrad Heiden, *Der Fuehrer: Hitler's Rise to Power* (Boston, 1944), pp. 1–5, 16–18. Reprinted by permission of Houghton Mifflin Company. This and other readings in this book appear without the footnotes which are found in the original publications.

first by a book in which "respect of the ancient traditions and symbols stands side by side with a bold and thorough radicalism in social and political problems . . . absolute individualism with an ardent fidelity to the common weal. . . ." Then, in Berlin, he will become ruler of the "United States of Europe"; he will conquer Asia and North Africa; America will submit to him voluntarily. He is an absolute genius, and he may, says Soloviev, wear a small mustache.

This is the demon who speaks out of the book.

"We shall talk with the people on the streets and squares," says the demon, "and teach them to take the view of political questions which at the moment we require. For what the ruler says to the people spreads through the whole country like wildfire, the voice of the people carries it to all four winds.

"We" — the demon always says "We" — "shall create unrest, struggle, and hate in the whole of Europe and thence in other continents. We shall at all times be in a position to call forth new disturbances at will, or to restore the old order.

"Unremittingly we shall poison the relations between the peoples and states of all countries. By envy and hatred, by struggle and warfare, even by spreading hunger, destitution, and plagues, we shall bring all peoples to such a pass that their only escape will lie in total submission to our domination.

"We shall stultify, seduce, ruin the youth.

"We shall not stick at bribery, treachery, treason, as long as they serve the realization of our plans. Our watchword is: force and hypocrisy!

"In our arsenal we carry a boundless ambition, burning avidity, a ruthless thirst for revenge, relentless hatred. From us emanates the specter of fear, all-embracing terror."

A gabbling demon, and self-conceited, too:

"We are the chosen, we are the true men.

Our minds give off the true power of the spirit; the intelligence of the rest is instinctive and animal. They can see, but they cannot foresee; their inventions are purely corporeal. Does it not follow clearly that Nature herself has predestined us to dominate the whole world?

"We shall not submit the unique greatness of our ultimate plan, the context of its particular parts, the consequences of each separate point, the secret meaning of which remains hidden, to the judgment and decision of the many, even, of those who share our thoughts; we shall not cast the gleaming thoughts of our leader before the swine, and even in more intimate circles we shall not permit them to be carped at.

"We shall paint the misdeeds of foreign governments in the most garish colors and create such an ill-feeling toward them that the peoples would a thousand times rather bear a slavery which guarantees them peace and order than enjoy their much-touted freedom. The peoples will tolerate any servitude we may impose on them, if only to avoid a return to the horrors of wars and insurrection. Our principles and methods will take on their full force when we present them in sharp contrast to the putrid old social order.

"Outwardly, however, in our 'official' utterances, we shall adopt an opposite procedure and always do our best to appear honorable and co-operative. A statesman's words do not have to agree with his acts. If we pursue these principles, the governments and peoples which we have thus prepared will take our IOU's for cash. One day they will accept us as the benefactors and saviors of the human race.

"If any state dares to resist us; if its neighbors make common cause with it against us, we shall unleash a world war."

And then the demon spreads his wings, conceals the sky, darkens the world:

"By all these methods we shall so wear down the nations that they will be forced to offer us world domination. We shall stretch out our arms like pincers in all directions, and introduce an order of such violence that all peoples will bow to our domination."

Who is this "we"? Who is it that brags so absurdly?

To the student it is not absurd. It sounds fantastic, but it is not a mere tissue of lies. He turns back the pages and discovers that all this accursed wisdom, all these diabolical plans, were hatched out by a group of old Jews, who met together in a back room in Basel, Switzerland, in the year 1897. The demon aiming to devour the world is a Jewish club. It stands there in black and white, described at length, with place and date. Twenty years had passed before this knowledge found the right man. And thus *The Protocols of the Wise Men of Zion,* since become so famous, fell into the hands of Alfred Rosenberg.

A mysterious occurrence. Rosenberg himself has often told how the unknown suddenly stepped into the room, laid down the book, and silently departed. To Rosenberg it was a sign from heaven. Both the place and the hour were significant. Moscow, 1917. Far to the west, the German-Russian phase of the First World War was drawing to an end in crumbling trenches; in the streets of the capital, the Russian Revolution was ebbing and flowing. Alfred Rosenberg, the son of a shoemaker, born in Reval (Tallinn) on the Baltic, was then twenty-four years old; he was of German descent but as an Esthonian, he was a subject of the Russian tsar. He had been raised in the German and Russian languages; he had first studied engineering and architecture at Riga, also on the Baltic; then, when the German army occupied Riga, he had fled. Now he was studying in Moscow.

The globe was afire. The tsar's empire was crumbling. Perhaps there would never again be peace. Perhaps this book would tell him why. The demon, who had incited the nations against each other, had spoken. Perhaps he, Alfred Rosenberg, understood him better than others; for in his own soul he could feel more strongly than others the mesh woven by hatred and love between the nations. He came from the tsar's Baltic

German provinces. He could scarcely say whether he was more Russian or more German. But today there were greater things concerning which he must achieve clarity. Here in Russia's holy city, in Russia's language, he had received a message. Judah, a book has brought forth thine innermost thoughts! He, the student, would close his eyes and believe it all his life, as firm as a rock. Was a new epoch of world history beginning in Moscow at that hour? Surely one of the most astounding, far-reaching, and bloody conspiracies of all time was bound to that hour. He who could read would go far.

"The nations," says the demon, "love and honor audacity in statesmen. Faced with an act of violence, they say: that was vile but clever! A scoundrel's trick, but wonderfully executed! With what insolence! Our leaders must move toward their goal with unparalleled boldness. Then we shall break all resistance in our path." The vision sends forth an icy chill and a breath of deadly truth.

The demon of world domination has spoken. He has proclaimed the great secret: the world can be dominated. Bowed with weariness, the peoples demand subjection. And those who resist will be tamed by terrible blows and sufferings. Modern society is charged with a magical current which in all men creates the same thoughts. The masses expect great things of their rulers. And for that reason, great things are easy.

This is the true sense of the secret writings which we today know as *The Protocols of the Wise Men of Zion.* Everything else in them develops from the basic idea that world domination is possible in our time: with sovereign contempt it is shown with what relative ease it can be achieved. Later, at third, fourth, and fifth hand, these profound thoughts were woven together with a figment of forgeries and purposeful lies which confused and obscured the whole document to the point of unintelligibility. But precisely in that condition it could be swallowed without understanding by millions of readers, and this gave it its great effect.

. . . For beneath the heavy coating of a clumsily exaggerated forgery, the *Protocols* contain a genuine element which might well carry a strong, mysterious appeal to the modern intellectual. This element is their radicalism. The *Protocols* are the work of a decadent, unscrupulous group of intellectuals, who pondered the problem of dominating the masses. They saw the modern mass in revolutionary motion. They set themselves the task of weaning the masses from their revolutionary leaders. See what these socialist agitators had succeeded in doing with a few revolutionary phrases and little apparent thought! Why couldn't we learn to do as well? We academicians would surely be a match for a band of trade-union secretaries! There is a technique of dominating the masses, and in principle technical problems can always be solved. The intellectual's envy of the demagogue gave birth to a new political technique.

And here history turns over a new leaf. The conspirators did not need to invent anti-Semitism; no, what they did was to create anti-Semitism as a weapon in the class struggle; something quite apart from the hostility which, since the beginning of the nineteenth century, had been aroused by the Jewish entrance into the bourgeois society of Europe. For now, in modern society, a new Jewish type had made its appearance — the Jewish intellectual; and it is predominantly he who became the target and victim of the most frightful outbursts of anti-Semitism in modern history. For it is his competitor, the non-Jewish intellectual, who incited and directed this anti-Semitism, and directed it chiefly, not against Jewish capital (though an outmoded propaganda says so), but against the Jewish intellectuals — the lawyers, doctors, government officials, and others who had made themselves, by their share in modern education, so influential a part of society.

We are living in the age of technology. Technology is more than the transforma-tion of heat into power. It is, in general, the domination of brute force by trained intelligence. Natural scientists have studied the soul, and vaudeville "professors" have demonstrated the power of hypnosis. The fakirs are not the only ones who can cast a spell over the masses. Here, this book shows what great things are possible, even with the simplest methods. Alfred Rosenberg is an engineer and architect, a young man who in a few months will take his examinations for registered engineer. The powers have laid this book on his desk and thereby given him the watchword that was to govern his life, the open sesame of technology: everything is possible.

With the book in his bag, he fled at the beginning of 1918 to his native city of Reval, later called Tallinn. German troops took the city. Rosenberg remembered that he was a German. He volunteered for the German army, to fight against the Bolsheviki who for some months had been in the saddle in Petersburg and Moscow. The German commandant distrusted the German Russian and rejected him. He remained a civilian, earning his living as a drawing instructor at the *Gymnasium*. His eyes were still fixed on Russia. The Bolsheviki had disbanded the Constituent Assembly, proclaimed the dictatorship of the proletariat and the advent of socialism, but at the same time had given the poor peasants land, or rather summoned them to take it; they had brutally suppressed all political freedom, all opposition parties. Those affected resisted; there were plots and assassinations. The Bolsheviki, in a desperate life-and-death struggle, always in power but always on the brink of catastrophe, struck down their enemies by ruthless, barbaric terror. They acted in accordance with the recommendations of *The Protocols of Zion*. . Were they not themselves the Wise Men of Zion? Hadn't they Jewish leaders? Isn't Lenin, their top leader, a Jew? In this, to be sure, Rosenberg was mistaken. Lenin was no more a Jew than Rykov, Kalinin, Krassin, Bucharin, and other Bolshevik leaders of the old guard; but Trotzky, Zinoviev,

Radek were Jews. The Bolsheviki exterminated the Jewish bourgeoisie of Russia as heartlessly as the Christian; from time to time some little Jewish community cursed and excommunicated a Bolshevik leader who arose in its midst; for Rosenberg, however, Russia was ruled by the Jewish Antichrist which Nilus had prophesied. Rosenberg himself has a little drop of Jewish blood in his veins; let us assume that he did not know it at the time. The world in which his great experiences took place remains in any case Russia. It was there that he met the demon. It was there that the dice governing the destiny of nations were falling. There the Antichrist held sway over a field of corpses. From there the plague was moving on Europe. It was on Russia that we should march, when the time came, to tumble Satan from his throne. Our life work was to summon Europe to avenge our exile.

For at the end of 1918, Rosenberg was forced to leave Reval with the remnants of the withdrawing, disbanding German army. The Bolsheviki pressed after them, occupied Reval, took Riga, approached the German border. He fled from them, crying:

The plague is coming! An infected army, on the point of mutiny, flowed homeward, carrying him along. Thus he left Russia, came to Germany, bearing with him a treasure, the message of the Russian Antichrist, the *Protocols*. In a swarm of Russian fugitives, officers, intellectuals, barons and princes, Rosenberg reached Berlin, then Munich. At the same time other refugees reached Constantinople, London, Paris; Russians, Germans, but also Englishmen, Frenchmen, even Americans, members of those Allied expeditionary armies who, after the outbreak of the Bolshevik revolution, had occupied, for a time, Russian territory in Siberia, in the North, in the Crimea. And with this flow of fugitives not a few copies of the *Protocols* reached Western Europe.

A pity that General Ratchkovsky never lived to see the day. The shadow of Russia fell over Europe. From the Kremlin, Lenin exhorted the world to revolution, holding aloft the *Communist Manifesto*. Rosenberg comes, a humble fugitive, with the textbook of world domination in his battered suitcase.

I. TOWARD A DEFINITION

Totalitarianism Is a Unique Type of Society

CARL FRIEDRICH AND ZBIGNIEW BRZEZINSKI

Friedrich and Brzezinski's *Totalitarian Dictatorship and Autocracy*, from which the following selection is taken, is still the clearest and most comprehensive treatment of totalitarianism. Both authors have had unusually successful careers and were among the first to fully work out a systematic conception of totalitarianism. Carl Friedrich was born in Germany and educated in that country's most prestigious universities. His teaching career has been spent mostly at Harvard University. In addition to a long list of important publications in the field of political science, he has also authored a widely praised work of history: *The Age of the Baroque.* Zbigniew Brzezinski has had an unusually active career for such a relatively young man. An outstanding interpreter of contemporary Russian and East European politics, he has served for some time as the Director of Columbia University's Research Institute on Communist Affairs. In addition, he has been an outspoken advisor on, and defender of, United States foreign policy.

BUT IT IS our contention in this volume that totalitarian dictatorship is historically unique and *sui generis* [of its own kind]. It is also our conclusion from all the facts available to us that fascist and communist totalitarian dictatorships are basically alike, or at any rate more nearly like each other than like any other system of government, including earlier forms of autocracy. These two theses are closely linked and must be examined together. They are also linked to a third, that totalitarian dictatorship as it actually developed was not intended by those who created it — Mussolini talked of it, but meant something different — but resulted from the political situations in which the anticonstitutionalist and antidemocratic revolutionary movements and their leaders found themselves. Let us take the third of these points first, treating the second and first afterward.

The fascist and communist systems evolved in response to a series of unprecedented crises, and they have shown a continuous, though intermittent, tendency to become more "totalitarian." There is no present reason to conclude that the existing totalitarian systems will disappear as a result of internal evolution, though this possibility cannot be excluded. The two totalitarian governments which have perished thus far have perished as the result of wars in which they had become involved with outside powers, but this does not mean that the Soviet Union necessarily will. We do not presuppose that totalitarian societies are fixed and static entities, but, on the contrary, that they have undergone and continue to undergo a steady evolution, presumably involving both growth and deterioration.

In terms of historical perspective, three points might be added. First, certain autocracies in the past have shown extraordinary capacity for survival. Not only the Roman but also several Oriental empires lasted for hundreds of years, at least as systems they did, though the dynasties changed. By contrast, the tyrannies of the Greek city states were usually short-lived, as Aristotle noted. Second, such autocracies have as a rule perished in consequence of foreign invasions. Third, their autocratic features have usually been intensified over long periods, the reason being that violence is readily available for dealing with the tensions and breakdowns that occur. In short, some of these autocracies were not stable, but lasting.

To the uncertainties about the end correspond the controversies about the beginning of totalitarian dictatorship. The debate about the causes or origins of totalitarianism has run all the way from a primitive bad-man theory to the "moral crisis of our time" kind of argument. A detailed inspection of the available evidence suggests that virtually every one of the factors which has been offered by itself as an explanation of the origin of totalitarian dictatorship has played its role. For example, in the case of Germany — Hitler's moral and personal defects, weaknesses in the German constitutional tradition, certain traits involved in the German "national character," the Versailles Treaty and its aftermath, the economic crisis and the "contradictions" of an aging capitalism, the "threat" of communism, the decline of Christianity and of such other spiritual moorings as the belief in the reason and the reasonableness of man — all have played a role in the total configuration of factors contributing to the over-all result. As in the case of other broad developments in history, only a multiple-factor analysis will do. But at the present time, we cannot fully explain the rise of totalitarian dictatorship. All we can do is to explain it partially by identifying some of the antecedent and concomitant conditions. Broadly speaking, totalitarian dictatorship is a new development; there has never been anything quite like it before.

Now concerning the second point, it is very important to explain somewhat at the outset why the totalitarian dictatorships, communist and fascist, are *basically alike*. What does this mean? In the first place, it means that they are *not wholly alike*. Popular and journalistic interpretation has oscillated between two extremes; some have said that the communist and fascist dictatorships are wholly alike, others that they are not at all alike. The latter view was the prevailing one during the popular-front days in Europe as well as in "liberal" circles in the United States. It was even more popular during the Second World War, especially among Allied propagandists. Besides, it was and is the official Soviet and Hitler party line. It is only natural that these regimes, conceiving of themselves as bitter enemies, dedicated to the task of liquidating each other, should take the view that they have nothing in common. This has happened before in history. When the Protestants and Catholics were fighting each other during the religious wars of the sixteenth and seventeenth centuries, they very commonly denied to each other the name of "Christians," and argued about each other that they were not "true churches." Actually, and from the viewpoint of the sectarians whom they both persecuted, they were indeed that.

The other view, that communist and fascist dictatorships are wholly alike, is presently favored in the United States and in Western Europe to an increasing extent. Yet they are obviously not wholly alike. For example, they differ in their proclaimed purposes and intentions. Everyone knows that the communists say they seek the world revolution of the proletariat, while the fascists proclaimed their determination to establish the world dominance of a particular nation or people, or at least their imperial predominance in a region, as in the case of the Italian Fascists. The communist and fascist dictatorships differ also in their historical antecedents: the fascist movements have arisen in reaction to the communist challenge and have offered themselves to a frightened middle class as the saviors from the communist danger. As we shall have occasion to show in the chapters which follow, there are many other differences which do not allow us to speak of the communist and fascist totalitarian dictatorships as wholly alike, but which suggest that they are sufficiently alike to class them together and contrast them not only with constitutional systems, but also with former types of autocracy.

Before we turn to these common features, however, there is another difference which used to be emphasized by many who wanted "to do business with Hitler" or who admired Mussolini and therefore argued that, far from being wholly like the communist dictatorship, the fascist regimes must really be seen as merely authoritarian forms of constitutional systems. It is indeed true that more of the institutions of the preceding liberal and constitutional society survived in the Italian Fascist than in the Russian Communist society. But this is due in part to the fact that no liberal, constitutional society preceded Soviet Communism. The promising period of the Duma came to naught as a result of the war and the disintegration of tsarism, while the Kerensky interlude was far too brief and too superficial to become meaningful for the future. In Czechoslovakia and in the Soviet Zone of Germany (German Democratic Republic) we find precisely such institutions as universities, churches, and schools surviving. It is likely that, were a communist dictatorship to be established in Great Britain or France, the situation would be similar, and that here even more such institutions of the liberal era would continue to operate for a considerable initial period at least. Precisely this argument has been advanced by such British radicals as Sidney and Beatrice Webb. The tendency of isolated fragments of the preceding state of society to survive has been a significant source of misinterpretation of the fascist totalitarian society, especially in the case of Italy. In the twenties, Italian totalitarianism was very commonly misinterpreted as being "merely" an author-

itarian form of middle class rule, with the trains running on time, and the beggars off the street. In the case of Germany, this sort of misinterpretation took a slightly different form. In the thirties, various authors tried to interpret German totalitarianism as either "the end phase of capitalism" or as "militarist imperialism." These interpretations stress the continuance of a "capitalist" economy whose leaders are represented as dominating the regime. The facts as we know them do not correspond to this view. For one who sympathized with socialism or communism it was very tempting to try and depict the totalitarian dictatorship of Hitler as nothing but a capitalist society and therefore totally at variance with the "new civilization" that was arising in the Soviet Union. These few remarks have suggested, it is hoped, why it may be wrong to consider the totalitarian dictatorships under discussion as either wholly alike or basically different. Why they are basically alike remains to be shown, and to this key argument we now turn.

The basic features or traits which we suggest as generally recognized to be common to totalitarian dictatorships are six in number. The "syndrome," or pattern of interrelated traits, of the totalitarian dictatorship consists of an ideology, a single party typically led by one man, a terroristic police, a communications monopoly, a weapons monopoly, and a centrally directed economy. Of these, the last two are also found in constitutional systems: Socialist Britain had a centrally directed economy, and all modern states possess a weapons monopoly. . . .

These six basic features, which we think constitute the character of totalitarian dictatorship, form a cluster of interrelated traits, intertwined and mutually supporting each other, as usual in "organic" systems. They should therefore not be considered in isolation or be made the focal point of comparisons, such as "Caesar developed a terroristic secret police, therefore he was the first totalitarian dictator," or "the Catholic

Church has practised ideological thought control, therefore . . ."

The totalitarian dictatorships all possess the following:

1. an official ideology, consisting of an official body of doctrine covering all vital aspects of man's existence to which everyone living in that society is supposed to adhere, at least passively; this ideology is characteristically focused and projected toward a perfect final state of mankind, that is to say, it contains a chiliastic claim, based upon a radical rejection of the existing society and conquest of the world for the new one;

2. a single mass party led typically by one man, the "dictator," and consisting of a relatively small percentage of the total population (up to 10 per cent) of men and women, a hard core of them passionately and unquestioningly dedicated to the ideology and prepared to assist in every way in promoting its general acceptance, such a party being hierarchically, oligarchically organized, and typically either superior to, or completely intertwined with the bureaucratic government organization;

3. a system of terroristic police control, supporting but also supervising the party for its leaders, and characteristically directed not only against demonstrable "enemies" of the regime, but against arbitrarily selected classes of the population; the terror of the secret police systematically exploiting modern science, and more especially scientific psychology;

4. a technologically conditioned near-complete monopoly of control, in the hands of the party and its subservient cadres, of all means of effective mass communication, such as the press, radio, motion pictures;

5. a similarly technologically conditioned near-complete monopoly of control (in the same hands) of all means of effective armed combat;

6. a central control and direction of the entire economy through the bureaucratic co-ordination of its formerly independent corporate entities, typically including most other associations and group activities.

The enumeration of these six traits or trait clusters is not meant to suggest that there might not be others, now insufficiently recognized, but that these are universally acknowledged to be the features of totalitarian dictatorship to which the writings of students of the most varied backgrounds, including totalitarian writers, bear witness.

Within this broad pattern of similarities, there are many significant variations to which the analysis of this book will give detailed attention. To offer a few random illustrations, at present the party zealots play less of a role in the Soviet Union than the party bureaucrats, as contrasted with an earlier stage; the ideology of the Soviet Union is more specifically committed to certain assumptions, because of its Marx-Engels bible, than that of Italian or German fascism, where ideology was formulated by the leader of the party himself; the corporate entities of the fascist economy remained in private hands, as far as property claims are concerned, whereas they become public property in the Soviet Union.

Let us now turn to our first point, namely, that these systems are historically "unique"; that is to say, that no government like totalitarian dictatorship has ever before existed, even though it bears a resemblance to autocracies of the past. It may be interesting to consider briefly some data which show that the six traits we have just identified are to a large extent lacking in historically known autocratic regimes. Neither the Oriental despotisms of the more remote past, nor the absolute monarchies of modern Europe, neither the tyrannies of the ancient Greek cities, nor the Roman Empire, nor yet the tyrannies of the city states of the Italian Renaissance and the Bonapartist military dictatorships of the last century exhibit this design, this combination of features, though they may possess one or another of its constituent traits. For example, efforts have often been made to organize some kind of secret police, but they have not been even horse-and-buggy affairs compared with the terror of the Gestapo or of the OGPU (MVD today). Similarly, there have been both military and propagandistic concentrations of power and control, but the limits of technology prevented any thoroughgoing development along totalitarian lines. It is very evident, we trust, that the six distinctive features here sketched, and to be developed in what follows, sharply differentiate contemporary totalitarian dictatorships from past autocratic regimes. Certainly neither the Roman emperor nor the absolute monarch sought or needed a party to support him nor an ideology in the modern party sense, and the same is obviously true of oriental despots. The tyrants of Greece and Italy may have had a party — that of the Medicis in Florence was called *lo stato* — but they had no ideology to speak of. And, of course, all of these autocratic regimes were far removed from the very distinctive features which are rooted in modern technology, from the terror to the centrally directed economy.

Something more should perhaps be added on the subject of technology. This technological aspect of totalitarianism is, of course, particularly striking in the matter of weapons and communications, but it is involved also in the secret police terror, depending as it does upon technically enhanced possibilities of supervision and control of the movement of persons. In addition, the centrally directed economy presupposes the reporting, cataloging, and calculating devices provided by modern technology. In short, four of the six traits are technologically conditioned. To envisage what this technological advance means in terms of political control, one has to think only of the weapons field. The Constitution of the United States guarantees to every citizen the "right to bear arms" (Fourth Amendment). In the days of the minutemen, this was a very important right, and the freedom of the citizen was indeed symbolized by the gun over the hearth, as it

is in Switzerland to this day. But who can "bear" such arms as a tank, a bomber, or a flame-thrower, let alone an atom bomb? The citizen as an individual, and indeed in larger groups, is simply defenseless against the overwhelming technological superiority of those who can centralize in their hands the means with which to wield these modern arms and thereby physically to coerce the mass of the citizenry. Similar observations are easy to make regarding the press, the radio, and so forth. "Freedom" does not have the same potential, resting as it did upon individual effort, which it had a hundred and fifty years ago. With few exceptions, the trend of technological advance implies the trend toward greater and greater size of organization. In the perspective of these four traits, therefore, totalitarian societies appear to be merely exaggerations, but nonetheless logical exaggerations, of the technological state of modern society.

The same cannot be said with respect to the first two distinctive features of totalitarian dictatorships, for neither ideology nor party have any significant relation to the state of technology. (This may not be strictly true, since the mass conversion continually attempted by totalitarian propaganda through its effective use of the communications monopoly could not be carried through without it.) However, the party, its leader(s), and the ideology link the totalitarian dictatorship to modern democracy. It is the perversion of democracy. Not only did Hitler, Mussolini, and Lenin build typical parties within a constitutional, if not a democratic, context but the connection is plain between the stress on ideology and the role which platforms and other types of ideological goal-formation play in democratic parties. To be sure, totalitarian parties developed a pronounced authoritarian pattern while organizing themselves into effective revolutionary instruments of action; but, at the same time, its leaders, beginning with Marx and Engels, saw themselves as constituting the vanguard of the democratic movement of their day, and Stalin always talked of the

Soviet totalitarian society as the "perfect democracy"; Hitler and Mussolini made similar statements. Both the world brotherhood of the proletariat and the folk community were conceived of as supplanting the class divisions of past societies by a complete harmony — the classless society of the socialist tradition.

Not only the party but also its ideology harkens back to the democratic context within which the totalitarian movements arose. Ideology generally, but more especially totalitarian ideology, involves a high degree of convictional certainty. As has been indicated, totalitarian ideology consists of an official doctrine which radically rejects the pre-existing society in terms of a chiliastic proposal for a new one. As such it contains strongly utopian elements, some kind of notion of a paradise on earth. This utopian and chiliastic outlook of totalitarian ideologies gives them a pseudoreligious quality. In fact, they often elicit in the less critical followers a depth of conviction and a fervor of devotion usually found only among persons inspired by a transcendent faith. Whether these aspects of totalitarian ideologies bear some sort of relationship to the religions which they seek to replace is arguable. Marx denounced religion as "the opium of the people." It would seem that this is rather an appropriate way of describing totalitarian ideologies. In place of the more or less sane platforms of regular political parties, critical of the existing state of affairs in a limited way, totalitarian ideologies are perversions of such programs. They substitute faith for reason, magic exhortation for scientific knowledge. And yet, it must be recognized that there is enough of these same elements in the operations of democratic parties to attest to the relation between them and their perverted descendants, the totalitarian movements. That is why these movements must be seen and analyzed in their relationship to the democracy which they seek to supplant.

In summary, these regimes could have arisen only within the context of mass democracy and modern technology.

Totalitarianism Is One Possible Aspect of Any Society

N. S. TIMASHEFF

N. S. Timasheff is an outstanding sociologist, distinguished for the extensive and remarkable contributions which he made to Pitirim Sorokin's monumental, if controversial and unduly pessimistic, *Social and Cultural Dynamics*.
Chosen for this task because of his detailed knowledge of the field of law,
Timasheff reveals this interest clearly in the selection which follows. More recently, Timasheff has devoted the major part of his research to the study of
the place of revolutions and wars in modern society. The reader should carefully compare the views of Timasheff with those of Friedrich and Brzezinski in
the preceding article. Before coming to a conclusion about which of the methods
of visualizing totalitarianism is more correct, the reader must first inquire if the
difference between the two views is merely semantic, or whether there is a
fundamental distinction of practical import.

THE TERM "totalitarian society" is applied in two closely related but
nevertheless distinct meanings. In the first
meaning it connotes a *type* of society characterized by a number of traits such as concentration of power in the hands of a few;
the absence of rights ascribed to the individuals *vs.* the collectivity; and an unlimited extension of the functions of the
state making the state almost tantamount
with society. Other combinations of traits
are possible; for example, the addition of
the ideocratic nature of the state, of imperialism, of the organization of atomized
men. In another meaning the term connotes one definite *trait*, namely the unlimited extension of state functions; then,
the term designates not a concrete type of
society, but a trait isolated by means of abstraction and apt to appear in societies of
various types.

Definitions, as is well known, cannot be
proved to be right or wrong. They are verbal equations equalizing the term with a
combination of attributes; the formula is:
N is that which possesses traits or properties
A, B, C. These verbal equations can be
tested from the point of view of their adequacy. The test of adequacy must establish (1) whether the traits chosen coincide
with clusters of traits observable in reality;
(2) whether the meaning ascribed to the
term approximately coincides with common
speech and etymology; (3) whether the
definition is a satisfactory tool for scientific
inquiry.

Since this is an exploratory paper, no assertion is made that one of the two definitions is more adequate than the other. But
the position is hypothetically taken that the
second definition, identifying totalitarianism with one definite trait appearing in
society rather than identifying it with a
type of society, is at least plausible and
fruitful.

Let us begin by establishing a few differences which obtain depending on the definition chosen. If the first definition is
chosen, totalitarian society may be considered as a unique phenomenon having
appeared in our day, though this is subject
to doubt. G. Ferrero applies the term "totalitarian" to the Consulate and Empire
while Pitirim Sorokin points to totalitarian
periods in the history of Ancient Egypt, the
late Roman Empire (since Diocletian),
China, and the state of the Incas.

If the second definition is chosen, the

term "totalitarian" may be applied to a society which differs significantly from the concrete totalitarian societies of our day, Communist, Fascist, and National Socialist. One could then combine the term "totalitarian" with the term "democratic," which is obviously impossible if Definition 1 is chosen. There recently appeared a book, by Professor J. L. Talmon, entitled *The Rise of Totalitarian Democracy*. This combination of terms is used to designate the type of society which was being created in France under the Jacobins. Finally, if Definition 2 is chosen, correlations of isolated traits may be studied, while under the first definition, comparative study of total social configurations is the adequate approach.

Definition 2, to be explored in this paper, is logically connected with the requirements of a multidimensional analysis of the political phase of social life. This multidimensional analysis must be logically embedded in the essential properties of the structure and functions of the state.

The organization of the state presents enormous variations. For our purposes, these variations may be reduced to a formula expressing the basis of the political status of those in power, in other words, answering the question: why are these men and not other ones in power, while the other ones obey orders issued by the former? The foundation of the political status of those in power may be, first, explicit and periodically checked consent of the governed; then, the government is democratic. Second, the foundation of the political status of those in power may be implicit but unchecked consent of the ruled, derived from the fact that obedience to those in power and their predecessors is consecrated by tradition; then, the government is traditional. Or, third, the political status of those in power may be based upon the seizure of power by the rulers and their ability to maintain it against attempts to dislodge them. Then, the government is dictatorial.

It is obvious that the three types are ideal or pure types. In concrete situations, there may be mixtures of two or even all the three. The government of this country is primarily democratic, but secondarily traditional since the rules of the democratic game have been received into America's culture tradition. The government of the Soviet Union is dictatorial, but it makes attempts to invoke, in its favor, both the results of elections and the millennial tradition of Russia. The government of Napoleon also was dictatorial; but it made attempts to restore in its favor the tradition of the *ancien régime* and to strengthen itself by democratic consent in the form of plebiscites.

Other lines of analysis must be related to the three main divisions of the functions of the state. Two of them cover the state's essential functions, i.e., functions without which the state cannot exist.

The first of them is self-assertion in the framework of the greater society consisting of bodies politic in interaction. The second is maintenance of law and order which is manifested mainly in criminal and civil justice and is a substitute for conflict solution by means of violence; later on, it will be called protective. The two functions, by inner necessity, must be carried on by one organization or, eventually, a system of organizations forming a hierarchy. This is so because each function can be adequately performed only by an organization possessing overwhelming power — that is, power sufficient to break the resistance of reluctant individuals. It is obvious that, in a given area, there cannot be two overwhelmingly strong organizations, for each of them would be deprived of this attribute by the very existence of the other.

The third division of the state's functions is residual. It covers all functions which are not ramifications of the self-assertive and protective functions. These functions which can be called auxiliary arise on the background of the principle of the heterogeny of ends. An organization exists and is endowed with overwhelming power. It is there primarily for self-assertion and maintenance of law and order. Then, under most diversified conditions, part of its energy is diverted to achieve other ends. This happens if their achievement receives positive social evaluation, and the possibility and/or desirability of their achievement in nonpolitical ways is questioned.

Depending on the scope and modalities of the exertion of the three types of functions, the politically organized societies may be distributed along continua, each, in principle, independent of the others.

With respect to the self-assertive function, the states may be distributed along a continuum beginning with peace-loving societies and finishing by warlike, highly aggressive, morbidly nationalistic or imperialistic societies. This position of the individual units (states) can be measured. Such a measurement has been carried out, with interesting results, by L. T. Hobhouse and associates relating to primitive societies, and by Pitirim Sorokin and Q. Wright relating to advanced societies. The latter measurement could be refined if the individual wars counted in the two works were divided into defensive and aggressive ones.

Concerning the protective function of the state, units can be distributed along a continuum beginning with that which, in German, is called *Rechtsstaat* and, in English, is covered by the phrase, "due process of law," and ending by the despotic state. A society is despotic if, in the relationship between the state and the citizens, the state ascribes to itself all the rights and imposes on its citizens a heavy burden of duties. A society is legalistic (let us use tentatively this term), if the opposite is the case. The position of the individual states can be indirectly measured by comparing the average intensity of the criminal sanctions they use.

Concerning the auxiliary functions of the state, the units can be distributed along a continuum beginning with liberal society and finishing with totalitarian society. A society is totalitarian if the number of the auxiliary functions of the state is so high that almost all human activities are regulated by it. A society is liberal if the number of the auxiliary functions is so small that the state's activities are almost confined

to its logical minimum. The contradistinction between the two extreme positions on the continuum can be best illustrated by two quotations, one from Jefferson, another from Mussolini. Jefferson advocates a government "which shall restrain men from injuring one another, which shall leave them otherwise free to regulate their own pursuits of industry and improvement." Mussolini declares that everything must be done within the nation (in the meaning of the state), nothing against the nation or outside the nation; the individuals are related to each other through the medium of the whole, or of one of its spheres (political, economic, and so on).

It is noteworthy that the exertion of the auxiliary functions of the state can appear in at least three forms: (1) state regulation of activities of individuals or corporations carrying out a function; (2) licensing of individuals or corporations desirous to perform a function; or (3) absorption of the function, manifested in the annexation of the corresponding organizations by the bureaucratic machinery of the state.

This is a continuum relating to which indirect measurement is possible. The auxiliary functions of the state must be enforced, and the main instrument of enforcement is, of course, criminal law. Consequently, the larger the scope of the auxiliary functions, the larger is the number of types of conduct punished by criminal law.

The scientific problem which arises when confronting and correlating the distribution of the units (i.e., states) among the classes or positions in the four-dimensional space just traced is this: are, or are not, the positions of the units in the four dimensions related in such a way that, from the position along one of the dimensions, positions along the other dimensions can be predicted? This is of course an enormous problem, the solution of which would require years of team work. At this place only a tentative answer can be given: There are incompatible locations; there are, on the other hand, frequent and naturally recurring combinations; there is, however, also a significant area of freedom characterized by the appearance of diverse combinations.

We observe, or have recently observed, a number of political units whose position on the four coördinates must be termed as dictatorial, highly aggressive, despotic, and totalitarian (in the meaning of Definition 2), and we are inclined to construct, to cover them, an historical, or concrete, type (totalitarian in the meaning of Definition 1). Such are, or have been, Communist Russia, now also Communist China, National Socialist Germany, Fascist Italy, perhaps also Franco's Spain. But relating to the Western satellites, the classification would not be exactly the same. These societies are dictatorial and despotic, but they cannot be aggressive (since they are themselves victims of aggression), and they have not yet reached the climax of totalitarianism. Salazar's Portugal is a dictatorship; it is far advanced toward totalitarianism (but without reaching the limit); it is not aggressive and is not so much despotic as authoritarian, a position midway between legalism and despotism. In the twenties, thirties, and early forties, there were in Europe many semifascist societies, such as Spain under Primo de Rivera, Poland under Pilsudski and his successors, Lithuania under Waldemaras and his successors, Latvia under Ulmanis, Rumania under Carol II and Antonescu, Bulgaria under K. Gueorguiev and his successors, Greece under Metaxas, Vichy France. They all were dictatorships, close to despotism, inclined to aggression (*vide* Lithuania vs. the Memelland, Poland vs. Lithuania and Teschen, Hungary vs. the provinces lost in 1918, Rumania vs. Bessarabia and a vast area East of it, Bulgaria vs. the lands granted her by the treaty of San Stefano, but lost through the treaty of Berlin). They were also inclined to totalitarianism without going, however, more than halfway.

As a contrast to these combinations, let us mention the combination of democracy, legalism, and liberalism in the United States, Belgium, and Switzerland, and the combination of democracy, legalism, and significant expansion of the functions of the state toward totalitarianism in Great Britain, Australia, New Zealand, France, Italy, and many other, formerly liberal countries.

If we leave the contemporary European scene, we find other combinations. France, under the Jacobins, was a combination of democracy (the convention having been elected by universal suffrage!), aggressiveness, despotism, and far-advanced totalitarianism (tendency to regulate everything, including religion). The mercantilistic states of continental Europe in the seventeenth and eighteenth centuries were also well advanced toward the totalitarian regulation of life (especially, economic life); they were however traditional in their organization, but despotic as to the relations between the state and the individuals, with a few striking exceptions: Frederick the Great's Prussia approximated the ideal of legalism. At the same time England was a traditional body politic with incipient concessions toward democracy, as inclined to totalitarianism as the continental nations, but, like Prussia, approximating legalism. Some of the English colonies in America presented peculiar combinations of democracy, legalism, and quasi-totalitarianism, especially relative to religion and the connected regulations of everyday life.

Russia under Nicholas I was traditional, despotic, aggressive, and inclined to totalitarianism, as were the Western states fifty years earlier. Under Nicholas II, Russia was traditional, but with significant concessions to democracy; closer to legalism than to despotism; aggressive, but closer to the liberal than to the totalitarian position on the fourth continuum.

The Latin American dictatorships are commonly despotic (sometimes only authoritarian), but little inclined to totalitarianism: life is politically regulated only so far as it is relevant for the maintenance in power of those who hold it. But Paraguay under the Jesuits was close to totalitarianism; Peron's Argentina is midway between the liberal and totalitarian positions.

The Ancient World presents instances of combinations closely resembling totalitarian society (Definition 1) of our day, but also combinations of democracy with despotism and inclination toward totalitarianism.

It is worth while to conclude this survey by comparing the lists of actions considered criminal in the Middle Ages, the climax of liberalism (from the French Revolution up to the last quarter of the nineteenth century), and the postliberal period characterized by the rise of modern totalitarianism (Definition 1). This comparison shows that (1) there is a hard core of such actions perpetuated from period to period and approximately corresponding to the "maintenance of law and order" function of the state; (2) in the Middle Ages, and well into the eighteenth century, such actions appeared punishable as apostasy, heresy, schism, conversion to another religion, sorcery, nonperformance of the rites of the official religion, contact with Jews, fornication, sodomy, wearing of prohibited apparel (thus violating the symbolic separation of the social classes), infringement of government regulations concerning the production of specified commodities; (3) in the postliberal period, many subtle types of sexual abuse and many complex modalities of the violation of the order of production and exchange made their appearance, even in nontotalitarian societies. But even the totalitarian societies do not penalize many of the actions enumerated above, thus testifying to the fact that they are not interested in the corresponding activities; of course,

they punish deviations from their secular ideologies and the principles of action derived therefrom. The number of types of action punishable in modern totalitarian societies and in typical medieval societies is perhaps not very much different.

Of course, this survey is very superficial. It proves, however, that the extreme positions along the four dimensions disussed above do not necessarily go together. In the survey, some of the theoretically possible combinations are conspicuous by their absence. No traditional society has been simultaneously despotic *and* liberal; no democratic society either; no dictatorial society has been legalistic. But this is not sufficient evidence in favor of the proposition that such combinations are impossible.

For further study of totalitarian society as of an historical type these conclusions may be drawn: (1) it is worth while analyzing it into elements; (2) it is desirable to establish, throughout history, the fluctuations of concrete societies along the types of organization and the continua corresponding to the three divisions of the functions of the state, applying, whenever possible, quantitative methods; (3) it is desirable to find out the conditions directing societies toward the choice of dictatorship and of extreme positions on each of the continua; (4) it is desirable to reach, by case study, the understanding of conditions favorable to the *simultaneous* movement of a society in the directions just stated. This is, perhaps, the most promising way to understand the compound which is totalitarian society (Definition 1), and eventually to control movements conducive to its emergence and expansion.

Plato as a Totalitarian Ideologist

KARL POPPER

Karl Popper is an Austrian-born philosopher who has spent the greater part of his academic career in England. His work has been mainly concerned with questions of methodology and epistemology, and he has made important contributions both to social science and to physical science with his highly influential study, *The Logic of Scientific Discovery*. One of Popper's main concerns has been to demonstrate both the fallacy and the danger of misunderstanding the nature of social science by assuming that its chief task is that of prediction or by allowing it to become a scientism which attempts to substitute for human responsibility. His attack on Plato, which constitutes a major section of *The Open Society and Its Enemies*, has been much criticized by many ardent defenders of Plato's thought. Professor Popper has, however brought an impressive degree of scholarship to his work and has supported his analysis of Plato with extensive historical documentation and full annotations which deepen and extend his arguments. Despite the controversial nature of his work, Popper's criticisms of Plato are most important, for they call attention to the role which pseudo-social science, transformed into prophecy, has played in totalitarian movements.

THE ANALYSIS of Plato's sociology makes it easy to present his political programme. His fundamental demands can be expressed in either of two formulæ, the first corresponding to his idealist theory of change and rest, the second to his naturalism. The idealist formula is: *Arrest all political change!* Change is evil, rest divine. All change can be arrested if the state is made an exact copy of its original, i.e. of the Form or Idea of the city. Should it be asked how this is practicable, we can reply with the naturalistic formula: *Back to nature!* Back to the original state of our forefathers, the primitive state founded in accordance with human nature, and therefore stable; back to the tribal patriarchy of the time before the Fall, to the natural class rule of the wise few over the ignorant many.

I believe that practically all the elements of Plato's political programme can be derived from these demands. They are, in turn, based upon his historicism; and they have to be combined with his sociological doctrines concerning the conditions for the stability of class rule. The principal elements I have in mind are:

(A) The strict division of the classes; i.e. the ruling class consisting of herdsmen and watch-dogs must be strictly separated from the human cattle.

(B) The identification of the fate of the state with that of the ruling class; the exclusive interest in this class, and in its unity; and subservient to this unity, the rigid rules for breeding and educating this class, and the strict supervision and collectivization of the interests of its members.

From these principal elements, others can be derived, for instance the following:

(C) The ruling class has a monopoly of things like military virtues and training, and of the right to carry arms and to receive education of any kind; but it is excluded from any participation in economic activi-

From Karl Popper, *The Open Society and Its Enemies*, 4th edition (Princeton, N.J., 1963), pp. 86–87, 89, 120–121, 122, 136–137, 155–156, 165–166, 168. Reprinted by permission of Princeton University Press; Routledge and Kegan Paul, Ltd.; and the author.

ties, and especially from earning money.

(*D*) There must be a censorship of all intellectual activities of the ruling class, and a continual propaganda aiming at moulding and unifying their minds. All innovation in education, legislation, and religion must be prevented or suppressed.

(*E*) The state must be self-sufficient. It must aim at economic autarchy; for otherwise the rulers would either be dependent upon traders, or become traders themselves. The first of these alternatives would undermine their power, the second their unity and the stability of the state.

This programme can, I think, be fairly described as totalitarian. And it is certainly founded upon a historicist sociology.

But is that all? Are there no other features of Plato's programme, elements which are neither totalitarian nor founded upon historicism? What about Plato's ardent desire for Goodness and Beauty, or his love of Wisdom and of Truth? What about his demand that the wise, the philosophers, should rule? What about his hopes of making the citizens of his state virtuous as well as happy? And what about his demand that the state should be founded upon Justice? Even writers who criticize Plato believe that his political doctrine, in spite of certain similarities, is clearly distinguished from modern totalitarianism by these aims of his, the happiness of the citizens, and the rule of justice. Crossman, for instance, whose critical attitude can be gauged from his remark that "Plato's philosophy is the most savage and most profound attack upon liberal ideas which history can show," seems still to believe that Plato's plan is "the building of a perfect state in which every citizen is really happy." Another example is Joad who discusses the similarities between Plato's programme and that of fascism at some length, but who asserts that there are fundamental differences, since in Plato's best state "the ordinary man . . . achieves such happiness as appertains to his nature," and since this state is built upon the ideas of "an absolute good and an absolute justice."

In spite of such arguments I believe that Plato's political programme, far from being morally superior to totalitarianism, is fundamentally identical with it. I believe that the objections against this view are based upon an ancient and deep-rooted prejudice in favour of idealizing Plato. . . .

What do we really mean when we speak of "Justice"? I do not think that verbal questions of this kind are particularly important, or that it is possible to make a definite answer to them, since such terms are always used in various senses. However, I think that most of us, especially those whose general outlook is humanitarian, mean something like this: (*a*) an equal distribution of the burden of citizenship, i.e. of those limitations of freedom which are necessary in social life; (*b*) equal treatment of the citizens before the law, provided, of course, that (*c*) the laws show neither favour nor disfavour towards individual citizens or groups or classes; (*d*) impartiality of the courts of justice; and (*e*) an equal share in the advantages (and not only in the burden) which membership of the state may offer to its citizens. If Plato had meant by "justice" anything of this kind, then my claim that his programme is purely totalitarian would certainly be wrong and all those would be right who believe that Plato's politics rested upon an acceptable humanitarian basis. But the fact is that he meant by "justice" something entirely different.

What did Plato mean by "justice"? I assert that in the *Republic* he used the term "just" as a synonym for "that which is in the interest of the best state." And what is in the interest of this best state? To arrest all change, by the maintenance of a rigid class division and class rule. If I am right in this interpretation, then we should have to say that Plato's demand for justice leaves his political programme at the level of totalitarianism; and we should have to conclude that we must guard against the danger of being impressed by mere words.

*   *   *

We have seen that Plato's idea of justice demands, fundamentally, that the natural rulers should rule and the natural slaves should slave. It is part of the historicist demand that the state, in order to arrest all change, should be a copy of its Idea, or of its true "nature." This theory of justice indicates very clearly that Plato saw the fundamental problem of politics in the question: *Who shall rule the state?*

It is my conviction that by expressing the problem of politics in the form "Who should rule?" or "Whose will should be supreme?," etc., Plato created a lasting confusion in political philosophy. It is indeed analogous to the confusion he created in the field of moral philosophy by his identification, discussed in the last chapter, of collectivism and altruism. It is clear that once the question "Who should rule?" is asked, it is hard to avoid some such reply as "the best" or "wisest" or "the born ruler" or "he who masters the art of ruling" (or, perhaps, "The General Will" or "The Master Race" or "The Industrial Workers" or "The People"). But such a reply, convincing as it may sound — for who would advocate the rule of "the worst" or "the greatest fool" or "the born slave"? — is, as I shall try to show, quite useless.

First of all, such a reply is liable to persuade us that some fundamental problem of political theory has been solved. But if we approach political theory from a different angle, then we find that far from solving any fundamental problems, we have merely skipped over them, by assuming that the question "Who should rule?" is fundamental. For even those who share this assumption of Plato's admit that political rulers are not always sufficiently "good" or "wise" (we need not worry about the precise meaning of these terms), and that it is not at all easy to get a government on whose goodness and wisdom one can implicitly rely. If that is granted, then we must ask whether political thought should not face from the beginning the possibility of bad government; whether we should not prepare for the worst leaders, and hope for the best. But this leads to a new approach to the problem of politics, for it forces us to replace the question: *Who should rule?* by the new question: *How can we so organize political institutions that bad or incompetent rulers can be prevented from doing too much damage?* . . .

My claim is that every theory of sovereignty omits to face a more fundamental question — the question, namely, whether we should not strive towards institutional control of the rulers by balancing their powers against other powers. This *theory of checks and balances* can at least claim careful consideration. The only objections to this claim, as far as I can see, are (*a*) that such a control is *practically* impossible, or (*b*) that it is *essentially* inconceivable since political power is essentially sovereign. Both of these dogmatic objections are, I believe, refuted by the facts; and with them fall a number of other influential views (for instance, the theory that the only alternative to the dictatorship of one class is that of another class).

*   *   *

It may be mentioned here that, in practice, Plato did not prove too successful as a selector of political leaders. I have in mind not so much the disappointing outcome of his experiment with Dionysius the Younger, tyrant of Syracuse, but rather the participation of Plato's Academy in Dio's successful expedition against Dionysius. Plato's famous friend Dio was supported in this adventure by a number of members of Plato's Academy. One of them was Callippus, who became Dio's most trusted comrade. After Dio had made himself tyrant of Syracuse he ordered Heraclides, his ally (and perhaps his rival), to be murdered. Shortly afterwards he was himself murdered by Callippus who usurped the tyranny, which he lost after thirteen months. (He was, in turn, murdered by the Pythagorean philosopher Leptines.) But this event was not the only one of its kind in Plato's career as a teacher. Clearchus, one of Plato's (and of Isocrates') disciples, made himself tyrant of Heraclea after having posed as a democratic leader. He was murdered by his relation, Chion, another member of Plato's Academy. (We cannot know how Chion, whom some represent as an idealist, would have developed, since he was soon killed.) These and a few similar experiences of Plato's — who could boast a total of at least nine tyrants among his one-time pupils and associates — throw light on the peculiar difficulties connected with the selection of men who are to be invested with absolute power. It is hard to find a man whose character will not be corrupted by it. As Lord Acton says — all power corrupts, and absolute power corrupts absolutely.

To sum up. Plato's political programme was much more institutional than personalist; he hoped to arrest political change by the institutional control of succession in leadership. The control was to be educational, based upon an authoritarian view of learning — upon the authority of the learned expert, and "the man of proven probity." This is what Plato made of Socrates' demand that a responsible politician should be a lover of truth and of wisdom rather than an expert, and that he was wise only if he knew his limitations.

*   *   *

I think we must face the fact that behind the sovereignty of the philosopher king stands the quest for power. The beautiful portrait of the sovereign is a self-portrait. When we have recovered from the shock of this finding, we may look anew at the awe-inspiring portrait; and if we can fortify ourselves with a small dose of Socrates' irony then we may cease to find it so terrifying. We may begin to discern its human, indeed, its only too human features. We may even begin to feel a little sorry for Plato, who had to be satisfied with establishing the first professorship, instead of the first kingship, of philosophy; who could never realize his dream, the kingly Idea which he had formed after his own image.

Fortified by our dose of irony, we may even find, in Plato's story, a melancholy resemblance to that innocent and unconscious little satire on Platonism, the story of the *Ugly Dachshund*, of Tono, the Great Dane, who forms his kingly Idea of "Great Dog" after his own image (but who happily finds in the end that he is Great Dog himself).

What a monument of human smallness is this idea of the philosopher king. What a contrast between it and the simplicity and humaneness of Socrates, who warned the statesman against the danger of being dazzled by his own power, excellence, and wisdom, and who tried to teach him what matters most — that we are all frail human beings. What a decline from this world of irony and reason and truthfulness down to Plato's kingdom of the sage whose magical powers raise him high above ordinary men; although not quite high enough to forgo the use of lies, or to neglect the sorry trade of every shaman — the selling of spells, of breeding spells, in exchange for power over his fellow-men.

*   *   *

It is interesting to observe the close relationship between Plato's utter radicalism, the demand for sweeping measures, and his æstheticism. The following passages are most characteristic. Plato, speaking about "the philosopher who has communion with the divine," mentions first that he will be "overwhelmed by the urge . . . to realize his heavenly vision in individuals as well as in the city," — a city which "will never know happiness unless its draughtsmen are artists who have the divine as their model." Asked about the details of their draughtsmanship, Plato's "Socrates" gives the following striking reply: "They will take as their canvas a city and the characters of men, and they will, first of all, *make their canvas clean* — by no means an easy matter. But this is just the point, you know, where they will differ from all others. They will not start work on a city nor on an individual (nor will they draw up laws) unless they are given a clean canvas, or have cleaned it themselves."

The kind of thing Plato has in mind when he speaks of canvas-cleaning is explained a little later. "How can that be done?" asks Glaucon. "All citizens above the age of ten," Socrates answers, "must be expelled from the city and deported somewhere into the country; and the children who are now free from the influence of the manners and habits of their parents must be taken over. They must be educated in the ways [of true philosophy], and according to the laws, which we have described." (The philosophers are not, of course, among the citizens to be expelled: they remain as educators, and so do, presumably, those non-citizens who must keep them going.) In the same spirit, Plato says in the *Statesman* of the royal rulers who rule in accordance with the Royal Science of Statesmanship: "Whether they happen to rule by law or without law, over willing or unwilling subjects; . . . and whether they purge the state for its good, by killing or by deporting [or "banishing"] some of its citizens . . . — so long as they proceed according to science and justice, and preserve . . . the state and make it better

than it was, this form of government must be declared the only one that is right."

This is the way in which the artist-politician must proceed. This is what canvas-cleaning means. He must eradicate the existing institutions and traditions. He must purify, purge, expel, banish, and kill. ("Liquidate" is the terrible modern term for it.) Plato's statement is indeed a true description of the uncompromising attitude of all forms of out-and-out radicalism — of the æstheticist's refusal to compromise. The view that society should be beautiful like a work of art leads only too easily to violent measures. But all this radicalism and violence is both unrealistic and futile. . . .

Aestheticism and radicalism must lead us to jettison reason, and to replace it by a desperate hope for political miracles. This irrational attitude which springs from an intoxication with dreams of a beautiful world is what I call Romanticism. It may seek its heavenly city in the past or in the future; it may preach "back to nature" or "forward to a world of love and beauty"; but its appeal is always to our emotions rather than to reason. Even with the best intentions of making heaven on earth it only succeeds in making it a hell — that hell which man alone prepares for his fellow-men.

Oriental Despotism

KARL A. WITTFOGEL

Karl Wittfogel was born in Germany in 1896 and was educated at several leading German universities at a time when the prestige of German sociology and historiography was at its height. He served for a time as a research associate at the famous *Institut für Sozialforschung*, a distinction shared by several other authors in this volume. Now living in the United States, Professor Wittfogel has taught at Columbia University and at the University of Washington, which has established a world-wide reputation in the field of Asian studies. Wittfogel's original interest in oriental studies was significantly motivated by the work of the great German sociologist and historian, Max Weber, who pioneered in the study of oriental society and religion.

Wittfogel's views on totalitarianism arise from a conviction that developments in twentieth century Russia are not to be explained merely by referring to the logic of Marxism, but rather, are largely attributable to Asiatic influences. His discussion of various oriental despotisms introduces a new element, for these despotisms arose in what Wittfogel identifies as "Hydraulic Societies" — political systems dependent on the maintenance of large-scale irrigation for their survival. Thus totalitarianism might be seen as arising, at least to a large extent, from the demands which an advancing technology imposes on a society.

THE DESPOTIC CHARACTER of hydraulic government is not seriously contested. The term "Oriental despotism," which is generally used for the Old World variants of this phenomenon, connotes an extremely harsh form of absolutist power.

But those who admit the ruthlessness of Oriental despotism often insist that regimes of this type were limited by institutional and moral checks which made them bearable and at times even benevolent. How bearable and how benevolent was hydraulic despotism? Obviously this question can be answered only by a comparative and reasoned examination of the pertinent facts.

The existence of constitutional regulations does not necessarily involve the existence of a constitutionally restricted government. All governments that persist over time — and many others as well — have a certain pattern (constitution). This pattern may be expressed in written form.

Under advanced cultural conditions, this is usually done, and at times in an orderly collection, a code.

The development of a written constitution is by no means identical with the development of a "constitutionally" restricted government. Just as a law may be imposed by the government (*lex data*) or agreed upon both by governmental authority and independent nongovernmental forces (*lex rogata*), so a constitution may also be imposed or agreed upon. The term *constitutiones* originally referred to edicts, rescripts, and mandates that were one-sidedly and autocratically issued by the Roman emperors.

Even a highly systematized law code does not bind the autocratic lawgivers by restrictions other than those inherent in all self-imposed norms. The ruler who exercises complete administrative, managerial, judicial, military, and fiscal authority may use his power to make whatever laws he and

From Karl A. Wittfogel, *Oriental Despotism: A Comparative Study of Total Power* (New Haven, 1957), pp. 101–108, 137–139, 141–143, 154–156. Reprinted by permission of Yale University Press.

his aides deem fit. Expediency and inertia favor the perpetuation of most of these laws, but the absolutist regime is free to alter its norms at any time; and the history of hydraulic civilizations testifies to the periodic promulgation of new laws and new codes. The "Collected Regulations" (*hui yao*) of imperial China, the Law Books (*dharma shāstra*) of India, and the administrative and judicial writings of the Byzantine and Islamic East are all cases in point.

Having been imposed one-sidedly, constitutional regulations are also changed one-sidedly. In China "all legislative, executive and judicial powers belonged to him [the emperor]." In Hindu India "constitutionally the king was in a position to accept or repudiate the laws accepted by his predecessor." In Byzantium "there was no organ in the state that had a right to control him [the emperor]." Or, more specifically: "For his legislative and administrative acts, the monarch was responsible to none, except to Heaven."

In Islamic society the caliph, like all other believers, was expected to submit to the Sacred Law, and generally he was quite ready to uphold it as part of the dominant religious order. But he asserted his power whenever he thought it desirable by establishing (administrative) secular courts and by directing them through special decrees (*qānūn* or *siyāsa*). And the religious judges, the *kadis*, were eager to support a government that appointed and deposed them at will. Thus the theoretical absence of a legislature modified the appearance but not the substance of Islamic absolutism. "The Caliphate . . . was a despotism which placed unrestricted power in the hands of the ruler."

In these and other comparable instances the regime represents a definite structural and operational pattern, a "constitution." But this pattern is not agreed upon. It is given from above, and the rulers of hydraulic society create, maintain, and modify it, not as the controlled agents of society but as its masters.

Of course, the absence of formal constitutional checks does not necessarily imply the absence of societal forces whose interests and intentions the government must respect. In most countries of postfeudal Europe the absolutist regimes were restricted not so much by official constitutions as by the actual strength of the landed nobility, the Church, and the towns. In absolutist Europe all these nongovernmental forces were politically organized and articulate. They thus differed profoundly from the representatives of landed property, religion, or urban professions in hydraulic society.

Some of these groups were poorly developed in the Orient, and none of them congealed into political bodies capable of restricting the hydraulic regime. The Indian scholar, K. V. Rangaswami, correctly describes the situation when, in his discussion of Hindu absolutism, he defines genuine absolutism as "a form of government in which all the powers *must* be vested in the hands of the Ruler, there being *no other concurrent and independent authority*, habitually obeyed by the people as much as he is obeyed, and which lawfully resist him or call him to account."

The lack of lawful means for resisting the government is indeed a significant feature of despotism. When such means are not available, discontented and desperate men have time and again taken up arms against their government, and under extreme conditions they have succeeded in overthrowing it altogether. Subsequently the new rulers justified their procedure by juxtaposing the worthiness of their cause to the unworthiness of the former regime; and the historians and philosophers have in the same manner explained periodic dynastic changes. It is from events and ideas of this kind that the so-called right of rebellion has been derived.

The term "right of rebellion" is unfortunate in that it confuses a legal and a moral issue. The official discussions on the rise and fall of dynastic power were presented as warnings against rebellious action rather than as guides for it; and they were certainly not incorporated into any official constitutional regulations or laws. The right of rebellion could be exercised only when the existing laws were violated and at the risk of total destruction for whoever asserted it.

Traces of the so-called right of rebellion can be found in virtually all hydraulic societies. Pueblo folklore proudly relates successful action against unworthy *caciques* [tribal chiefs], and revolutions in Bali have been so justified. Hindu and Muslim rulers have been similarly warned — and similarly challenged. The fact that in China the right of rebellion was formulated in the Confucian classics did as little to check total power as does the presence in the USSR of Marx' and Lenin's writings, which postulate revolutionary action against oppression.

Nor does the regime become less despotic because the ruler attains his position through election rather than through inheritance. The transfer of title and authority to a close relative of the deceased sovereign, preferably to the oldest son, favors political stability, while election favors gifted leadership. The first principle prevails among the indigenous rulers of hydraulic societies, the second among pastoral or other peoples who, as conquerors of such societies, frequently perpetuated their original patterns of succession.

The Byzantine custom of determining the emperor through election goes back to republican Rome. It suited the conditions of the early empire, which, being largely controlled by military officials, chose its sovereigns more often through "the army" than through the top-ranking body of civil officials. When, from Diocletian on, the Senate took a more prominent part in the election of the emperor, the political center of gravity shifted from the military to the civil branch of the officialdom. Election was not the best method by which to establish a new emperor, but wrapped in the cloak of tradition and legitimacy it proved definitely compatible with the requirements of bu-

reaucratic absolutism. And the frequent changes in the person of the supreme leader deprived neither his position nor the bureaucratic hierarchy, which he headed, of its despotic character.

In ancient Mexico and in most Chinese dynasties of conquest the new ruler was elected from members of the ruling kin group. The procedure combined the principle of inheritance with the principle of limited choice; and, as in the case of Byzantium, those who made the choice were top-ranking members of the political hierarchy. This arrangement increased the political opportunities among the masters of the apparatus, but it did not increase the authority of the nongovernmental forces of society.

Two nonhydraulic parallels may aid in dispelling the misconception that despotic power is democratized by an elective system of succession. The regime of Chingis Khan, which was perpetuated through limited election, remains one of the most terrifying examples of total power. And the transfer of leadership from one member of the Bolshevik Politburo to another makes the Soviet government temporarily less stable but certainly not more democratic.

Mommsen called the state of Eastern Rome "an autocracy tempered by a revolution which is legally recognized as permanent." Bury translates Mommsen's unwieldy formulation as "an autocracy tempered by the legal right of revolution." Both phrasings are problematic because they imply that the subjects were legally entitled to replace one emperor by another. Actually no such right existed. Diehl recognizes this by speaking of "an autocracy tempered by revolution and assassination"; and Bury admits that "there was no formal process of deposing a sovran." But he adds, "the members of the community had the means of dethroning him, if the government failed to give satisfaction, by proclaiming a new emperor."

This was indeed the pattern established by the military officials of Eastern Rome; and congruent with it, usurpation was considered legitimate if and when it was successful. That is, rebellion becomes legal — *post festum* [after the event]. Says Bury: "If he [the pretender] had not a sufficient following to render the proclamation effective and was suppressed, *he was treated as a rebel*."

Thus, in Byzantium as in other states of the hydraulic world, anyone might try to usurp power; and the elective nature of sovereignty combined with the temporary dominance of military leadership inspired frequent attempts of this kind. But no law protected such actions while they were being undertaken. In Byzantium persons attacking the existing government were punished with barbarous brutality. In China persons caught while trying to exercise the right of rebellion were executed. Under the last three dynasties they were cut to pieces.

If armed conflict, rebellion, and the assassination of weak rulers do not make Oriental despotism more democratic, do they not at least give the populace some relief from oppression? The argument has less validity than may appear at first glance. Such diversions rarely reduce in any decisive way the traditional administrative and judicial pressures; and the inclination to assert supreme leadership through open violence is more than likely to intensify the tendency to brutality among those in power. Furthermore, the devastations of any major civil war generally lay increased economic burdens on the commoners. The frequent occurrence of violence within the ruling circles, far from tempering despotism, tends to make it more oppressive.

But are there perhaps forces inside the government that mitigate the ruthlessness of agromanagerial despotism? This question focuses attention on the relation between absolutism and autocracy. Absolutism and autocracy are not identical, but they interlock closely. A government is absolutist when its rule is not effectively checked by nongovernmental forces. The ruler of an absolutist regime is an autocrat when his decisions are not effectively checked by intragovernmental forces.

The absolutist regimes of hydraulic society are usually headed by a single individual in whose person is concentrated all the power over major decisions. Why is this so? Do the great water works, which characterize the core areas of the hydraulic world and which indeed require centralized direction, necessitate autocratic leadership? After all, controlled (democratic or aristocratic) governments also initiate and maintain huge public enterprises. They muster large and disciplined armies and/or fleets; and they operate thus, for substantial periods of time, without developing autocratic patterns of rulership.

Manifestly, the rise of autocratic power depends on more than the existence of large state enterprises. In all hydraulic societies proper such enterprises play a considerable role; and there, as well as in the institutional margin, we always find disciplined armies and almost always, also, comprehensive organizations of communication and intelligence. But there is no technical reason why these various enterprises could not be headed by several leading officials. This is indeed the case in controlled governments, whose department chiefs are carefully separated from, and balanced against, one another.

However, despotic states lack appropriate mechanics of outside control and internal balance. And under such conditions there develops what may be called a *cumulative tendency of unchecked power*. This tendency could be countered if all major subsections of authority were more or less equally powerful. It could be countered if the chiefs of the public works, of the army, of the intelligence service, and of the revenue system were more or less equally strong in terms of organizational, communicational, and coercive power. In such a case, the absolutist regime might be headed by a balanced oligarchy, a "politburo," whose members would actually, and more or less equally, participate in the exercise of supreme authority. However, the organizational, communicational, and coercive power of the major sectors of any government is rarely, if ever, so balanced; and under absolutist conditions the holder of the strongest position, benefiting from the cumulative tendency of unchecked power, tends to expand his authority through alliances, maneuvers, and ruthless schemes until, having conquered all other centers of supreme decision, he alone prevails.

The point at which the growth of government functions precludes effective outside control differs in different institutional configurations. But it may safely be said that whenever this critical point is passed, the cumulative strength of superior power tends to result in a single autocratic center of organization and decision making.

The crucial importance of this center is not negated by the fact that the supreme power-holder may delegate the handling of his affairs to a top-ranking assistant, a vizier, chancellor, or prime minister. Nor is it negated by the fact that he and/or his aide may lean heavily for advice and speedy action on selected groups of strategically placed and carefully tested officials. The governmental apparatus as a whole does not cease to be absolutist because the actual center of decision making temporarily, and often in a veiled manner, shifts to persons or groups below the ruler.

The sovereign of an agrobureaucratic state may be completely under the influence of his courtiers or administrators; but such influence differs qualitatively from the institutional checks of balanced power. In the long run the head of a controlled government must adjust to the effective nongovernmental forces of society, while the head of an absolutist regime is not similarly restricted. Simple self-interest urges any intelligent despot to listen to experienced persons. Councillors have existed in most agromanagerial civilizations, and not infrequently councils were a standard feature of government. But the ruler was under no compulsion to accept their suggestions.

Whether the sovereign was his own chief executive, whether he delegated many of his functions to a vizier, or whether he or his vizier largely followed the advice of official and nonofficial advisors depended, in addition to custom and circumstance, on the personalities of the ruler and his aides. But despite significant bureaucratic attempts to subordinate the absolutist sovereign to the control of his officialdom, the ruler could always *rule,* if he was determined to do so. The great monarchs of the Oriental world were almost without exception "self-rulers" — autocrats.

Serious observers do not generally contest these facts. However, not a few among them seek to minimize their significance by reference to mores and beliefs, which are assumed to restrict even the most tyrannical regime.

Mores and beliefs do indeed play a role; and so, for that matter, do the laws of nature. However, the potential victims of despotic power seem to find little consolation in either fact. They know that their masters' behavior, like their own, is affected by the laws of nature and by more or less firmly established cultural circumstances. But they know also that, nevertheless and in the last analysis, their fate will be determined by the will of those who wield total power.

The mechanics of administration and coercion depend on man's insight into the laws of nature and his ability to use them. A despotic regime will proceed in one way in the neolithic period, in another in the iron age, and in still another in our own time. But in each case the ruling group asserts its total superiority under the then actual natural conditions and by means of the then available technology. The victim of a crude form of despotism does not consider his persecutors less powerful because, under more advanced technical conditions, they may catch and destroy him by different methods or with greater speed.

Nor does he doubt their absolute superiority because they act in conformity with prevailing cultural patterns. Such patterns always shape the manner in which the ruler (and his subjects) act; and occasionally they mitigate or prolong governmental procedures at particular stages. But they do not prevent the government from ultimately achieving its goal. The fact that in many countries persons under sentence of death are normally not executed in certain seasons or on certain days does not mean that they escape their doom. And the fact that a dominant religion praises acts of mercy does not mean that it refrains from invoking measures of extreme harshness.

The potential victim of despotic persecution knows full well that the natural and cultural settings, whatever temporary respites they may provide, do not prevent his final destruction. The despotic ruler's power over his subjects is no less total because it is limited by factors that mold human life in every type of society.

    *   *   *

Man is no ant. His efforts to escape from freedom show him ambivalently attracted by what he ambivalently abandons. The urge to act independently is an essential attribute of *homo sapiens,* and a highly complex one. Not all of its components are socially valuable; but among them is man's most precious motivating force: the urge to obey his conscience, all external disadvantages notwithstanding.

What happens to man's desire for autonomy under the conditions of total power? One variant of total power, hydraulic despotism, tolerates no relevant political forces besides itself. In this respect it succeeds on the institutional level because it blocks the development of such forces; and it succeeds on the psychological level, because it discourages man's desire for independent political action. In the last analysis, hydraulic government is government by intimidation.

Man is no ant. But neither is he a stone. A policy that upholds the rulers' publicity optimum confuses the people's mind, without however eliminating their feelings of frustration and unhappiness. Unchecked, these feelings may lead to rebellious action. To counter this dangerous trend the hydraulic regime resorts to intimidation.

Terror is the inevitable consequence of the rulers' resolve to uphold their own and not the people's rationality optimum.

Many spokesmen of hydraulic despotism have emphasized the need for rule by punishment. Such a policy may be justified by the argument that guiltless people are few. Confucius preferred education to punishment; yet he, too, believed that it would take a hundred years of good government "to transform the violently bad and to dispense with capital punishment."

Thus with varying arguments, punishment has been viewed as an essential tool of successful statecraft. The Hindu law book of Manu establishes fear-inspiring punishment as the foundation of internal peace and order. Punishment, which — of course — must be just, makes everyone behave properly. Without it caste barriers would be crossed; and all men would turn against their fellows. "Where Punishment with a black hue and red eye stalks about," subjects live at peace. *"The whole world is kept in order by punishment."*

By punishment the ruler protects the weak against the strong, sacrifice against animal violation, property against its (nongovernmental) enemies and social superiority against assaults from below. "If the king did not, without tiring, inflict punishment on those worthy to be punished, the stronger would roast the weaker, like fish on a spit: The crow would eat the sacrificial cake and the dog would lick the sacrificial viands, and ownership would not remain with any one, the lower ones would (usurp the place of) the higher ones." Thus "punishment alone governs all created beings, punishment alone protects them, punishment watches over them while they sleep." Indeed, "punishment is . . . the king."

The rulers of ancient Mesopotamia claimed that they received their power from the great Enlil. This terrifying god symbolizes "the power of force, of compulsion. Opposing wills are crushed and beaten into submission." Although he is supposed to use his cruel might judiciously, "man can never be fully at ease with Enlil but feels a lurking fear." This being so, the sovereign's readiness to identify himself with Enlil or with deities descended from him is deeply significant. The Sumerian kings usually identified themselves with Enlil directly. The Babylonians upheld the basic idea, but modified it. Hammurabi pictured himself as having been "called" by Enlil; and he names Enlil's son, Sin, as his divine father. In both cases the Mesopotamian rulers stressed the terroristic quality of their position.

The terror inherent in Pharaonic despotism is symbolized by the poisonous Uraeus snake, which lies coiled on the ruler's forehead and threatens his enemies with destruction. The king's actions are also compared with those of the fear-inspiring lion goddess, Sekhmet.

Chinese statecraft learned to express its need for terifying punishment in the rational and moral form of Confucianism. But punishment was the primary weapon of the so-called Legalists and of such Legalist-influenced Confucianists as Hsün Tsŭ. And it remained a cornerstone of official policy throughout the imperial period. What we would call the Ministry of Justice was known in traditional China as the Ministry of Punishments.

The Islamic ruler saw to it that he was both respected and feared. The *Arabian Nights,* which depicts Harun al-Rashīd usually accompanied by his executioner, presents in fictional dress a historic truth. The executioner was a standard feature of the Abbassid court. . . .

Like the tiger, the engineer of power must have the physical means with which to crush his victims. And the agromanagerial despot does indeed possess such means. He exercises unchecked control over the army, the police, the intelligence service; and he has at his disposal jailers, torturers, executioners, and all the tools that are necessary to catch, incapacitate, and destroy a suspect.

Furthermore, he can employ these devices with maximum psychological effect.

Everywhere persons wielding great governmental or proprietary power like to shroud certain of their acts in secrecy; but the procedures of a despotic government are enigmatic because of the very nature of the regime. Accountable only to themselves, the men of the apparatus tend to handle even insignificant matters with secretiveness; and they raise mystification to an art when they want to intimidate and surprise. Unpredictability is an essential weapon of absolute terror. . . .

A chief or ruler does not necessarily override the laws of his hydraulic community when he himself commits — or gives orders to commit — acts of terrifying brutality.

In smaller hydraulic tribes autocratic cruelty is no issue, because the chief, being close to his fellow tribesmen, is unable to exert power over and above his directing functions. This is the case among the Suk and their hydraulic neighbors and throughout the American Pueblos.

In larger hydraulic tribes the chief may seek to bolster his incipient autocracy by the employment of spectacular terror. A Chagga chief, for instance, may commit all manner of cruelties against his subjects. Ndeserno is said to have torn the hearts from his victims' bodies while they were still alive and to have had them roasted for his children. A chieftain who went to such extremes was contemplated with grave apprehension, but, according to Gutmann, "such cruelties against individuals did not harm his prestige." On the contrary, the fear they inspired cemented the stability of the regime.

The spectacular terror directed by the rulers of ancient Hawaii may well have served the same purpose; and the so-called Cannibal Texts of the Old Kingdom suggest a similar situation in prehistoric Egypt. One of these texts, found in a pyramid, reveals a dead ruler killing, dissecting, and cooking human beings in the nether world for his gustatory pleasure; and another reveals him as taking "the wives from their husbands whenever he wants to and according to his heart's desire."

In more differentiated hydraulic civilizations, there is less need to bulwark the ruler's exalted position by spectacular acts of autocratic ruthlessness. Although such acts do not completely cease, they are now initiated mainly by excessively cruel (and/or insecure) sovereigns and by the heads of dynasties which operate below the rulers' rationality maximum. Gaudefroy-Demombynes describes the irrationally terroristic quality of the Abbassid caliphate as follows: "Improvised executions and the exhibition of heads are part of the regular life of the Abbassid court. Beginning with the reign of El Mançour, when a person is urgently summoned to the palace by the guards of the caliph, he feels that he has a good chance not to return alive. He makes his testament, says farewell to his family, and carries his shroud under his arm."

In these and other instances, the ruler's terroristic behavior was above rather than against the law. On the other hand, officials who resorted to extreme brutalities often went beyond even the broadest possible interpretation of the law. At times they might be held accountable. But many "lawless" bureaucratic terrorists were criticized only after they were dead.

The excesses of autocratic and bureaucratic terror are an extreme manifestation of human behavior under total power. Institutionally, however, they are probably less important than the innumerable acts of terror that were perpetrated as a matter of routine and within the flexible frame of despotic law. It was this routine terror in managerial, fiscal, and judicial procedures that caused certain observers to designate the government of hydraulic despotism as "government by flogging."

*   *   *

Demonstrative and total submission is the only prudent response to total power. Manifestly, such behavior does not gain a superior's respect; but other ways of proceeding invite disaster. Where power is polarized, as it is in hydraulic society, human relations are equally polarized. Those who have no control over their government quite reasonably fear that they will be crushed in any conflict with its masters.

And the formidable might of the state apparatus can destroy not merely objectionable nongovernmental forces — with equal thoroughness it may also overwhelm individual members of the ruling group, the ruler himself included. Many anxieties darken the path of life; but perhaps none is as devastating as the insecurity created by polarized total power.

The ruler, being most illustrious, is also most to be envied. Among those near him, there are always some who long to replace him. And since constitutional and peaceful change is out of the question, replacement usually means one thing and one thing only: physical annihilation. The wise ruler therefore trusts no one.

For obvious reasons the innermost thoughts of despots have been little publicized. But observable behavior and utterances confirm our assumption. Egyptian papyri preserve what is said to be a Pharaoh's advice to his son. The message reads: "Hold thyself apart from those subordinate to (thee), lest that should happen to whose terrors no attention has been given. Approach them not in thy loneliness. Fill not thy heart with a brother, nor know a friend. . . . (EVEN) WHEN THOU SLEEPEST, GUARD THY HEART THYSELF, because no man has adherents on the day of distress."

The *Arthashāstra* [an Indian work on political theory of the 4th century B.C.] specifies the dangers which surround the ruler, and it discusses the many means by which they can be averted. His residence must be made safe. Measures must be taken against poisoning. All members of his entourage must be watched and controlled. The king must spy on his prime minister. He must beware of his close friends, of his wives, of his brothers, and most particularly of his heir apparent. According to an authority frequently quoted in the classic of Indian despotism, "Princes, like crabs, have a notorious tendency of eating up their begetter." To prevent this from happening, the manual lists numerous ways by which a ruler can protect himself against his son.

Nor does the official live securely. "Self-protection shall be the first and constant thought of a wise man; for the life of a man under the service of a king is aptly compared to life in fire; whereas fire burns a part or the whole of the body, if at all, the king has the power either to destroy or to advance the whole family."

A Persian variant stresses particularly the danger that lurks behind seeming bureaucratic safety and success: Should [the ruler] at any time pretend to you that you are completely secure with him, begin from that moment to feel insecure; if you are being fattened by someone, you may expect very quickly to be slaughtered by him."

And the need for eternal suspicion is by no means confined to those occupying the top of the bureaucratic pyramid. In traditional China, as in other hydraulic civilizations, "high officials cannot but be jealous of those below them, for it is from that quarter that their rivals are to be dreaded. The lower officials, on the other hand, are not less suspicious of those above them, for it is from that quarter that their removal may be at any moment effected."

The commoner is confronted with problems of a very different kind. He is not worried by the pitfalls inherent in autocratic or bureaucratic power, but by the threat which this power presents to all subjects. A regime that proceeds unchecked in the fields of taxation, corvé, and jurisprudence is capable of involving the commoners in endless predicaments. And caution teaches them to avoid any unnecessary contacts with their government.

Smith ascribes the mutual distrust that, according to him, prevails in traditional China to the people's fear of getting involved. In the *Arabian Nights*, a corpse is shoved from door to door, because each house owner is convinced that the authorities will hold him responsible for the death of the unknown man. The frequently observed reluctance to help a drowning stranger is caused by similar reasoning: If I fail to rescue the poor devil, how shall I prove to the authorities that I did not plan his submersion?

Those who walk away when they can be of help are neither different from nor worse than other human beings. But their behavior makes it clear that voluntary participation in public matters, which is encouraged in an open society, is extremely risky under conditions of total power. The fear of getting involved with an uncontrollable and unpredictable government confines the prudent subject to the narrow realm of his personal and professional affairs. This fear separates him effectively from other members of the wider community to which he also belongs.

Is Totalitarianism a Meaningful Concept?

STANISLAV ANDRESKI

Stanislav Andreski is a noted British sociologist who has recently published an important study on *The Uses of Comparative Sociology*. In the article which follows, which is reprinted in full, Andreski expresses serious methodological reservations concerning the concept of totalitarianism. It is to be noted, however, that Andreski himself uses the term in a manner quite similar to the position taken by Timasheff.

Andreski's article first appeared in the *Dictionary of the Social Sciences*. This work, prepared by a group of British and American scholars under the auspices of the United Nations' Educational, Scientific, and Cultural Organization (UNESCO), attempts to provide clear definitions of a great number of concepts of central importance to the various social sciences. The individual articles in the *Dictionary* are notable not only for their clarity, but also for showing how the meanings of various terms and concepts have evolved historically.

TOTALITARIANISM is the extension of permanent governmental control over the totality of social life. A movement or an ideology may be called totalitarian if it advocates such an extension. Totalitarianism in this sense is, of course, an ideal type to which concrete cases can only approximate, since no government can control every instance of social interaction. The qualification "permanent" is important because it excludes a large number of cases, such as various sultanates and primitive kingdoms, where sporadic interference with all aspects of life of the subjects was common, but where there was little of systematic regulation.

In *Wörterbuch der Soziologie* (ed. by W. Bernsdorf & F. Bülow, Stuttgart: F. Enke Verlag, 1955, p. 551) O. Stammer says: "we can speak of totalitarianism only where a centralistically oriented mass movement, led by a political minority in an authoritarian manner, relying on the monopoly of power, and with the aid of a dictatorially ruled state, builds an apparatus of power which bears upon all parts of the society." Z. Brzezinski (*The Permanent Purge: Politics in Soviet Totalitarianism*, Cambridge, Mass.: Harvard University Press, 1956, p. 7) writes: "Totalitarianism can, therefore, be defined as a system where technologically advanced instruments of political power are wielded without restraint by centralized leadership of an elite movement, for the purpose of effecting a total social revolution, on the basis of certain arbitrary ideological assumptions proclaimed by the leadership, in an atmosphere of coerced unanimity of the entire population." These definitions, which are fairly typical, raise a general methodological issue.

A scientific term can be useful only if it is sufficiently general to be applied to a number of cases: there is hardly much to be gained by having a term so highly specified that it merely replaces one or two proper names. Stammer's definition fits only Hitler's regime in Germany: the Bolsheviks were never a mass movement, and neither they nor the Chinese communists received help from a "dictatorially ruled state" in building up their apparatus of power. Brzezinki's definition fits only Soviet Russia be-

Reprinted with permission of The Free Press from *A Dictionary of the Social Sciences* edited by William L. Kolb and Julius Gould, pp. 719–720. Copyright 1964 by the United Nations Educational, Scientific and Cultural Organization. Reprinted also by permission of Tavistock Publications, London.

fore 1935: the efforts of the Soviet rulers of today are aimed rather at preventing than at effecting a revolution, and the party could hardly be called "a movement" nowadays; the Chinese communists turned from a mass movement into an elite, but were never "an elite movement"; Hitler never attempted to carry out a total social revolution. Many other definitions of totalitarianism could be likewise accused of unprofitable restrictiveness. Secondly, scientific thought proceeds by decomposing complex individual entities into simpler units (material or conceptual), among whose mutual relations some uniformity might be detected: our concepts should enable us to analyse concrete cases — not merely to name them.

The definition proposed in . . . [the first paragraph] above leaves entirely open the question of antecedents, determinants, consequences and correlates of totalitarianism, though it does imply the absence of any independent centres of power. In fact, a very high degree of totalitarianism can go together with very primitive technology (e.g. the Inca empire or Egypt under the Ptolemies). The late Roman Empire as well as Tokugawa Japan were both highly totalitarian without the aid of any revolutionary ideas. Calvin's Geneva provided an example of theocratic totalitarianism. Whereas effective control over the totality of social life must produce outward unanimity, the reverse is not true: in Spain under the Inquisition there was forced unanimity without totalitarianism. Moreover, there are reasons for thinking that totalitarianism is compatible with considerable variations in the distribution of power within the governmental apparatus, and in the methods of governing.

II. CHARACTERISTICS OF TOTALITARIAN RULE

The Institutionalization of Anxiety

FRANZ NEUMANN

The selection which follows is taken from the work of Franz Neumann and was intended as part of a comprehensive work on dictatorship which remained unfinished because of the author's premature death at the age of fifty-five. Neumann, a native German and a respected expert in the field of labor law, served for some time as legal adviser to the German Social Democratic Party. Arrested in 1933 when the Nazis came to power, he managed to escape and emigrated to the United States where he followed an academic career and also served for a time with the United States' State Department as an adviser on Germany. His *Behemoth* still remains one of the most successful studies of National Socialism, although as Neumann himself later realized it placed too much stress on the economic factors in the rise of Nazism. As a humanist and devoted democrat Neumann, like many others, was shaken by the political developments of the twentieth century and spent the later years of his life grappling with the problems which dictatorship has posed for modern society.

IN HIS LETTERS "Ueber die aesthetische Erziehung des Menschen," ["Concerning the Aesthetic Education of Man"] Schiller has magnificently described man in modern society. "Man portrays himself," he writes, "and what a form is presented in the drama of the modern age? Barrenness here, license there; the two extremes of human decay, and both united in a single period." As Rousseau did before him, Schiller indicts civilization itself: "It was culture itself which inflicted this wound on modern humanity." And this wound was inflicted on man by the division of labor: "Gratification is separated from labor, means from ends, effort from reward. Eternally *fettered* only to a single little fragment of the whole, man fashions himself only as a fragment. . . ."

What Schiller describes so impressively is what Hegel and Marx were to characterize as alienation. Schiller contrasts the "polypus nature" of the Greek states, "where each individual enjoyed an independent existence and, if necessary, could become a whole," with modern society which is one of hierarchical division of labor. Modern society produces a fragmentation not only of social functions but of man himself who, as it were, keeps his different faculties in different pigeonholes — love, labor, leisure, culture — that are somehow held together by an externally operating mechanism that is neither comprehended nor comprehensible. One may — as I do — consider Schiller's (as also Hegel's) analysis of the Greek state as strongly unrealistic and one may, perhaps, even see certain dangers in the glorification of Greece; nevertheless his analysis of modern man, pointing far beyond his age, remains valid and it is perhaps only today that we have become fully conscious of how true Schiller's Letters are.

In his *Theologische Jugendschriften* [*Theological Books for the Young*] Hegel developed for the first time the concept of alienation. In his draft, entitled "Love," he defined love as the "whole," as "a feeling, but not a single feeling." "In it, life finds itself, as a duplication of its self, and as its unity." But this love is frequently shattered by the resistance of the outside world, the social world of property, a world indeed which man has created through his own labor and knowledge but which has become an alien, a dead world through property. Man is alienated from himself. Since we are here not concerned with the Hegelian concept of alienation, we may pass over the development of his concept.

It is equally unnecessary for us here to develop fully Marx's concept of alienation. For Marx it is the commodity that determines human activity, that is, the objects which are supposed to serve man become the tyrant of man. For according to Marx, who thus fully agrees with Schiller, Hegel, and Feuerbach, man is a universal being. Man is free if he "recognizes himself in a world he has himself made." But that does not happen. Since "alienating labor (1) alienates man from nature, (2) alienates him from himself, his own active function, his life's activity, it alienates man from his species." The separation of labor from the object is thus for him a threefold one: man is alienated from external nature, from himself, and from his fellow-men. The relations of men to one another are reified: personal relations appear as objective relations between things (commodities).

Man, (not only the worker, since the process of alienation affects society as a whole) is thus for Marx as for Schiller, Feuerbach and Hegel, a mutilated man.

But these theories of alienation are not adequate. While the principles developed by Hegel and Marx must not be given up, these theories need supplementation and deepening. Their inadequacy consists in this, that they oppose universal or nearly universal man (of ancient Greece in Schiller and Hegel) to the mutilated man of the modern world. But there is no historical form of society in which men have ever existed as universal beings; for slavery is not compatible with universality. My meaning may, perhaps, become clearer if I distinguish three strata of alienation. The stratum of psychology; that of society; and that of politics.

* * *

We have distinguished three strata of alienation. The psychological stratum remains no matter what social institutions man lives in. It creates potential anxiety which man in the mass attempts to overcome through ego-surrender. This affective identification with a leader is facilitated by the notion of false concreteness, the theory of conspiracy.

But so far we have not yet said when such regressive mass movements are activated; that is, when potential anxiety can be activated in such a manner that it can become a cruel weapon in the hands of irresponsible leaders.

In order to get at this problem we must take into account the two other strata of alienation: the social and political.

Alienation of labor: it is the separation of labor from the product of labor through hierarchical division of labor which characterizes modern industrial society. Probably no one doubts that the division of labor as well as the hierarchical organization of labor have shown a steady rise since the industrial revolution of the 18th century. German romantic psychology of labor calls this the "de-spiritualization of labor" (*Entseelung der Arbeit*). This concept as well as the various remedies are dangerous — for they cover up the inevitability of this process of alienation which must be admitted, understood, and accepted. If this does not happen, if one refuses to take account of the inevitability of the division of labor and of the hierarchical ordering of the process of labor and attempts to "spiritualize" labor instead of restricting it to a minimum, then social anxiety is deepened. The attitude of the so-called "new middle class" (salaried employees) can be understood from this process.

While the so-called new middle class does labor which — to remain with the language of German psychology of labor — is "more de-spiritualized than that of the industrial worker, and although his average income probably lies below that of the industrial worker, he yet holds fast to his middle class ideology and customs. Thus he refuses to take account of the inevitability of the process and — as in Germany before 1933 — becomes the social stratum most susceptible to Caesarism.

In a society which is constituted by competition, the competitor is supposed to be rewarded for his effort when he is competent; that is, when he exerts himself, is intelligent, and accepts risks. There is little doubt that the principle of competition dominates not only the economy but all social relations. Karen Horney, a representative of Freudian revisionism, claims that the destructive character of competition creates great anxiety in neurotic persons. Now this is not convincing when genuine competition really prevails, that is, competition in which relatively equally strong persons fight with fair methods; that is, the kind of competition which Adam Smith defines in his *Theory of Moral Sentiments* as follows: "One individual must never prefer himself so much even to any other individual as to hurt or injure that other in order to benefit himself, though the benefit of the one should be much greater than the hurt or injury to the other." And again, "In the race for wealth and honours and preferments, each may run as hard as he can and strain every nerve and every muscle in order to outstrip all his competitors. But if he jostle or throw down any of them, the indulgence of the spectator is entirely at an end. It is in violation of fair play, which they cannot admit of." I cannot here undertake a social analysis to show that this ethi-

cally circumscribed competition does not exist and perhaps never has existed, that in reality a monopolist struggle hides behind it, that, in other words, the efforts of the individual, his intelligence, his vision, his readiness to take risks, are easily shattered by the constellations of power.

Behind the mask of competition, which must not necessarily have destructive effects if it rationally organizes a society, there hide in fact relations of dependence. To be successful in present-day society, it is much more important to stand in well with the powerful than to preserve oneself through one's own strength. Modern man knows this. It is precisely the impotence of the individual who has to accommodate himself to the technological apparatus which is destructive and anxiety-creating.

But even where genuine competition is effective, no effort will help if crises ruin the merchant. The inability to understand the process of crises, and the frequent need to ascribe blame for them to sinister powers, is an additional factor in the destruction of ego. This psychological process operated in the so-called "old middle class" of Germany before 1933. But — to repeat — it is hard to see why fair competition must have destructive functions.

In every society that is composed of antagonistic groups there is an ascent and descent of groups. It is my contention that persecutory anxiety — but one that, as we said above, has a real basis — is produced when a group is threatened in its prestige, income, or even its existence; i.e., when it declines and does not understand the historical process or is prevented from understanding it. The examples are too numerous to be possibly mentioned here. German National Socialism and Italian Fascism are classical examples.

But not only social classes resist their degradation by means of such mass movements; religious and racial conflicts, too, frequently produce similar phenomena. The conflict between Negroes and whites in the southern states of the United States, the contemporary struggle of the South African government against the natives, take place in accord with the following scheme: the anxiety of a dominant white minority that it will be degraded through the economic and political rise of Negroes is used in propagandist fashion for the creation of affective mass movements, which frequently take on a fascist character.

Social alienation, i.e., the fear of social degradation, is not adequate by itself. The elements of political alienation must be added. . . . As a rule one is satisfied (above all, in the American literature) with defining abstention from voting at elections as political apathy. But I have pointed out elsewhere that the word "apathy" describes three different political reactions: first, the lack of interest in politics, say the opinion that politics is not the business of the citizen because it is after all only a struggle between small cliques and that therefore fundamentally nothing ever changes; then, the Epicurean attitude toward politics, the view that politics and state only have to supply the element of order within which man devotes himself to his perfection, so that forms of state and of government appear as secondary matters; and finally, as the third reaction, the conscious rejection of the whole political system which expresses itself as apathy because the individual sees no possibility of changing anything in the system through his efforts. Political life can, for example, be exhausted in the competition of political parties which are purely machines without mass participation, but which monopolize politics to such an extent that a new party cannot make its way within the valid rules of the game. This third form of apathy forms the core of what I characterize as political alienation. Usually this apathy, if it operates within social alienation, leads to the partial paralysis of the state and opens the way to a caesarist movement which, scorning the rules of the game, utilizes the inability of the citizen to make individual decisions and compensates for the loss of ego with identification with a Caesar.

The caesaristic movement is compelled not only to activate but to institutionalize anxiety. The institutionalization of anxiety is necessary because the caesaristic movement can never endure a long wait for power. This is precisely what follows from its affective basis. While the non-affective mass organization, such as a normal political party, can exist for a long time without disintegrating, the caesarist movement must hurry precisely because of the instability of the cement that holds it together: the libido-charged affectivity. After it has come to power it faces the need of institutionalizing anxiety as a means of preventing the extinction of its affective base by its bureaucratic structure.

The techniques are familiar: propaganda and terror, i.e., the incalculability of sanctions. I do not need to discuss this here. Montesquieu, building on Aristotle and Machiavelli, distinguished between three constitutional and one tyrannical governmental and social system. According to him, monarchy rests on the honor of the monarch; aristocracy, on the moderation of the aristocrats; democracy, on virtue (i.e., with him, patriotism); but tyranny, on fear. It must, however, not be overlooked —and our introductory remarks about alienation and anxiety had no other meaning—that every political system is based on anxiety. But there is more than a quantitative difference between the anxiety which is institutionalized in a totally repressive system and that which is the basis of a halfway liberal one. These are qualitatively different states of affairs. One may perhaps say that the totally repressive system institutionalizes depressive and persecutory anxiety, the halfway liberal system, true anxiety.

Once the connection between anxiety and guilt is seen, it will at once become obvious that these are different states of affairs.

In his *Peloponnesian War*, Thucydides reports the following about Sparta: "Indeed fear of their [the Helots'] numbers and obstinacy even persuaded the Lacedaemonians to the action which I shall now relate.

. . . The Helots were invited by a proclamation to pick out those of their number who claimed to have most distinguished themselves against the enemy, in order that they might receive their freedom; the object being to test them, as it was thought that the first to claim their freedom would be the most high-spirited and the most apt to rebel. As many as two thousand were selected accordingly, who crowned themselves and went round the temples, rejoicing in their new freedom. The Spartans however, soon afterwards did away with them, and no one ever knew how each of them perished."

With his customary psychological penetration this greatest of all historians saw clearly the connection of anxiety and collective guilt. And then we read Plutarch's description of the terrible Cryptia, the Spartan secret police: "By this ordinance, the magistrates [i.e., the Ephors] despatched privately some of the ablest of the young men into the country, from time to time, armed only with their daggers, and taking a little necessary provision with them; in the daytime, they hid themselves in out-of-the-way places, and there lay close, but in the night issued out into the highways and killed all the helots they could light upon." Here is a striking example of what we have in mind.

Who does not here think of Dostoyevsky's *The Possessed,* when Stavrogin gives the following piece of advice: "All that business of titles and sentimentalism is a very good cement, but there is something better; persuade four members of the circle to do for a fifth on the pretence that he is a traitor, and you'll tie them all together with the blood they've shed as though it were a knot. They'll be your slaves, they won't dare to rebel or call you to account. Ha ha ha!" This famous passage in Dostoyevsky is important not only because it verifies our psychological theory, but also because it shows at the same time that the leader activates anxiety through guilt for his own advantage, not for the sake of the led.

I do not wish here to discuss the psychological theory concerning the relation of anxiety and guilt. According to Freud man's feeling of guilt stems from the Oedipus complex. It is this aggression that the child represses and thus effects an unconscious feeling of guilt. The feeling of guilt is the superego, man's conscience. But that is precisely why the intensification of the unconscious feeling of guilt permits man to become a criminal.

If one examines the Spartan example, Stavrogin's advice, the Fehme-murders, and the collective crimes of the SS, one may perhaps undertake the following psychological analysis:

There are anxiety and an unconscious feeling of guilt. It is the task of the leader, by creating neurotic anxiety, to tie the led so closely to the leader that they would perish without identification with him. Then the leader orders the commission of crimes; but these are, in accord with the morality that prevails in the group—with the Lacedaemonians, the Nihilists, the SS — no crimes, but fundamentally moral acts. But the conscience — the superego — protests against the morality of the crimes, for the old moral convictions cannot simply be extirpated. The feeling of guilt is thus repressed and makes anxiety a nearly panicky one, which can be overcome only through unconditional surrender to the leader and compels the commission of new crimes.

Totalitarian Propaganda

GEORGE ORWELL

George Orwell, a prominent British author, was born in 1903 and educated at Eton. In addition to his literary career, Orwell led an active life. In the 1920s he served with the Indian Imperial Police in Burma and in the 1930s he fought for a short time in the Spanish Civil War as a member of the Trotskyite P.O.U.M. Orwell died in 1950 after having turned his talents more and more to political writing which, he said, he wanted to make an art. Orwell remained a socialist until the end of his life. Yet, in spite of this, he was highly critical of Russian Communism. Indeed, in his *Animal Farm: A Fairy Story* — next to *1984* the most famous of his political writings — he created a savage parody on the decay of the Russian Revolution. At the same time, however, Orwell did not detect the dangers of totalitarianism only in communist societies. Rather, as *1984* makes clear, he feared its development in the West as well.

Orwell's understanding of the psychology of totalitarian propaganda is amply demonstrated in his description of the "Two Minutes Hate." The propaganda which is directed at Winston depends more on its ability to threaten him than it does on any extravagant promises. Even more significant is the fact that the propaganda effectively utilizes his most private emotions and translates his frustrations, and even his hatred of the regime, into a reliance on the protective figure of "Big Brother."

IT WAS NEARLY eleven hundred, and in the Records Department, where Winston worked, they were dragging the chairs out of the cubicles and grouping them in the center of the hall, opposite the big telescreen, in preparation for the Two Minutes Hate. Winston was just taking his place in one of the middle rows when two people whom he knew by sight, but had never spoken to, came unexpectedly into the room. One of them was a girl whom he often passed in the corridors. He did not know her name, but he knew that she worked in the Fiction Department. . . . She was a bold-looking girl of about twenty-seven, with thick dark hair, a freckled face, and swift, athletic movements. A narrow scarlet sash, emblem of the Junior Anti-Sex League, was wound several times around the waist of her overalls, . . . Winston had disliked her from the very first moment of seeing her. He knew the

reason. It was because of the atmosphere of hockey fields and cold baths and community hikes and general clean-mindedness which she managed to carry about with her. He disliked nearly all women, and especially the young and pretty ones. It was always the women, and above all the young ones, who were the most bigoted adherents of the Party, . . . But this particular girl gave him the impression of being more dangerous than most. Once when they passed in the corridor she had given him a quick sidelong glance which seemed to pierce right into him and for a moment had filled him with black terror. The idea had even crossed his mind that she might be an agent of the Thought Police. That, it was true, was very unlikely. Still, he continued to feel a peculiar uneasiness, which had fear mixed up in it as well as hostility, whenever she was anywhere near him.

The other person was a man named

O'Brien, a member of the Inner Party and holder of some post so important and remote that Winston had only a dim idea of its nature. A momentary hush passed over the group of people round the chairs as they saw the black overalls of an Inner Party member approaching. O'Brien was a large, burly man with a thick neck and a coarse, humorous, brutal face. In spite of his formidable appearance he had a certain charm of manner. He had a trick of resettling his spectacles on his nose which was curiously disarming — in some indefinable way, curiously civilized. It was a gesture which, if anyone had still thought in such terms, might have recalled an eighteenth-century nobleman offering his snuff-box. Winston had seen O'Brien perhaps a dozen times in almost as many years. He felt deeply drawn to him, and not solely because he was intrigued by the contrast between O'Brien's urbane manner and his prizefighter's physique. Much more it was because of a secretly held belief — or perhaps not even a belief, merely a hope — that O'Brien's political orthodoxy was not perfect. Something in his face suggested it irresistibly. And again, perhaps it was not even unorthodoxy that was written in his face, but simply intelligence. But at any rate he had the appearance of being a person that you could talk to, if somehow you could cheat the telescreen and get him alone. Winston had never made the smallest effort to verify this guess; indeed, there was no way of doing so. At this moment O'Brien glanced at his wristwatch, saw that it was nearly eleven hundred, and evidently decided to stay in the Records Department until the Two Minutes Hate was over. He took a chair in the same row as Winston, a couple of places away. A small, sandy-haired woman who worked in the next cubicle to Winston was between them. The girl with dark hair was sitting immediately behind.

The next moment a hideous, grinding screech, as of some monstrous machine running without oil, burst from the big telescreen at the end of the room. It was a noise that set one's teeth on edge and bristled the hair at the back of one's neck. The Hate had started.

As usual, the face of Emmanuel Goldstein, the Enemy of the People, had flashed onto the screen. There were hisses here and there among the audience. The little sandy-haired woman gave a squeak of mingled fear and disgust. Goldstein was the renegade and backslider who once, long ago (how long ago, nobody quite remembered), had been one of the leading figures of the Party, almost on a level with Big Brother himself, and then had engaged in counterrevolutionary activities, had been condemned to death, and had mysteriously escaped and disappeared. The program of the Two Minutes Hate varied from day to day, but there was none in which Goldstein was not the principal figure. He was the primal traitor, the earliest defiler of the Party's purity. All subsequent crimes against the Party, all treacheries, acts of sabotage, heresies, deviations, sprang directly out of his teaching. Somewhere or other he was still alive and hatching his conspiracies: perhaps somewhere beyond the sea, under the protection of his foreign paymasters; perhaps even — so it was occasionally rumored — in some hiding place in Oceania itself.

Winston's diaphragm was constricted. He could never see the face of Goldstein without a painful mixture of emotions. It was a lean Jewish face, with a great fuzzy aureole of white hair and a small goatee beard — a clever face, and yet somehow inherently despicable, with a kind of senile silliness in the long thin nose near the end of which a pair of spectacles was perched. It resembled the face of a sheep, and the voice, too, had a sheeplike quality. Goldstein was delivering his usual venomous attack upon the doctrines of the Party — an attack so exaggerated and perverse that a child should have been able to see through it, and yet just plausible enough to fill one with an alarmed feeling that other people, less level-headed than oneself, might be taken in by it. He was abusing Big Brother, he was denouncing the dictatorship of the Party, he was demanding the immediate conclusion of peace with Eurasia, he was advocating freedom of speech, freedom of the press, freedom of assembly, freedom of thought, he was crying hysterically that the revolution had been betrayed — and all this in rapid polysyllabic speech which was a sort of parody of the habitual style of the orators of the Party, and even contained Newspeak words: . . . And all the while, lest one should be in any doubt as to the reality which Goldstein's specious claptrap covered, behind his head on the telescreen there marched the endless columns of the Eurasian army — row after row of solid-looking men with expressionless Asiatic faces, who swam up to the surface of the screen and vanished, to be replaced by others exactly similar. The dull, rhythmic tramp of the soldiers' boots formed the background to Goldstein's bleating voice.

Before the Hate had proceeded for thirty seconds, uncontrollable exclamations of rage were breaking out from half the people in the room. The self-satisfied sheeplike face on the screen, and the terrifying power of the Eurasian army behind it, were too much to be borne; besides, the sight or even the thought of Goldstein produced fear and anger automatically. He was an object of hatred more constant than either Eurasia or Eastasia, since when Oceania was at war with one of these powers it was generally at peace with the other. But what was strange was that although Goldstein was hated and despised by everybody, although every day, and a thousand times a day, on platforms, on the telescreen, in newspapers, in books, his theories were refuted, smashed, ridiculed, held up to the general gaze for the pitiful rubbish that they were — in spite of all this, his influence never seemed to grow less. Always there were fresh dupes waiting to be seduced by him. A day never passed when spies and saboteurs acting under his directions were not unmasked by the Thought Police. He was the commander of a vast shadowy army, an underground network of conspirators dedicated to the overthrow of the State. The Brotherhood, its name was supposed to be. There were also whispered stories of a terrible book, a compendium of all the heresies, of which Goldstein was the author and which circulated clandestinely here and there. It was a book without a title. People referred to it, if at all, simply as *the book*. But one knew of such things only through vague rumors. Neither the Brotherhood nor *the book* was a subject that any ordinary Party member would mention if there was a way of avoiding it.

In its second minute the Hate rose to a frenzy. People were leaping up and down in their places and shouting at the tops of their voices in an effort to drown the maddening bleating voice that came from the screen. The little sandy-haired woman had turned bright pink, and her mouth was opening and shutting like that of a landed fish. Even O'Brien's heavy face was flushed. He was sitting very straight in his chair, his powerful chest swelling and quivering as though he were standing up to the assault of a wave. The dark-haired girl behind Winston had begun crying out "Swine! Swine! Swine!" and suddenly she picked up a heavy Newspeak dictionary and flung it at the screen. . . . In a lucid moment Winston found that he was shouting with the others and kicking his heel violently against the rung of his chair. The horrible thing about the Two Minutes Hate was not that one was obliged to act a part, but that it was impossible to avoid joining in. Within thirty seconds any pretense was always unnecessary. A hideous ecstasy of fear and vindictiveness, a desire to kill, to torture, to smash faces in with a sledge hammer, seemed to flow through the whole group of people like an electric current, turning one even against one's will into a grimacing, screaming lunatic. And yet the rage that one felt was an abstract, undirected emotion which could be switched from one object to another like the flame of a blowlamp. Thus, at one moment Winston's hatred was not turned against Goldstein at all, but, on the contrary, against Big Brother, the Party, and the Thought Police; and at such moments his heart went out to the lonely, derided heretic on the screen, sole guardian of truth and sanity in a world of lies. And yet the very next instant he was at one with the people about him, and all that was said of Goldstein seemed to him to be true. At those moments his secret loathing of Big Brother changed into adoration, and Big Brother seemed to tower up, an invincible, fearless protector, standing like a rock against the hordes of Asia, and Goldstein, in spite of his isolation, his helplessness, and the doubt that hung about his very existence, seemed like some sinister enchanter, capable by the mere power of his voice of wrecking the structure of civilization.

It was even possible, at moments, to switch one's hatred this way or that by a voluntary act. Suddenly, by the sort of violent effort with which one wrenches one's head away from the pillow in a nightmare, Winston succeeded in transferring his hatred from the face on the screen to the dark-haired girl behind him. Vivid, beautiful hallucinations flashed through his mind. He would flog her to death with a rubber truncheon. He would tie her naked to a stake and shoot her full of arrows like Saint Sebastian. He would ravish her and cut her throat at the moment of climax. Better than before, moreover, he realized *why* it was that he hated her. He hated her because she was young and pretty and sexless, because he wanted to go to bed with her and would never do so, because round her sweet supple waist, which seemed to ask you to encircle it with your arm, there was only the odious scarlet sash, aggressive symbol of chastity.

The Hate rose to its climax. The voice of Goldstein had become an actual sheep's bleat, and for an instant the face changed into that of a sheep. Then the sheepface melted into the figure of a Eurasian soldier who seemed to be advancing, huge and terrible, his submachine gun roaring and seeming to spring out of the surface of the screen, so that some of the people in the front row actually flinched backwards in their seats. But in the same moment, draw-

ing a deep sigh of relief from everybody, the hostile figure melted into the face of Big Brother, black-haired, black-mustachio'd, full of power and mysterious calm, and so vast that it almost filled up the screen. Nobody heard what Big Brother was saying. It was merely a few words of encouragement, the sort of words that are uttered in the din of battle, not distinguishable individually but restoring confidence by the fact of being spoken. Then the face of Big Brother faded away again, and instead the three slogans of the Party stood out in bold capitals:

WAR IS PEACE

FREEDOM IS SLAVERY

IGNORANCE IS STRENGTH

But the face of Big Brother semed to persist for several seconds on the screen, as though the impact that it had made on everyone's eyeballs were too vivid to wear off immediately. The little sandy-haired woman had flung herself forward over the back of the chair in front of her. With a tremulous murmur that sounded like "My Savior!' she extended her arms toward the screen. Then she buried her face in her hands. It was apparent that she was uttering a prayer.

At this moment the entire group of people broke into a deep, slow, rhythmical chant of "B-B! . . . B-B! . . . B-B!" over and over again, very slowly, with a long pause between the first "B" and the second —a heavy, murmurous sound, somehow curiously savage, in the background of which one seemed to hear the stamp of naked feet and the throbbing of tom-toms. For perhaps as much as thirty seconds they kept it up. It was a refrain that was often heard in moments of overwhelming emotion. Partly it was a sort of hymn to the wisdom and majesty of Big Brother, but still more it was an act of self-hypnosis, a deliberate drowning of consciousness by means of rhythmic noise. Winston's entrails seemed to grow cold. In the Two Minutes

Hate he could not help sharing in the general delirium, but this subhuman chanting of "B-B! . . . B-B!" always filled him with horror. Of course he chanted with the rest: it was impossible to do otherwise. To dissemble your feelings, to control your face, to do what everyone else was doing, was an instinctive reaction.

Totalitarian Ideology

HANNAH ARENDT

Hannah Arendt today occupies the role of one of the leading social and political thinkers of the twentieth century. A student of both Karl Jaspers and Martin Heidegger, two of the most influential philosophers of our age, Miss Arendt received her Ph.D. from the University of Heidelberg. During the 1930s she was a social worker in Paris. Coming to the United States in 1941 she served as both the Executive Director of Jewish Cultural Reconstruction and, later, as a professor at the University of Chicago. Professor Arendt's works, of which *The Origins of Totalitarianism* is still the most important, display her amazing range of knowledge in all fields of social and philosophical thought. In the selection which follows, Professor Arendt develops her concept of the nature of a totalitarian ideology, an area in which her contributions have been both original and stimulating. Her views on this question, as on other issues, have led some critics of Professor Arendt to argue that she over-emphasizes certain characteristics of totalitarianism beyond their objective importance. But despite the fact that many of her views are controversial and sometimes difficult to comprehend, her study must be regarded as a classic of twentieth-century political thought.

IDEOLOGIES — ISMS which to the satisfaction of their adherents can explain every thing and every occurrence by deducing it from a single premise — are a very recent phenomenon and, for many decades, played a negligible role in political life. Only with the wisdom of hindsight can we discover in them certain elements which have made them so disturbingly useful for totalitarian rule. Not before Hitler and Stalin were the great political potentialities of the ideologies discovered.

Ideologies are known for their scientific character: they combine the scientific approach with results of philosophical relevance and pretend to be scientific philosophy. The word "ideology" seems to imply that an idea can become the subject matter of a science just as animals are the subject matter of zoology, and that the suffix-*logy* in ideology, as in zoology, indicates nothing but the *logoi*, the scientific statements made on it. If this were true, an ideology would indeed be a pseudo-science and a pseudo-philosophy, transgressing at the same time the limitations of science and the limitations of philosophy. Deism, for example, would then be the ideology which treats the idea of God, with which philosophy is concerned, in the scientific manner of theology for which God is a revealed reality. (A theology which is not based on revelation as a given reality but treats God as an idea would be as mad as a zoology which is no longer sure of the physical, tangible existence of animals.) Yet we know that this is only part of the truth. Deism, though it denies divine revelation, does not simply make "scientific" statements on a God which is only an "idea," but uses the idea of God in order to explain the course of the world. The "ideas" of isms — race in racism, God in deism, etc. — never form the subject matter of the ideologies and the suffix *-logy* never indicates simply a body of "scientific" statements.

An ideology is quite literally what its name indicates: it is the logic of an idea. Its subject matter is history, to which the "idea" is applied; the result of this application is not a body of statements about something that *is,* but the unfolding of a process which is in constant change. The ideology treats the course of events as though it followed the same "law" as the logical exposition of its "idea." Ideologies pretend to know the mysteries of the whole historical process — the secrets of the past, the intricacies of the present, the uncertainties of the future — because of the logic inherent in their respective ideas.

Ideologies are never interested in the miracle of being. They are historical, concerned with becoming and perishing, with the rise and fall of cultures, even if they try to explain history by some "law of nature." The word "race" in racism does not signify any genuine curiosity about the human races as a field for scientific exploration, but is the "idea" by which the movement of history is explained as one consistent process.

The "idea" of an ideology is neither Plato's eternal essence grasped by the eyes of the mind nor Kant's regulative principle of reason but has become an instrument of explanation. To an ideology, history does not appear in the light of an idea (which would imply that history is seen *sub specie* [under the species] of some ideal eternity which itself is beyond historical motion) but as something which can be calculated by it. What fits the "idea" into this new role is its own "logic," that is a movement which

is the consequence of the "idea" itself and needs no outside factor to set it into motion. Racism is the belief that there is a motion inherent in the very idea of race, just as deism is the belief that a motion is inherent in the very notion of God.

The movement of history and the logical process of this notion are supposed to correspond to each other, so that whatever happens, happens according to the logic of one "idea." However, the only possible movement in the realm of logic is the process of deduction from a premise. Dialectical logic, with its process from thesis through antithesis to synthesis which in turn becomes the thesis of the next dialectical movement, is not different in principle, once an ideology gets hold of it; the first thesis becomes the premise and its advantage for ideological explanation is that this dialectical device can explain away factual contradictions as stages of one identical, consistent movement.

As soon as logic as a movement of thought — and not as a necessary control of thinking — is applied to an idea, this idea is transformed into a premise. Ideological world explanations performed this operation long before it became so eminently fruitful for totalitarian reasoning. The purely negative coercion of logic, the prohibition of contradictions, became "productive" so that a whole line of thought could be initiated, and forced upon the mind, by drawing conclusions in the manner of mere argumentation. This argumentative process could be interrupted neither by a new idea (which would have been another premise with a different set of consequences) nor by a new experience. Ideologies always assume that one idea is sufficient to explain everything in the development from the premise, and that no experience can teach anything because everything is comprehended in this consistent process of logical deduction. The danger in exchanging the necessary insecurity of philosophical thought for the total explanation of an ideology and its *Weltanschauung* [world view], is not even so much the risk of falling for some usually vulgar, always uncritical assumption as of exchanging the freedom inherent in man's capacity to think for the straitjacket of logic with which man can force himself almost as violently as he is forced by some outside power.

The *Weltanschauungen* and ideologies of the nineteenth century are not in themselves totalitarian, and although racism and communism have become the decisive ideologies of the twentieth century they were not, in principle, any "more totalitarian" than the others; it happened because the elements of experience on which they were originally based — the struggle between the races for world domination, and the struggle between the classes for political power in the respective countries — turned out to be politically more important than those of other ideologies. In this sense the ideological victory of racism and communism over all other isms was decided before the totalitarian movements took hold of precisely these ideologies. On the other hand, all ideologies contain totalitarian elements, but these are fully developed only by totalitarian movements, and this creates the deceptive impression that only racism and communism are totalitarian in character. The truth is, rather, that the real nature of all ideologies was revealed only in the role that the ideology plays in the apparatus of totalitarian domination. Seen from this aspect, there appear three specifically totalitarian elements that are peculiar to all ideological thinking.

First, in their claim to total explanation, ideologies have the tendency to explain not what is, but what becomes, what is born and passes away. They are in all cases concerned solely with the element of motion, that is, with history in the customary sense of the word. Ideologies are always oriented toward history, even when, as in the case of racism, they seemingly proceed from the premise of nature; here, nature serves merely to explain historical matters and reduce them to matters of nature. The claim to total explanation promises to explain all historical happenings, the total explanation of the past, the total knowledge of the present, and the reliable prediction of the future. Secondly, in this capacity ideological thinking becomes independent of all experience from which it cannot learn anything new even if it is a question of something that has just come to pass. Hence ideological thinking becomes emancipated from the reality that we perceive with our five senses, and insists on a "truer" reality concealed behind all perceptible things, dominating them from this place of concealment and requiring a sixth sense that enables us to become aware of it. The sixth sense is provided by precisely the ideology, that particular ideological indoctrination which is taught by the educational institutions, established exclusively for this purpose, to train the "political soldiers" in the *Ordensburgen* [Nazi training schools for future leaders] of the Nazis or the schools of the Comintern and the Cominform. The propaganda of the totalitarian movement also serves to emancipate thought from experience and reality; it always strives to inject a secret meaning into every public, tangible event and to suspect a secret intent behind every public political act. Once the movements have come to power, they proceed to change reality in accordance with their ideological claims. The concept of enmity is replaced by that of conspiracy, and this produces a mentality in which reality — real enmity or real friendship — is no longer experienced and understood in its own terms but is automatically assumed to signify something else.

Thirdly, since the ideologies have no power to transform reality, they achieve this emancipation of thought from experience through certain methods of demonstration. Ideological thinking orders facts into an absolutely logical procedure which starts from an axiomatically accepted premise, deducing everything else from it; that is, it proceeds with a consistency that exists nowhere in the realm of reality. The deducing may proceed logically or dialectically; in either case it involves a consistent process of argumentation which, because it thinks in terms of a process, is supposed to be able to comprehend the movement of the suprahuman, natural or historical processes. Comprehension is achieved by the mind's imitating, either logically or dialectically, the laws of "scientifically" established movements with which through the process of imitation it becomes integrated. Ideological argumentation, always a kind of logical deduction, corresponds to the two aforementioned elements of the ideologies — the element of movement and of emancipation from reality and experience — first, because its thought movement does not spring from experience but is self-generated, and, secondly, because it transforms the one and only point that is taken and accepted from experienced reality into an axiomatic premise, leaving from then on the subsequent argumentation process completely untouched from any further experience. Once it has established its premise, its point of departure, experiences no longer interfere with ideological thinking, nor can it be taught by reality.

The device both totalitarian rulers used to transform their respective ideologies into weapons with which each of their subjects could force himself into step with the terror movement was deceptively simple and inconspicuous: they took them dead seriously, took pride the one in his supreme gift for "ice cold reasoning" (Hitler) and the other in the "mercilessness of his dialectics," and proceeded to drive ideological implications into extremes of logical consistency which, to the onlooker, looked preposterously "primitive" and absurd: a "dying class" consisted of people condemned to death; races that are "unfit to live" were to be exterminated. Whoever agreed that there are such things as "dying classes" and did not draw the consequence of killing their members, or that the right to live had something to do with race and did not draw the consequence of killing "unfit races," was plainly either stupid or a coward. This stringent logicality as a guide to action permeates the whole structure of totalitarian movements and governments. It is exclusively the work

of Hitler and Stalin who, although they did not add a single new thought to the ideas and propaganda slogans of their movements, for this reason alone must be considered ideologists of the greatest importance.

What distinguished these new totalitarian ideologists from their predecessors was that it was no longer primarily the "idea" of the ideology — the struggle of classes and the exploitation of the workers or the struggle of races and the care for Germanic peoples — which appealed to them, but the logical process which could be developed from it. According to Stalin, neither the idea nor the oratory but "the irresistible force of logic thoroughly overpowered [Lenin's] audience." The power, which Marx thought was born when the idea seized the masses, was discovered to reside, not in the idea itself, but in its logical process which "like a mighty tentacle seizes you on all sides as in a vise and from whose grip you are powerless to tear yourself away; you must either surrender or make up your mind to utter defeat." Only when the realization of the ideological aims, the classless society or the master race, was at stake, could this force show itself. In the process of realization, the original substance upon which the ideologies based themselves as long as they had to appeal to the masses — the exploitation of the workers or the national aspirations of Germany — is gradually lost, devoured as it were by the process itself: in perfect accordance with "ice cold reasoning" and the "irresistible force of logic," the workers lost under Bolshevik rule even those rights they had been granted under Tsarist oppression and the German people suffered a kind of warfare which did not pay the slightest regard to the minimum requirements for survival of the German nation. It is in the nature of ideological politics — and is not simply a betrayal committed for the sake of self-interest or lust for power — that the real content of the ideology (the working class or the Germanic peoples), which originally had brought about the "idea" (the struggle of classes as the law of history or the struggle of races as the law of nature), is devoured by the logic with which the "idea" is carried out.

The preparation of victims and executioners which totalitarianism requires in place of Montesquieu's principle of action is not the ideology itself—racism or dialectical materialism—but its inherent logicality. The most persuasive argument in this respect, an argument of which Hitler like Stalin was very fond, is: You can't say A without saying B and C and so on, down to the end of the murderous alphabet. Here, the coercive force of logicality seems to have its source; it springs from our fear of contradicting ourselves. To the extent that the Bolshevik purge succeeds in making its victims confess to crimes they never committed, it relies chiefly on this basic fear and argues as follows: We are all agreed on the premise that history is a struggle of classes and on the role of the Party in its conduct. You know therefore that, historically speaking, the Party is always right (in the words of Trotsky: "We can only be right with and by the Party, for history has provided no other way of being in the right.") At this historical moment, that is in accordance with the law of history, certain crimes are due to be committed which the Party, knowing the law of history, must punish. For these crimes, the Party needs criminals; it may be that the Party, though knowing the crimes, does not quite know the criminals; more important than to be sure about the criminals is to punish the crimes, because without such punishment, History will not be advanced but may even be hindered in its course. You, therefore, either have committed the crimes or have been called by the Party to play the role of the criminal—in either case, you have objectively become an enemy of the Party. If you don't confess, you cease to help History through the Party, and have become a real enemy.—The coercive force of the argument is: if you refuse, you contradict yourself and, through this contradiction, render your whole life meaningless; the A which you said dominates your whole life through the consequences of B and C which it logically engenders.

Totalitarian rulers rely on the compulsion with which we can compel ourselves, for the limited mobilization of people which even they still need; this inner compulsion is the tyranny of logicality against which nothing stands but the great capacity of men to start something new. The tyranny of logicality begins with the mind's submission to logic as a never-ending process, on which man relies in order to engender his thoughts. By this submission, he surrenders his inner freedom as he surrenders his freedom of movement when he bows down to an outward tyranny. Freedom as an inner capacity of man is identical with the capacity to begin, just as freedom as a political reality is identical with a space of movement between men. Over the beginning, no logic, no cogent deduction can have any power, because its chain presupposes, in the form of a premise, the beginning. As terror is needed lest with the birth of each new human being a new beginning arise and raise its voice in the world, so the self-coercive force of logicality is mobilized lest anybody ever start thinking—which as the freest and purest of all human activities is the very opposite of the compulsory process of deduction. Totalitarian government can be safe only to the extent that it can mobilize man's own will power in order to force him into that gigantic movement of History or Nature which supposedly uses mankind as its material and knows neither birth nor death.

The compulsion of total terror on one side, which, with its iron band, presses masses of isolated men together *and* supports them in a world which has become a wilderness for them, and the self-coercive force of logical deduction on the other, which prepares each individual in his lonely isolation against all others, correspond to each other and need each other in order to set the terror-ruled movement into motion and keep it moving. Just as terror, even in its pre-total, merely tyrannical form ruins all relationships between men, so the self-compulsion of ideological thinking ruins all relationships with reality. The preparation has succeeded when people have lost contact with their fellow men as well as the reality around them; for together with these contacts, men lose the capacity of both experience and thought.

The ideal subject of totalitarian rule is not the convinced Nazi or the convinced Communist, but people for whom the distinction between fact and fiction (*i.e.,* the reality of experience) and the distinction between true and false (*i.e.,* the standards of thought) no longer exist.

Totalitarian Terror

CARL FRIEDRICH AND ZBIGNIEW BRZEZINSKI

All governments depend to some extent on the ability to use coercion. But dictatorships expand the range of coercion far more than would be allowed in a constitutional political system. Similarly, those who argue that totalitarian regimes must be distinguished from traditional dictatorships point out that under totalitarianism, coercion becomes terror. In the selection which follows, Friedrich and Brzezinski argue that totalitarian terror is not merely a way of suppressing active opponents of the regime, but rather that it is an essential ingredient of totalitarian rule which operates on the entire population. Moreover, they point out that totalitarian terror — unlike the coercion practiced by dictatorship which tends to let up when opposition has been crushed — expands and grows as the movement becomes more entrenched in power.

W E CAN SEE CLEARLY why totalitarian terror and total unanimity are thus interdependent. The passion for unanimity, characteristic of a mass movement, demands tools to enforce it. And according to totalitarian ideology all "normal" members of the society will naturally be part of that unanimity. Only scattered social misfits — be they bourgeoisie (historically doomed) or Jews (racially deformed) — remain outside that unanimity, joined possibly by a few traitors. The terror makes certain that the masses are not infected, while the "social misfits" are liquidated. In this way, all the brutal, premeditated violence of the terror becomes rationally justified to the totalitarian.

Totalitarian terror has not only this negative function to perform. Operating within the context of enforced unanimity, it becomes a stimulant to more enthusiastic expressions of support for the regime. It classifies men's behavior according to degrees of loyalty, and mere absence of opposition to the regime becomes insufficient as proof of devotion to it. Positive action is demanded, and men compete in loyalty. It is no accident that secret police files in the USSR stress, first of all, whether a given individual is passive or active. Needless to add, one can be active in a totalitarian society only on behalf of the regime. A remark on someone's *kharakteristika* [file] that he is passive represents a major question mark as to his loyalty. The Communist Party of the Soviet Union particularly

Reprinted by permission of the publishers from Carl Friedrich and Zbigniew Brzezinski, *Totalitarian Dictatorship and Autocracy,* Cambridge, Mass.: Harvard University Press, pp. 135–138, Copyright, 1956, by the President and Fellows of Harvard College.

stresses the fact that *partiinost* (literally "party-ness") demands active, very active support of the regime, measured by concrete achievements.

The same was true in the Fascist and Nazi dictatorships. In the election campaign after the murder of Matteotti there was a great deal of pressure, of violence, of the parade of uniformed force. Whether one agrees with Finer that these "secured the triumph of the party," there is no question that he is right in stressing the extent to which party activity was made the test for remaining after the victory had been won. "No compromise, no quietism, no cowardice in the face of the responsibilities imposed by the party" — thus Finer sums up the party member's role. Outward conformity to certain changes in style of speaking and eating were made the test of party enthusiasm and members who did not conform were not only rebuffed, but at times expelled, beaten up, or imprisoned.

In National Socialist Germany, the party was so large that its membership failed to display some of the characteristics of complete dedication just described. As a consequence, the elite guard (SS) increasingly stepped into this role of being the unquestioning, enthusiastic supporter of the regime. It was the SS in its three distinct formations that embodied, for the masses of the subject people, the terroristic apparatus of the regime, symbolized by the dagger that every member received upon his initiation into this "elite." From a recent careful analysis it becomes clear that the SS embodied a more satanic outlook on life and politics than was represented by the ordinary Nazi and SA men. Indeed, there was at work a distinctly anti-intellectual trend in the SS which was fully shared by Himmler, their boss. These anti-intellectuals infiltrated the government, the military and economic cadres, and the party which they sought to control. After the abortive *putsch* of the underground opposition, the SS succeeded in taking over the key controls of the armed forces. Its style of "the marching column" triumphed.

The SS was essentially an "order." Its attitude was pointedly summed up in the demand, "Believe, obey, fight!" All ideas were reduced to the sloganized framework of an ossified ideology to be enunciated, and perhaps restated, by the Führer at his pleasure. Any dissent must be ferreted out and crushed with ruthless terror.

It is a curious and frightening fact that totalitarian terror increases in scope and violence as the totalitarian system becomes more stable and firm. In the initial period after the seizure of power, the major energy of the machinery of terror is directed at the obvious enemies — such as the Social Democrats in Germany, the Mensheviks or "bourgeoisie" in Russia, the democratic parties in Eastern Europe. Only when these are destroyed is the sword of the regime turned against the broad masses; only then does mass terror gradually develop. Hannah Arendt observed that

the end of the first stage comes with the liquidation of open and secret resistance in any organized form; it can be set at about 1935 in Germany and approximately 1930 in Soviet Russia. Only after the extermination of real enemies has been completed and the hunt for "potential enemies" begun does terror become the actual content of totalitarian regimes. Under the pretext of building socialism in one country, or using a given territory as a laboratory for a revolutionary experiment, or realizing the *Volksgemeinschaft* [National Community], the second claim of totalitarianism, the claim to total domination, is carried out.

It is at this latter stage that totalitarian terror comes into its own. It aims to fill everyone with fear and vents in full its passion for unanimity. Terror embraces the entire society, searching everywhere for actual or potential deviants from the totalitarian unity. Indeed to many it seems as if they are hunted, even though the secret police may not touch them for years, if at all. Total fear reigns.

The total scope and the pervasive and sustained character of totalitarian terror are accordingly its unique qualities. By operating with the latest technological devices, by allowing no refuge from its reach, and by penetrating even the innermost sanctums of the regimes, it achieves a scope unprecedented in history. The atmosphere of fear it creates easily exaggerates the strength of the regime and helps it achieve and maintain its façade of unanimity. Scattered opponents of the regime, if still undetected, become isolated and feel themselves cast out of society. This sense of loneliness, which is the fate of all, but more especially of an opponent of the totalitarian regime, tends to paralyze resistance and makes it much less appealing. It generates a universal longing to "escape" into the anonymity of the collective whole. Unanimity, even if coerced, is a source of strength for the regime.

Of course, it would be a gross over-simplification to claim therefore that in all places and at all times the citizens of a totalitarian regime are subject to immediate arrest and live in a spine-chilling fear for their lives. First of all, terror can become internalized; the people become familiar with a pattern of conformance, they know how to externalize a behavior of loyalty, they learn what not to say and do. Second, reliance on force can decrease as a new generation, brought up in loyalty and fully indoctrinated, takes its place in the totalitarian society. But terror as a last resort is always present in the background, and the potentiality of its uninhibited use does not disappear. That seems to be, for instance, the situation in the USSR in 1956.

It should be apparent from the preceding analysis that totalitarian terror cannot be compared to the occasional outbursts of violence and terrorism which occur sometimes in constitutional societies. Such outbursts, unfortunate as they are, usually represent sporadic responses to specific crises. Even when institutionalized by legislative process, they operate with a definite goal in view and apply to a small and sharply delimited segment of society. Such situations are open to abuse and, indeed, history tells of many cases of injustice. Yet to compare these outbursts, as some are inclined to do, to totalitarian terror is to underestimate the latter and grossly exaggerate the former. The total scope of totalitarian terror and its pervasive and sustained character, operating in an atmosphere of ideological compulsion, makes it a unique feature of modern totalitarianism.

The Shapelessness of the System

HANNAH ARENDT

In examining the selection which follows, the reader should remember that the bureaucratic confusion to which Professor Arendt points is not the only characteristic of totalitarianism which she identifies. Like other authorities, Arendt also notes such distinguishing features as one-party rule, adherence to ideology, and reliance on terror. But neither does she consider the bureaucratic complexity of the Nazi and Soviet systems merely accidental. Rather, she argues that it is a basic tool of totalitarian rule serving to keep the system flexible and thus responsive to the will of the leader who presides over the entire organization like a ventriloquist manipulating passive puppets.

WHAT STRIKES the observer of the totalitarian state is certainly not its monolithic structure. On the contrary, all serious students of the subject agree at least on the co-existence (or the conflict) of a dual authority, the party and the state. Many, moreover, have stressed the peculiar "shapelessness" of the totalitarian government. Thomas Masaryk saw early that "the so-called Bolshevik system has never been anything but a complete absence of system"; and it is perfectly true that "even an expert would be driven mad if he tried to unravel the relationships between Party and State" in the Third Reich. It has also been frequently observed that the relationship between the two sources of authority, between state and party, is one of ostensible and real authority, so that the government machine is usually pictured as the powerless façade which hides and protects the real power of the party.

All levels of the administrative machine in the Third Reich were subject to a curious duplication of offices. With a fantastic thoroughness, the Nazis made sure that every function of the state administration would be duplicated by some party organ: the Weimar division of Germany into states and provinces was duplicated by the Nazi division into *Gaue* whose borderlines, how-ever, did not coincide, so that every given locality belonged, even geographically, to two altogether different administrative units. Nor was the duplication of functions abandoned when, after 1933, outstanding Nazis occupied the official ministries of the state; when Frick, for instance, became Minister of the Interior or Guerthner Minister of Justice. These old and trusted party members, once they had embarked upon official nonparty careers, lost their power and became as uninfluential as other civil servants. Both came under the factual authority of Himmler, the rising chief of the police, who normally would have been subordinate to the Minister of the Interior. Better known abroad has been the fate of the old German Foreign Affairs Office in the Wilhelmstrasse. The Nazis left its personnel nearly untouched and of course never abolished it; yet at the same time they maintained the prepower Foreign Affairs Bureau of the Party, headed by Rosenberg; and since this office had specialized in maintaining contacts with Fascist organizations in Eastern Europe and the Balkans, they set up another organ to compete with the office in the Wilhelmstrasse, the so-called Ribbentrop Bureau, which handled foreign affairs in the West, and survived the departure of its chief as Ambassador to

From *The Origins of Totalitarianism*, copyright, 1951, 1958, by Hannah Arendt, pp. 395–405. Reprinted by permission of Harcourt, Brace & World, Inc., and George Allen & Unwin Ltd.

England, that is, his incorporation into the official apparatus of the Wilhelmstrasse. Finally, in addition to these party institutions, the Foreign Office received another duplication in the form of an SS Office, which was responsible "for negotiations with all racially Germanic groups in Denmark, Norway, Belgium and the Netherlands." These examples prove that for the Nazis the duplication of offices was a matter of principle and not just an expedient for providing jobs for party members.

The same division between a real and an ostensible government developed from very different beginnings in Soviet Russia. The ostensible government originally sprang from the All-Russian Soviet Congress, which during the civil war lost its influence and power to the Bolshevik party. This process started when the Red Army was made autonomous and the secret political police re-established as an organ of the party, and not of the Soviet Congress; it was completed in 1923, during the first year of Stalin's General Secretaryship. From then on, the Soviets became the shadow government in whose midst, through cells formed by Bolshevik party members, functioned the representatives of real power who were appointed and responsible to the Central Committee in Moscow. The crucial point in the later development was not the conquest of the Soviets by the party, but the fact that "although it would have presented no difficulties, the Bolsheviks did not abolish the Soviets and used them as the decorative outward symbol of their authority."

The co-existence of an ostensible and a real government therefore was partly the outcome of the revolution itself and preceded Stalin's totalitarian dictatorship. Yet while the Nazis simply retained the existing administration and deprived it of all power, Stalin had to revive his shadow government, which in the early thirties had lost all its functions and was half forgotten in Russia; he introduced the Soviet constitution as the symbol of the existence as well as the powerlessness of the Soviets.

(None of its paragraphs ever had the slightest practical significance for life and jurisdiction in Russia.) The ostensible Russian government, utterly lacking the glamour of tradition so necessary for a façade, apparently needed the sacred halo of written law. The totalitarian defiance of law and legality (which "in spite of the greatest changes . . . still [remain] the expression of a permanently desired order") found in the written Soviet constitution, as in the never-repudiated Weimar constitution, a permanent background for its own lawlessness, the permanent challenge to the non-totalitarian world and its standards whose helplessness and impotence could be demonstrated daily.

Duplication of offices and division of authority, the co-existence of real and ostensible power, are sufficient to create confusion but not to explain the "shapelessness" of the whole structure. One should not forget that only a building can have a structure, but that a movement — if the word is to be taken as seriously and as literally as the Nazis meant it — can have only a direction, and that any form of legal or governmental structure can be only a handicap to a movement which is being propelled with increasing speed in a certain direction. Even in the prepower stage the totalitarian movements represented those masses that were no longer willing to live in any kind of structure, regardless of its nature; masses that had started to move in order to flood the legal and geographical borders securely determined by the government. Therefore, judged by our conceptions of government and state structure, these movements, so long as they find themselves physically still limited to a specific territory, necessarily must try to destroy all structure, and for this willful destruction a mere duplication of all offices into party and state institutions would not be sufficient. Since duplication involves a relationship between the façade of the state and the inner core of the party, it, too, would eventually result in some kind of structure, where the relationship between party and state would automatically end in a legal regulation which restricts and stabilizes their respective authority.

As a matter of fact, duplication of offices, seemingly the result of the party-state problem in all one-party dictatorships, is only the most conspicuous sign of a more complicated phenomenon that is better defined as multiplication of offices than duplication. The Nazis were not content to establish *Gaue* in addition to the old provinces, but also introduced a great many other geographical divisions in accordance with the different party organizations: the territorial units of the SA were neither coextensive with the *Gaue* nor with the provinces; they differed, moreover, from those of the SS and none of them corresponded to the zones dividing the Hitler Youth. To this geographical confusion must be added the fact that the original relationship between real and ostensible power repeated itself throughout, albeit in an ever-changing way. The inhabitant of Hitler's Third Reich lived not only under the simultaneous and often conflicting authorities of competing powers, such as the civil services, the party, the SA, and the SS; he could never be sure and was never explicitly told whose authority he was supposed to place above all others. He had to develop a kind of sixth sense to know at a given moment whom to obey and whom to disregard.

Those, on the other hand, who had to execute the orders which the leadership, in the interest of the movement, regarded as genuinely necessary — in contradistinction to governmental measures, such orders were of course entrusted only to the party's elite formations — were not much better off. Mostly such orders were "intentionally vague, and given in the expectation that their recipient would recognize the intent of the order giver, and act accordingly"; for the elite formations were by no means merely obligated to obey the orders of the Fuehrer (this was mandatory for all existing organizations anyway), but "to execute the *will* of the leadership." And, as can be gathered from the lengthy proceedings concerning "excesses" before the party courts, this was by no means one and the same thing. The only difference was that the elite formations, thanks to their special indoctrination for such purposes, had been trained to understand that certain "hints meant more than their mere verbal contents."

Technically speaking, the movement within the apparatus of totalitarian domination derives its mobility from the fact that the leadership constantly shifts the actual center of power, often to other organizations, but without dissolving or even publicly exposing the groups that have thus been deprived of their power. In the early period of the Nazi regime, immediately after the Reichstag fire, the SA was the real authority and the party the ostensible one; power then shifted from the SA to the SS and finally from the SS to the Security Service. The point is that none of the organs or power was ever deprived of its right to pretend that it embodied the will of the Leader. But not only was the will of the Leader so unstable that compared with it the whims of Oriental despots are a shining example of steadfastness; the consistent and ever-changing division between real secret authority and ostensible open representation made the actual seat of power a mystery by definition, and this to such an extent that the members of the ruling clique themselves could never be absolutely sure of their own position in the secret power hierarchy. Alfred Rosenberg, for instance, despite his long career in the party and his impressive accumulation of ostensible power and offices in the party hierarchy, still talked about the creation of a series of Eastern European States as a security wall against Moscow at a time when those invested with real power had already decided that no state structure would succeed the defeat of the Soviet Union and that the population of the Eastern occupied territories had become definitely stateless and could therefore be exterminated. In other words, since knowledge of whom to obey and a comparatively permanent settlement of hierarchy would introduce an element of stability which is essentially absent from totalitarian rule, the Nazis constantly disavowed real authority whenever it had come into the open and created new instances of government compared with which the former became a shadow government — a game which obviously could go on indefinitely. One of the most important technical differences between the Soviet and the National Socialist system is that Stalin, whenever he shifted the power emphasis within his own movement from one apparatus to another, had the tendency to liquidate the apparatus together with its staff, while Hitler, in spite of his contemptuous comments on people who "are unable to leap across their own shadows," was perfectly willing to continue using these shadows even though in another function.

The multiplication of offices was extremely useful for the constant shifting of power; the longer, moreover, a totalitarian regime stays in power, the greater becomes the number of offices and the possibility of jobs exclusively dependent upon the movement, since no office is abolished when its authority is liquidated. The Nazi regime started this multiplication with an initial co-ordination of all existing associations, societies, and institutions. The interesting thing in this nation-wide manipulation was that co-ordination did not signify incorporation into the already existing respective party organizations. The result was that up to the end of the regime, there were not one, but two National Socialist student organizations, two Nazi women's organizations, two Nazi organizations for university professors, lawyers, physicians, and so forth. It was by no means sure, however, that in all cases the original party organization would be more powerful than its co-ordinated counterpart. Nor could anybody predict with any assurance which party organ would rise in the ranks of the internal party hierarchy.

A classical instance of this planned shapelessness occurred in the organization of scientific antisemitism. In 1933, an institute for study of the Jewish question (Institut zur Erforschung der Judenfrage) was founded in Munich which, since the Jewish question presumably had determined the whole of German history, quickly enlarged into a research institute for modern German history. Headed by the well-known historian Walter Frank, it transformed the traditional universities into seats of ostensible learning or façades. In 1940, another institute for the study of the Jewish question was founded in Frankfurt, headed by Alfred Rosenberg, whose standing as a party member was considerably higher. The Munich institute consequently was relegated to a shadowy existence; the Frankfurt, not the Munich institution was supposed to receive the treasures from looted European Jewish collections and become the seat of a comprehensive library on Judaism. Yet, when these collections actually arrived in Germany a few years later, their most precious parts went not to Frankfurt, but to Berlin, where they were received by Himmler's special Gestapo department for the liquidation (not merely the study) of the Jewish question, which was headed by Eichmann. None of the older institutions was ever abolished, so that in 1944 the situation was this: behind the façades of the universities' history departments stood threateningly the more real power of the Munich institute, behind which rose Rosenberg's institute in Frankfurt, and only behind these three façades, hidden and protected by them, lay the real center of authority, the *Reichssicherheitshauptamt,* a special division of the Gestapo.

The façade of the Soviet government, despite its written constitution, is even less impressive, erected even more exclusively for foreign observation than the state administration which the Nazis inherited and retained from the Weimar Republic. Lacking the Nazis' original accumulation of offices in the period of co-ordination, the Soviet regime relies even more on constant creation of new offices to put the former centers of power in the shadow. The gigantic increase of the bureaucratic apparatus, inherent in this method, is checked by repeated liquidation through purges. Nevertheless, in Russia, too, we can distinguish at least three strictly separate organizations: the Soviet or state apparatus, the party apparatus, and the NKVD apparatus, each of which has its own independent department of economy, a political department, a ministry of education and culture, a military department, etc.

In Russia, the ostensible power of the party bureaucracy as against the real power of the secret police corresponds to the original duplication of party and state as known in Nazi Germany, and the multiplication becomes evident only in the secret police itself, with its extremely complicated, widely ramified network of agents, in which one department is always assigned to supervising and spying on another. Every enterprise in the Soviet Union has its special department of the secret police, which spies on party members and ordinary personnel alike. Co-existent with this department is another police division of the party itself, which again watches everybody, including the agents of the NKVD, and whose members are not known to the rival body. Added to these two espionage organizations must be the unions in the factories, which must see to it that the workers fulfill their prescribed quotas. Far more important than these apparatuses, however, is "the special department" of the NKVD which represents "an NKVD within the NKVD," *i.e.*, a secret police within the secret police. All reports of these competing police agencies ultimately end up in the Moscow Central Committee and the Politburo. Here it is decided which of the reports is decisive and which of the police divisions shall be entitled to carry out the respective police measures. Neither the average inhabitant of the country nor any one of the police departments knows, of course, what decision will be made; today it may be the special division of the NKVD, tomorrow the party's network of agents; the day after,

it may be the local committees or one of the regional bodies. Among all these departments there exists no legally rooted hierarchy of power or authority; the only certainty is that eventually one of them will be chosen to embody "the will of the leadership."

The only rule of which everybody in a totalitarian state may be sure is that the more visible government agencies are, the less power they carry, and the less is known of the existence of an institution, the more powerful it will ultimately turn out to be. According to this rule, the Soviets, recognized by a written constitution as the highest authority of the state, have less power than the Bolshevik party; the Bolshevik party, which recruits its members openly and is recognized as the ruling class, has less power than the secret police. Real power begins where secrecy begins. In this respect the Nazi and the Bolshevik states were very much alike; their difference lay chiefly in the monopolization and centralization of secret police services in Himmler on one hand, and the maze of apparently unrelated and unconnected police activities in Russia on the other.

If we consider the totalitarian state solely as an instrument of power and leave aside questions of administrative efficiency, industrial capacity, and economic productivity, then its shapelessness turns out to be an ideally suited instrument for the realization of the so-called Leader principle. A continuous competition between offices, whose functions not only overlap but which are charged with identical tasks, gives opposition or sabotage almost no chance to become effective; a swift change of emphasis which relegates one office to the shadow and elevates another to authority can solve all problems without anybody's becoming aware of the change or of the fact that opposition had existed, the additional advantage of the system being that the opposing office is likely never to learn of its defeat, since it is either not abolished at all (as in the case of the Nazi regime) or it is liquidated much later and without any apparent connection with the specific matter. This can be done all the more easily since nobody, except those few initiated, knows the exact relationship between the authorities. Only once in a while does the nontotalitarian world catch a glimpse of these conditions, as when a high official abroad confesses that an obscure clerk in the Embassy had been his immediate superior. In retrospect it is often possible to determine why such a sudden loss of power occurred, or, rather, that it occurred at all. For instance, it is not hard to understand today why at the outbreak of war people like Alfred Rosenberg or Hans Frank were removed to state positions and thus eliminated from the real center of power, namely, the Fuehrer's inner circle. The important thing is that they not only did not know the reasons for these moves, but presumably [had] not even suspected that such apparently exalted positions as Governor General of Poland or Reichsminister for all Eastern territories did not signify the climax but the end of their National Socialist careers.

The Leader principle does not establish a hierarchy in the totalitarian state any more than it does in the totalitarian movement; authority is not filtered down from the top through all intervening layers to the bottom of the body politic as is the case in authoritarian regimes. The factual reason is that there is no hierarchy without authority and that, in spite of the numerous misunderstandings concerning the so-called "authoritarian personality," the principle of authority is in all important respects diametrically opposed to that of totalitarian domination. Quite apart from its origin in Roman history, authority, no matter in what form, always is meant to restrict or limit freedom, but never to abolish it. Totalitarian domination, however, aims at abolishing freedom, even at eliminating human spontaneity in general, and by no means at a restriction of freedom no matter how tyrannical.

III. PICTURES OF THE TOTALITARIAN MAN

The Old Revolutionary and the Technician of Power

ARTHUR KOESTLER

Arthur Koestler, a novelist of worldwide reputation, was born in Budapest in 1905 and educated at the University of Vienna. A correspondent for a leading liberal Berlin newspaper during the troubled Weimar period, Koestler joined the Communist Party in 1931. Like many other intellectuals similarly attracted to communism, Koestler was ultimately unable to stomach the fanaticism of a party which attacked even its closest allies in the name of ideological conformity. After visiting civil war Spain and after imprisonment by the Franco forces, Koestler eventually escaped to England where he served in the British army. His most famous novel, *Darkness at Noon*, from which the following selection is taken, is based on the famous Moscow purge trials of the 1930s. Koestler secured his knowledge of the purges not only from such records as existed and from his personal knowledge of communism, but also from the information which he gained from Eva Weissberg, a close friend who personally went through the experience of being implicated and involved in the trials. Despite more recent, and strictly scholarly, studies of the purges, Koestler's treatment still remains an outstanding explanation of the motivations of both the purgers and their victims.

TOWARDS MORNING, when Rubashov still had not given in over the question of sabotage in the aluminum trust, Gletkin's voice acquired an undertone of nervousness — just as in the beginning, when Hare-lip had brought out the wrong answer. He turned the lamp on more sharply, which had not happened for a long time; but he turned it down again when he saw Rubashov's ironic smile. He put a few more questions, which had no effect, and said conclusively:

"So you definitely deny having committed any wrecking or subversive acts in the industry entrusted to you — or to have even planned such acts?"

Rubashov nodded — with a sleepy curiosity as to what would happen. Gletkin turned to the stenographer:

"Write: the examining magistrate recommends that this charge be dropped for lack of evidence."

Rubashov quickly lit a cigarette to conceal the movement of childish triumph which overcame him. For the first time he had won a victory over Gletkin. Certainly it was a pathetic little local victory in a lost battle, but yet a victory; and it had been so many months, even years, since he had last known this feeling. . . . Gletkin took the day's record from the secretary and dismissed her, according to the ritual which had latterly developed between them.

When they were alone, and Rubashov

From Arthur Koestler, *Darkness at Noon* (New York, 1941), pp. 223–227, 232–240. Reprinted by permission of the author.

had stood up to sign the protocol, Gletkin said, passing him his fountain pen:

"Industrial sabotage is, according to experience, the most effective means for the opposition to create difficulties for the Government, and to produce discontent amongst the workers. Why do you so stubbornly maintain that you did not use — or intend to use — just this method?"

"Because it is a technical absurdity," said Rubashov. "And this perpetual harping on the *saboteur* as a bogyman produces an epidemic of denunciation which revolts me."

The long-missed sensation of triumph caused Rubashov to feel fresher and speak louder than usual.

"If you hold sabotage for a mere fiction, what, in your opinion, are the real causes of the unsatisfactory state of our industries?"

"Too low piece-work tariffs, slave-driving and barbaric disciplinary measures," said Rubashov. "I know of several cases in my Trust in which workers were shot as *saboteurs* because of some trifling negligence caused by over-tiredness. If a man is two minutes late at clocking-in, he is fired, and a stamp is put in his identity-papers which makes it impossible for him to find work elsewhere."

Gletkin looked at Rubashov with his usual expressionless gaze, and asked him, in his usual expressionless voice:

"Were you given a watch as a boy?"

Rubashov looked at him in astonishment. The most conspicuous trait of the Neanderthal character was its absolute humourlessness, or more exactly, its lack of frivolity.

"Don't you want to answer my question?" asked Gletkin.

"Certainly," said Rubashov, more and more astonished.

"How old were you when the watch was given you?"

"I don't quite know," said Rubashov; "eight or nine probably."

"I," said Gletkin in his usual correct voice, "was sixteen years old when I learnt that the hour was divided into minutes. In my village, when the peasants had to travel to town, they would go to the railway station at sunrise and lie down to sleep in the waiting-room until the train came, which was usually at about midday; sometimes it only came in the evening or next morning. These are the peasants who now work in our factories. For example, in my village is now the biggest steel-rail factory in the world. In the first year, the foremen would lie down to sleep between two emptyings of the blast furnace, until they were shot. In all other countries, the peasants had one or two hundred years to develop the habit of industrial precision and of the handling of machines. Here they only had ten years. If we didn't sack them and shoot them for every trifle, the whole country would come to a standstill, and the peasants would lie down to sleep in the factory yards until grass grew out of the chimneys and everything became as it was before. Last year a women's delegation came to us from Manchester in England. They were shown everything, and afterwards they wrote indignant articles, saying that the textile workers in Manchester would never stand such treatment. I have read that the cotton industry in Manchester is two hundred years old. I have also read, what the treatment of the workers there was like two hundred years ago, when it started. You, Comrade Rubashov, have just used the same arguments as this women's delegation from Manchester. You, of course, know better than these women. So one may wonder at your using the same arguments. But then, you have something in common with them: you were given a watch as a child. . . ."

Rubashov said nothing and looked at Gletkin with a new interest. What was this? Was the Neanderthaler coming out of his shell? But Gletkin sat stiffly on his chair, as expressionless as ever.

"You may be right in some ways," Rubashov said finally. "But it was you who started me off on this question. What use is it to invent scapegoats for difficulties, the natural causes of which you have just so convincingly described?"

"Experience teaches," said Gletkin, "that the masses must be given for all difficult and complicated processes a simple, easily grasped explanation. According to what I know of history, I see that mankind could never do without scapegoats. I believe it was at all times an indispensable institution; your friend Ivanov taught me that it was of religious origin. As far as I remember, he explained that the word itself came from a custom of the Hebrews, who once a year sacrificed to their god a goat, laden with all their sins." Gletkin paused and shoved his cuffs into place. "Besides, there are also examples in history of voluntary scapegoats. At the age when you were given a watch, I was being taught by the village priest that Jesus Christ called himself a lamb, which had taken on itself all sin. I have never understood in what way it could help mankind if someone declares he is being sacrificed for its sake. But for two thousand years people have apparently found it quite natural."

Rubashov looked at Gletkin. What was he aiming at? What was the object of this conversation? In what labyrinth was the Neanderthaler straying?

"However that may be," said Rubashov, "it would be more in accordance with our ideas to tell the people the truth, instead of populating the world with *saboteurs* and devils."

"If one told the people in my village," said Gletkin, "that they were still slow and backward in spite of the Revolution and the factories, it would have no effect on them. If one tells them that they are heroes of work, more efficient than the Americans, and that all evil only comes from devils and *saboteurs,* it has at least *some* effect. Truth is what is useful to humanity, falsehood what is harmful. In the outline of history published by the Party for the evening classes for adults, it is emphasized that during the first few centuries the Christian religion realized an objective progress for mankind. Whether Jesus spoke the truth or not, when he asserted he was the son of God and of a virgin is of no interest to any sensible person. It is said to be symbolical, but the peasants take it literally. We have the same right to invent useful symbols which the peasants take literally."

*   *   *

He was not taken back to his cell as he had hoped, but straight to Gletkin's room. Gletkin was sitting at his desk, in the same position as Rubashov had left him in — how long ago? He looked as though he had not moved during Rubashov's absence. The curtains were drawn, the lamp burning; time stood still in this room, as in a putrefying pond. While sitting down again opposite Gletkin, Rubashov's glance fell on a damp patch on the carpet. He remembered his sickness. So it was, after all, but an hour since he had left the room.

"I take it that you feel better now," said Gletkin. "We left off at the concluding question of the motive for your counterrevolutionary activities."

He stared in slight surprise at Rubashov's right hand, resting on the arm of the chair and still clenching a tiny lump of snow. Rubashov followed his glance; he smiled and lifted his hand to the lamp. They both watched the little lump melting on his hand in the warmth of the bulb.

"The question of motive is the last," said Gletkin. "When you have signed that, we will have finished with one another."

The lamp radiated a sharper light than it had for a long time. Rubashov was forced to blink.

". . . And then you will be able to rest," said Gletkin.

Rubashov passed his hand over his temples, but the coolness of the snow was gone. The word "rest," with which Gletkin had ended his sentence, remained suspended in the silence. Rest and sleep. Let us choose a captain and return into the land of Egypt. . . . He blinked sharply through his pince-nez at Gletkin:

"You know my motives as well as I do,"

he said. "You know that I acted neither out of a 'counter-revolutionary mentality,' nor was I in the service of a foreign Power. What I thought and what I did, I thought and did according to my own conviction and conscience."

Gletkin had pulled a dossier out of his drawer. He went through it, pulled out a sheet and read in his monotonous voice:

"'. . . For us the question of subjective good faith is of no interest. He who is in the wrong must pay; he who is in the right will be absolved. That was our law. . . .' You wrote that in your diary shortly after your arrest."

Rubashov felt behind his eye-lids the familiar flickering of the light. In Gletkin's mouth the sentence he had thought and written acquired a peculiarly naked sound — as though a confession, intended only for the anonymous priest, had been registered on a gramophone record, which now was repeating it in its cracked voice.

Gletkin had taken another page out of the dossier, but read only one sentence from it, with his expressionless gaze fixed on Rubashov:

"'Honour is: to serve without vanity, and unto the last consequence.'"

Rubashov tried to withstand his gaze.

"I don't see," he said, "how it can serve the Party that her members have to grovel in the dust before all the world. I have signed everything you wanted me to sign. I have pleaded guilty to having pursued a false and objectively harmful policy. Isn't that enough for you?"

He put on his pince-nez, blinked helplessly past the lamp, and ended in a tired, hoarse voice:

"After all, the name N. S. Rubashov is itself a piece of Party history. By dragging it in dirt, you besmirch the history of the Revolution."

Gletkin looked through the dossier.

"To that I can also reply with a citation from your own writings. You wrote:

"'It is necessary to hammer every sentence into the masses by repetition and simplification. What is presented as right must shine like gold; what is presented as wrong must be black as pitch. For consumption by the masses, the political processes must be coloured like ginger-bread figures at a fair.'"

Rubashov was silent. Then he said:

"So that is what you are aiming at: I am to play the Devil in your Punch and Judy show — howl, grind my teeth and put out my tongue — and voluntarily, too. Danton and his friends were spared that, at least."

Gletkin shut the cover of the dossier. He bent forward a bit and settled his cuffs:

"Your testimony at the trial will be the last service you can do the Party."

Rubashov did not answer. He kept his eyes shut and relaxed under the rays of the lamp like a tired sleeper in the sun; but there was no escape from Gletkin's voice.

"Your Danton and the Convention," said the voice, "were just a gallant play compared to what is at stake here. I have read books about it: those people wore powdered pigtails and declaimed about their personal honour. To them, it only mattered to die with a noble gesture, regardless of whether this gesture did good or harm."

Rubashov said nothing. There was a buzzing and humming in his ears; Gletkin's voice was above him; it came from every side of him; it hammered mercilessly on his aching skull.

"You know what is at stake here," Gletkin went on. "For the first time in history, a revolution has not only conquered power, but also kept it. We have made our country a bastion of the new era. It covers a sixth of the world and contains a tenth of the world's population."

Gletkin's voice now sounded at Rubashov's back. He had risen and was walking up and down the room. It was the first time this had happened. His boots creaked at every step, his starched uniform crackled and a sourish smell of sweat and leather became noticeable.

"When our Revolution had succeeded in our country, we believed that the rest of the earth would follow suit. Instead, came a wave of reaction, which threatened to swamp us. There were two currents in the Party. One consisted of adventurers, who wanted to risk what we had won to promote the revolution abroad. You belonged to them. We recognized this current to be dangerous, and have liquidated it."

Rubashov wanted to raise his head and say something. Gletkin's steps resounded in his skull. He was too tired. He let himself fall back, and kept his eyes shut.

"The leader of the Party," Gletkin's voice went on, "had the wider perspective and the more tenacious tactics. He realized that everything depended on surviving the period of world reaction and keeping the bastion. He had realized that it might last ten, perhaps twenty, perhaps fifty years, until the world was ripe for a fresh wave of revolution. Until then we stand alone. Until then we have only one duty: not to perish."

A sentence swam vaguely in Rubashov's memory: "It is the Revolutionary's duty to preserve his own life." Who had said that? He, himself? Ivanov? It was in the name of that principle that he had sacrificed Arlova. And where had it led him?

". . . Not to perish," sounded Gletkin's voice. "The bulwark must be held, at any price and with any sacrifice. The leader of the Party recognized this principle with unrivalled clearsightedness, and has consistently applied it. The policy of the International had to be subordinated to our national policy. Whoever did not understand this necessity had to be destroyed. Whole sets of our best functionaries in Europe had to be physically liquidated. We did not recoil from crushing our own organizations abroad when the interests of the Bastion required it. We did not recoil from co-operation with the police of reactionary countries in order to suppress revolutionary movements which came at the wrong moment. We did not recoil from betraying our friends and compromising with our enemies, in order to preserve the Bastion. That was the task which history had given us, the representatives of the first victorious revolution. The shortsighted, the æsthetes, the moralists did not understand. But the leader of the Revolution understood that all depended on one thing: to be the better stayer."

Gletkin interrupted his pacing through the room. He stopped behind Rubashov's chair. The scar on his shaven skull shone sweatily. He panted, wiped his skull with his handkerchief, and seemed embarrassed at having broken his customary reserve. He sat down again behind the desk and settled his cuffs. He turned down the light a little, and continued in his usual expressionless voice:

"The Party's line was sharply defined. Its tactics were determined by the principle that the end justifies the means — all means, without exception. In the spirit of this principle, the Public Prosecutor will demand your life, Citizen Rubashov.

"Your faction, Citizen Rubashov, is beaten and destroyed. You wanted to split the Party, although you must have known that a split in the Party meant civil war. You know of the dissatisfaction amongst the peasantry, which has not yet learnt to understand the sense of the sacrifices imposed on it. In a war which may be only a few months away, such currents can lead to a catastrophe. Hence the imperious necessity for the Party to be united. It must be as if cast from one mould — filled with blind discipline and absolute trust. You and your friends, Citizen Rubashov, have made a rent in the Party. If your repentance is real, then you must help us to heal this rent. I have told you, it is the last service the Party will ask of you.

"Your task is simple. You have set it yourself: to gild the Right, to blacken the Wrong. The policy of the opposition is wrong. Your task is therefore to make the opposition contemptible; to make the masses understand that opposition is a crime and that the leaders of the opposition are criminals. That is the simple language which the masses understand. If you begin to talk of your complicated motives, you will only create confusion amongst them. Your task, Citizen Rubashov, is to avoid awakening sympathy and pity. Sympathy and pity for the opposition are a danger to the country.

"Comrade Rubashov, I hope that you have understood the task which the Party has set you."

It was the first time since their acquaintance that Gletkin called Rubashov 'Comrade.' Rubashov raised his head quickly. He felt a hot wave rising in him, against which he was helpless. His chin shook slightly while he was putting on his pince-nez.

"I understand."

"Observe," Gletkin went on, "that the Party holds out to you no prospect of reward. Some of the accused have been made amenable by physical pressure. Others, by the promise to save their heads — or the heads of their relatives who had fallen into our hands as hostages. To you, Comrade Rubashov, we propose no bargain and we promise nothing."

"I understand," Rubashov repeated.

Gletkin glanced at the dossier.

"There is a passage in your journal which impressed me," he went on. "You wrote: 'I have thought and acted as I had to. If I was right, I have nothing to repent of; if wrong, I shall pay.'"

He looked up from the dossier and looked Rubashov fully in the face:

"You were wrong, and you will pay, Comrade Rubashov. The Party promises only one thing: after the victory, one day when it can do no more harm, the material of the secret archives will be published. Then the world will learn what was in the background of this Punch and Judy show — as you called it — which we had to act to them according to history's textbook. . . ."

He hesitated a few seconds, settled his cuffs and ended rather awkwardly, while the scar on his skull reddened:

"And then you, and some of your friends of the older generation, will be given the sympathy and pity which are denied to you to-day."

While he was speaking, he had pushed the prepared statement over to Rubashov, and laid his fountain-pen beside it. Rubashov stood up and said with a strained smile:

"I have always wondered what it was like when the Neanderthalers became sentimental. Now I know."

"I do not understand," said Gletkin, who had also stood up.

Rubashov signed the statement, in which he confessed to having committed his crimes through counter-revolutionary motives and in the service of a foreign Power. As he raised his head, his gaze fell on the portrait of No. 1 hanging on the wall, and once again he recognized the expression of knowing irony with which years ago No. 1 had taken leave of him — that melancholy cynicism which stared down on humanity from the omnipresent portrait.

"It does not matter if you don't understand," said Rubashov. "There are things which only that older generation, the Ivanovs, Rubashovs and Kieffers have understood. That is over now."

"I will give orders that you are not to be troubled until the trial," said Gletkin after a short pause, again stiff and precise. Rubashov's smiling irritated him. "Have you any other particular wish?"

"To sleep," said Rubashov. He stood in the open door, beside the giant warder, small, elderly and insignificant with his pince-nez and beard.

"I will give orders that your sleep must not be disturbed," said Gletkin.

When the door had shut behind Rubashov, he went back to his desk. For a few seconds he sat still. Then he rang for his secretary.

She sat down in her usual place in the corner. "I congratulate you on your success, Comrade Gletkin," she said.

Gletkin turned the lamp down to normal.

"That," he said with a glance at the lamp, "plus lack of sleep and physical exhaustion. It is all a matter of constitution."

The SS Man: Idealist or Beast?

EUGEN KOGON

Eugen Kogon, a student of economics and sociology, established himself
as an active and determined opponent of Nazism during that movement's rise to
power in the 1930s. Arrested in March of 1938 he was taken to the infamous
Buchenwald in 1939. Slated to be sent to the death camp at Auschwitz, he
was saved from that fate partly by the efforts of influential friends. Liberated
in April of 1945, he settled with his family at Frankfurt-on-Main where he
resumed a literary career. His *Theory and Practice of Hell*, from which the following selection is taken, is a remarkable book, based on Kogon's own experiences and on those of other inmates of the camps, supplemented by official
records. The account is a marvel of objectivity, for Kogon was determined to
avoid the pitfall of sensationalism, on the one hand, and, at the same time, to
steer clear of any false squeamishness which would have prevented his account
from revealing the true, if unsavory, realities of the concentration camp system.

THE AIMS AND ORGANIZATION
OF THE SS SUPER STATE

LATE IN THE FALL of 1937, in Frankfurt,
I had occasion for an extended discussion with a leading SS man from Vogelsang Castle — a discussion that continued
over several afternoons.

It should be noted that Vogelsang, in
the Eiffel Mountains, was one of three cas-
tles — *Ordensburg* is the German term —
where the new Nazi elite was to be incu-
bated. *Ordensburg* really describes a castle
belonging to a medieval order, such as the
Knights Templar — and that is how the
Nazis thought of their elite. At the *Ordensburg*, young men chosen with care were
trained for several years under an austere
regimen of consecration.

My discussion with the SS officer was
very frank on both sides. It dealt with such
questions as the meaning of German history, the role of the Third Reich, and the
racial theories of the SS. The contrast between the views expressed was, of course,
extreme and gave me a wealth of insight,
confirming much that I had already sus-

pected. The SS officer was by no means
stupid, indeed he had a superior intellect,
for all that he was a thoroughgoing fanatic.
He made three remarkable statements:

*"What we trainers of the younger genera-
tion of Führers aspire to is a modern governmental structure on the model of the ancient
Greek city states. It is to these aristocratically
run democracies with their broad economic
basis of serfdom that we owe the great cultural
achievements of antiquity. From five to ten
per cent of the people, their finest flower, shall
rule; the rest must work and obey. In this way
alone can we attain that peak performance we
must demand of ourselves and of the German
people.*

*"The new Führer class is selected by the SS
—in a positive sense by means of the National
Political Education Institutes* (Napola) *as a
preparatory stage, of the Ordensburgen as the
academies proper of the coming Nazi aristocracy, and of a subsequent active internship in
public affairs; in a negative sense by the extermination of all racially and biologically in-
ferior elements and by the radical removal of
all incorrigible political opposition that refuses*

From *The Theory and Practice of Hell* by Eugen Kogon, pp. 15–16, 207–212. Translated by Heinz
Norden. Reprinted by permission of Farrar, Straus & Giroux, Inc., and Martin Secker & Warburg
Ltd. Published in 1950 by Farrar, Straus & Company, Inc.

on principle to acknowledge the philosophical basis of the Nazi State and its essential institutions.

"Within ten years at the latest it will be possible for us in this way to dictate the law of Adolf Hitler to Europe, put a halt to the otherwise inevitable decay of the continent, and build up a true community of nations, with Germany as the leading power keeping order."

* * *

SPECIAL PLACES OF EXECUTION
AND DISPOSAL OF THE DEAD

I am not exaggerating when I say that a separate book would have to be written on the concentration-camp prisons, called "Bunker." It would be a blood-curdling collection of documents. Each bunker in each individual camp had its own gruesome story, and it would be impossible for me to tell them all here, even if I knew all the details. They ranged from the "dog cells" at Dachau where the prisoners could only lie huddled on one side and had to bark for their food when it was passed to them; to unlighted solitary cells where German intellectuals were kept until they went almost blind; to the stand-up cells at Sachsenhausen, barely large enough to hold a man in upright position — it was impossible for him to wipe off the spittle if he was spat upon; and to every other imaginable form of torment.

It happened occasionally, though very exceptionally, that a prisoner was permanently kept in the bunker without being mistreated. Such an exception was Pastor Niemöller at Sachsenhausen. He spent his more than seven years in the concentration camps in solitary confinement, and saw virtually nothing of the rest of the camp. When it was necessary for him to visit the dental clinic, he had to climb into a wheelbarrow across which a tarpaulin was spread. The dental clinic was cleared and he was wheeled there and back in the same fashion. Niemöller, it is true, was visited by his wife. But the fact that he was for years kept in solitary confinement is significant enough.

Officially the bunker was called "The Cell Block." It was generally located in one wing of the gatehouse and consisted of a series of small concrete cells with raised bunks of stone and high window embrasures.

It was against this background that the prison wardens for years plied their dreadful trade. In Buchenwald it was Master Sergeant Sommer, a man who can be described only as a beast in human form — every camp knew his kind. Arrested in the course of the trial of Koch and Dr. Hoven, he admitted some 150 murders within a single half year. He tortured and killed during grillings, sometimes with the knowledge of the Political Department, as a form of "punishment," or simply "for fun." There are few methods that he failed to use. In the end the SS feared him no less than did the prisoners, for he was in a position to "rub out" anyone who got into his clutches.

Grillings in the bunker took place in the following manner: on admission the prisoner had to strip to the skin and his clothing was carefully searched. He was then taken to an unlighted cell and shackled to the radiator so that he was unable to move. At night the trusty Fischermann, a former Storm Trooper, made his rounds in felt-soled slippers. If he found the prisoner asleep, he would set upon him with a rubber truncheon. The prisoner's screams would bring Sommer, who would wield his whip until the victim was unconscious.

In the middle of the night Leclaire, an official of the Political Department, would arrive. The prisoner was revived with cold water. Leclaire would first of all beat him about the head, to refresh his memory: "You know, don't you, that you'll never leave this place alive? If you lie, we'll give you something to laugh about all right!" If the prisoner still refused to talk or did not tell enough, Commandant Koch would be requested to issue a written authorization that has become notorious: "The prisoner is to be examined until he confesses."

On the basis of this authorization Sommer would, for example, force the stripped prisoner to immerse his testicles in ice-cold and boiling water in turn, painting them with iodine when the skin came off in strips. Naturally this caused the most agonizing pain. Or Sommer would tie the prisoner's hands on his back and string him up by them from a set of rings mounted in a barred door in the central corridor of the cell block. The prisoner would hang suspended, his feet a foot or two off the floor. Sommer and Leclaire together would, in addition, place a rope around his neck and throttle him from time to time. Sometimes they would suspend themselves from the prisoner's legs. Few prisoners stood this treatment for more than twenty minutes without losing consciousness. They were then let down and revived with cold water, and the procedure was repeated. These tortures sometimes extracted confessions no man would have made under ordinary circumstances. Yet there were prisoners who never uttered a word. Food and water would be withdrawn and the examination repeated every day. There might be as many as three suspensions and starvation might be extended to as much as ten days. If the prisoner still failed to talk on the tenth day, there came the ultimate ordeal — suspension head down. If there were still no results, Sommer might release the prisoner or, if the Political Department regarded it as a "difficult case," he might offer the man a cup of tea that put him to sleep, whereupon Sommer would administer a fatal injection.

The next morning the public-address system would announce: "Corpse-carriers to the gatehouse!" The Camp Medical Officer would certify: "Death by circulatory failure." If the prisoner refused to drink the tea, Sommer would peer in through the peephole to see whether the man had fallen asleep yet. The next day poisoned food was brought to the cell. If this too failed, Sommer would affect a curious gesture — but only if the prisoner had not squealed on another! He would apply for the prisoner's discharge, which was always authorized —

that is, in those few cases in which a prisoner actually survived the tortures that have been described. When the prisoner was discharged from the bunker, Sommer would even present him with tobacco!

Fritz Männchen of Dresden, Kurt Leeser of Aachen, the bunker orderlies Richard Gritz of Antonienhütte near Kattowitz, Alfred Miller of Leonberg near Stuttgart, and Roman Hädelmeyer of Vienna all had long experience in the bunker and have recorded a wealth of factual information, all of which tallies.

The "simplest" death Sommer would pick for a prisoner was to hang him with his own hands from the window frame or radiator. Many prisoners, however, were simply beaten to death by Sommer with an iron bar. One case has become known, in which he applied an iron clamp to his victim's temples, screwing it shut until the skull was crushed.

To look out of a cell window meant certain death to any prisoner. If he was caught, Sommer would beat him to death or give him a fatal injection. The same punishment threatened anyone caught reading even the smallest fragment of newspaper issued as toilet paper. He was forbidden to pace the cell. The prisoner had to stand at attention from five o'clock in the morning to ten o'clock at night, staring at the door. The peephole in the door held a magnifying lens through which the slightest movement could be observed. Any violation was punished with twenty-five lashes. Food, when issued at all, consisted of half rations. In the wintertime, prisoners were commonly drenched with water, the clothing being allowed to dry on the body while the prisoner slept on the concrete floor.

One of the cells held seven Jews. One day Sommer appeared with a tin pail with which he beat two of the prisoners to death. He then ripped a piece of iron from the radiator and used it to kill the others. Of at least one hundred Jews who passed through the bunker between 1940 and 1941, not one left alive.

It was also customary to feed the prisoners cathartics in their food, until they fell sick with bloody stools. Of course there were no antidotes. There were two toilets in the bunker, one for the prisoners, the other for the SS. Whenever a prisoner received his twenty-five lashes, he had to bend over and immerse his head into the excrement-filled toilet bowl. When the punishment had been administered, he was not permitted to wipe the excrement from his face.

On one occasion Sommer shacked seven young Polish prisoners to their cots. Their diet was reduced to salt water and pickles, until they perished. Bunker orderly Gritz describes how their fearful screams, and finally moans, pierced his eardrums. A Czech Communist in Cell 11 was kept without food by Sommer for seven days. He was fond of inflicting death by starvation. He was in the habit of issuing the food himself, and would withhold it wholly or in part from his victims until they had slowly starved to death.

Some of the tortures inflicted by Sommer were nightmares of sadism. He liked to strangle prisoners with his bare hands. His greatest sport was to herd all his prisoners into the corridor, about four feet wide, where he had them do knee bends and hop about until they dropped from exhaustion. He would then trample them with his heels, until the blood spurted from ears and nose and at least a few were left dead. On one occasion he crowded fifteen prisoners into a single cell, giving them only a children's chamber pot which they were not permitted to empty for some ten days. The floor of the cell was ankle-deep in excrement. Subsequently Sommer murdered all fifteen men.

His own quarters were decorated with an illuminated skull. At night he would sometimes summon a victim from one of the cells and leisurely do away with him in the room. He would then place the body under his bed and fall asleep peacefully, his work well done.

And why were prisoners committed to the bunker? For any offense at all, big or little. It was largely a matter of caprice, like everything else in camp. A Jew might be admitted because he had smoked during working hours; another for alleged loafing, a third in order to be questioned by the Political Department or camp headquarters. If a prisoner looked up from his work as the wife of the Commandant, Ilse Koch, passed by, she might jot down his serial number. The hapless wretch was committed to the bunker, for having "stared shamelessly" at the Commandant's wife. He could almost count himself lucky if he got off with a fatal injection. The use of injections was, of course, properly the prerogative of the SS Medical Officers, but Sommer could not keep his fingers off this specialized medical field. Air, chloral hydrate and evipan were his favorite agents and he used them to kill many prisoners.

The Totalitarian Man: A Sociological Analysis

ZEVEDIE BARBU

Zevedie Barbu was born in Rumania and served for a time as a diplomat, visiting several Western capitols. He is now a lecturer on Social Psychology at the University of Glasgow. Having lived under various types of political regimes while in Rumania he was anxious to come to an understanding of the differences between democracy and dictatorship. To accomplish this task, however, he felt it was necessary to abandon a strictly political approach and to fuse both psychology and sociology into a common method in order to determine the "state of mind" of differing political systems. Convinced that one of the most important characteristics of any democratic society is its flexibility, he was led to note the rigidity so frequently demonstrated by totalitarian movements, whether fascist or communist. Moving to the conclusion that such rigidity frequently results from situations of stress, his analysis of those who follow a totalitarian movement leads him to the view that sociologically they consist for the most part of men under pressure by virtue of the fact that the changing structures of society deprive them of security, or of any settled place in society. These are the *"déclassés"* — the people who do not belong — who are described in the selection which follows.

Nazism and Social Classes

MOST STUDENTS of Nazism are inclined to look at the origins of this movement from a purely economic point of view. Lenin can be considered among the first who, from a Marxian viewpoint, foresaw a certain stage in the evolution of Western civilization which might be described as Fascism. The interests of various national economic systems will lead, according to Lenin, to an aggressive type of nationalism for which racial and nationalistic doctrines will be the most adequate ideological weapons. Basing his view on this thesis, Dr. F. Neumann writes: "German National Socialism is nothing but the dictatorship of a monopolized industry and of the big estate owners, the nakedness of which is covered by the mask of a corporative state." Charles Bettelheim sees the core of Nazism in the aggressive policy of the magnates of German industry, who have in their hands *"tous les leviers de commande"* [all the levers of power]. Often Nazism is called simply a "dictatorship of monopoly capitalism."

All these views imply that the structure of Nazism is closely related to the interests of the socially and economically upper strata of German Society. The main piece of evidence which is constantly produced by the supporters of this thesis is the fact that the Nazi movement was, particularly at its beginning, financed by many outstanding representatives of German industry. But today there is little doubt that this fact did not influence the structure of Hitler's movement, except in minor tactical points. In fact Hitler and his party could never be considered the "puppets" of the German upper classes. L. von Mises obviously speaks the truth when saying that "Thyssen and the rest paid him (Hitler), but they did not bribe him." On the contrary, the party organization, its aims, and the attitudes of its members could hardly fit into the interests and way of life of these social strata. Even Nazi bellicosity has little in common with the aggressive expansionistic attitude of the German industrialists. As we shall see later the two types of aggression are widely different in their sources and modes of manifestation.

Another opinion, also widespread, is that Nazism was a lower-middle-class movement. Karl Mannheim, amongst others, offered statistical evidence in its support. It is on this sociological view that Erich Fromm bases his psychological interpretation of Nazism. The main mental traits of the Nazi group, embodied in his concept of "authoritarian character," are characteristic features of the lower-middle classes. This point will be taken up at a later stage. For the moment it is enough to say that the statistical evidence on which this thesis is based is not conclusive. The membership list of 1935 shows the following figures: 32 per cent manual workers; 20.6 per cent, white collar employees; 20.2 per cent, independents; 13 per cent, officials; 10 per cent peasants; 3.4 per cent, others. The figures seem to show a certain preponderance of the middle-class element. But the point is that categories such as white collar employees, independents and officials can only arbitrarily be considered as together forming a social class. This type of approach to Nazism suffers from the ambiguity inherent in concepts such as the middle class, the lower-middle class, or petty bourgeoisie, which are often applicable only in very general terms. Many individuals who are believed to belong to these classes are in fact in a transitory state socially, and as such, they can better be described as classless. As will be seen later, classless individuals and groups have special significance for the structure of Nazism.

In conclusion we cannot see in the class approach to Nazism more than a comfortable hypothesis. As such it served the theoretical outlook of those intellectuals whose minds were tinted with an economistic or Marxian way of thinking. Any realistic approach to Nazism should, in our opinion, start by considering it as the outcome of an ethnic group — the German nation — living under conditions of stress caused by specific historical circumstances. . . .

THE SOCIAL COMPOSITION OF THE PARTY

It would be true to say that, sociologically, Nazism, as a political and spiritual movement, represents a cross-section of the German nation during the inter-war period. It answered a state of frustration and insecurity widespread in all strata of the population during this period. It would also be right to infer from this that the cadres, and particularly the leadership of the party, were made up of individuals and groups who suffered more than others from frustration and insecurity.

The core of the party was formed by socially nondescript people, frustrated in their efforts to achieve a certain status in their society, the prototype of whom is Hitler. The demobilized soldiers and officers, former members of the *Freikorps* [voluntary, paramilitary organizations common in Germany at the end of World War I], formed an important Nazi group. Goering and Röhm are typical. Unemployed youngsters, émigrés, and students also found a point of attraction in the movement. To this is added a number of intellectuals frustrated in their aspirations, as Goebbels was, or incapable of adjusting themselves to the cultural climate of their time and consequently escaping into the mythical world of the past, like those belonging to the Thule Society of Munich. From the historically constituted classes Nazism attracted in the first place the peripheral elements. From the working class it attracted "the flotsam, the strugglers living on the fringe of their own class, the workers of odd jobs, and the unemployed." In the upper classes the party appealed in particular to aristocrats who identified themselves with a highly inadequate concept of their own class; they joined the party in order to re-make the position once held by the Junkers in Imperial Germany. Peasants who were by their aspiration above their group, or by their poverty below it, were also attracted to the movement.

All the individuals and groups mentioned above have one trait in common: they all can be called *déclassés,* that is, people who failed completely or partly to integrate themselves with one of the institutionalized forms of their society. They also suffer from lack of social attachment. In this way the *déclassés* can, by analogy with psychopathic personality, be described as sociopathic personalities. As the psychopathics are liable to all forms of delinquency, so are the sociopathics liable to political delinquency in particular, that is, they are breakers of the political order of their own society. More will be said later about the connexion between psychopathic and sociopathic personality. For the moment we consider the sociopathic personality in itself. It should be mentioned in the first place that industrial society has a great capacity for creating sociopathic groups.

Its fluid character and its rapid growth are among the main causes of this phenomenon. The impersonal character of this society and the mechanical type of integration required by it have also contributed to this. The situation of post-war Germany is characteristic from this point of view. The instability of that period forms an additional factor contributing to the creation of non-integrated individuals and groups.

The Nazi movement can be considered as the meeting point of all individuals and groups with an unstable social status; it evolved as a result of the disrupting processes taking place in the post-war period. It is, therefore, the classless element, rather than a particular social class, that should first be considered in order to understand Nazism. As opposed to any socialist party — obviously a class party — and to any democratic party normally based on a particular social group, Nazism represents in its structure the entire nation on a reduced scale. This is one of the first factors determining its totalitarian character. . . .

The Political Articulation of Communism

THE PARTY

The Party is the totalitarian reality in a Communist society. It is "the whole," as Lenin calls it — the society itself becoming conscious of its unity. In the Soviet Union, the Party is referred to as "the organizing and guiding force of the Government," "the heart and the brain of the people," "the guide and the teacher of the workers." The Party can, at the same time, be conceived as an organism in its own right, a *corpus mysticum* [mystical body] of any Communist society.

In what follows we shall mark the main stages in the development of those political organizations which have finally crystallized in a Communist party of the Bolshevik type. Our attention is primarily concentrated on the gradual articulation of class consciousness into a specific political body.

This will prepare a certain basis for the psychological considerations following at a later stage.

THE SOCIAL BASIS OF THE PARTY

The fact that the Party has grown up as a political expression of the working class tells relatively little about its structure and particularly about its tactics and programmes. The working class is merely the raw material from which the Party is forged. For it is only a small section, the most "conscious" elements, or the *avantgarde* of the working class which acts decisively upon the structure of the Party. Therefore, the process of becoming conscious of the proletarian condition of one's own class constitutes a basic factor in the rise of the Party. This process implies in fact something much more than the spontaneous development of the industrial workers within the historical conditions of the last century, or of the Russian working class during the first decades of our century. It implies the damming up of a wide and diffuse historical process whose main stages can be outlined as follows: 1. The growth of the social importance of the industrial workers, which is a natural implication of industrialization. 2. The formation within the group of industrial workers of an upper stratum which used their "organizing" and political activities as a means to rise in the social scale, and thus to escape the condition of manual workers. Their main ambition was to become "leaders" within their own group. 3. The blend of this group of workers with middle-class intellectuals. 4. This was followed by the indoctrination of the industrial workers with a particular ideology, and by the development from within this group of a specific type of leadership, in which religious-messianic elements are intermingled with concrete political action. All this amounts to the "transfiguration" of the working class.

The first step in the building up of the Communist Party consisted in the transformation of the passive nihilism and anarchic mood which was, towards the mid-nineteenth century, a basic attitude of the industrial workers towards their society. In psychological terms this meant the transformation of a negative into a positive attitude. The early workers' movements, whether they were led by socialists, communists, or anarchists, were guided either by a mystic faith in their final victory, or by a purely anarchic drive. For the Blanquists there was no precise plane leading to socialism; all that was needed was a mystic faith in the outcome of a victory of the proletariat. Bakunin himself, though a typical representative of a combative anarchism, had no clear idea about the social meaning of anarchic action. He disapproved of Marx's attempt to impose upon the workers a Prussian type of organization. The Proudhonist and Bakuninist workers were against the use of strikes and against the

organization of the working class, even when these were initiated by recognized working-class authorities (The First International). On the whole, it would be adequate to describe this type of anarchism as regressive in a social sense, that is, as the individual's revolt against the super-rational type of integration required by industrial society. It might be that at the root of their revolt lay the golden era of a primitive society described by ideologues like Rousseau.

Marx was not alone in realizing the reactionary and regressive frame of mind of the industrial workers during the first half of the last century. Nor was he alone in demonstrating the necessity for workers' organizations against the employers and their society. He was, however, amongst the first who understood that this struggle could not be conducted on the basis of compromise and gradual improvements, but on the basis of revolutionary action; only revolution could satisfy the workers' desperate revolt. The meaning of revolution was, in Marx's mind, equal to social cataclysm. Workers have nothing of their own to secure and fortify; "their mission is to destroy all previous securities for, and insurance of, individual property."

Certain traits of Marx's personality explain the direction in which he interpreted the workers' state of mind. By his origins, and particularly by his personality structure, he was detached enough from his society to see a positive meaning in the workers' revolt. Moreover, he took the trouble to justify it. But what was important in his thought was not the justification of the proletariat's attitude in causal, but in teleological terms. The proletariat was right in its boycott of modern society, because it could create its own society; it was the treasurer of a new world. In this Marx was much more systematic and convincing than most political thinkers of his time. Knowing the depth of the proletariat's frustration and revolt he grasped the truth that the quickest relief would be brought by a mathematical demonstration of the proletariat's victory rather than by vague and partial promises.

Consequently he started to work out the proletariat's need for victory and its Messianic feelings into a rational system. He and Engels produced the scheme of the proletariat's mission, indicating the "necessary" stages in the evolution of human society and synchronizing all this process with the innermost wishes of the proletariat, i.e., total victory. At the same time they stressed the need for unity and struggle in the working class. Most important is their language, which is hortatory rather than explanatory.

Thus, the mind of the proletariat became gradually infused with a certain clear purpose — a new society — and with precise methods of achieving it. Its passive and destructive nihilism began to turn into a constructive attitude towards human history. This state of mind formed a basic factor leading to the formation of a new type of political party. This was a class party, less interested in society as a whole than in the fulfilment of a pre-established programme of evolution of the working class; less interested in progressive measures than in total revolution, and less interested in the present than in the future.

When Lenin, at the beginning of this century, built up the first party of a "new type" he based his action on these mental traits created in the proletariat by its own position in modern society, and by a series of ideologies instilled into the working class by various groups of intellectuals which had in common with the working class a deep revolt against the order of their society.

The party organized by Lenin has a class character only from the ideological point of view. Lenin had to choose between two extreme possibilities regarding the political action of the proletariat: courageous and revolutionary action carried out by isolated individuals, or slow action carried out by the working class as a whole in its "spontaneous" development towards a dominant political rôle. He solved this dilemma by creating the Party as a synthesis between these two extremes. The Party is conceived by Lenin as the organ of the most active and determined elements of the whole of society, united by their resentment against the existing social order, and by their belief in the historical mission of the proletariat. On this point Lenin writes: "We must have our men everywhere, in all social strata, in all positions which allow a knowledge of the resources and the mechanisms of the State." It is obvious that Lenin includes in his call also ". . . a portion of the bourgeois ideologists who have raised themselves to the level of comprehending theoretically the historical movement as a whole."

What Lenin wants most is a stable organization, at least a stable leadership composed of people trained in class struggle. He asks for full-time revolutionaries who should stop working in factories and live at the expense of the organization, "people whose profession consists in revolutionary action."

Here comes an important point. The party conceived by Lenin, though the party of the working class, consists of professional revolutionaries who have become conscious of the historical mission of the proletariat. This historical mission of the proletariat is in fact an idea existing in their minds for which there was no immediate need to consult the working class as a social body. Thus the Party is from the outset *for,* but not necessarily *of* the working class. It forms an advanced detachment in the struggle of the working class for its historical fulfilment.

Who formed the basis of the Party? To answer this question, one has to go back to the concept of sociopathic personality and to apply it in this specific context. The *avant-garde* of the working class is made up of people who, for one reason or another, failed to integrate themselves with their society. The *déclassés* in a broad sense, or the "disinherited," form the body of élite of the *avant-garde*. Though the feeling of disinheritance is wide-spread in the group of industrial workers, adherence to the Party cannot be considered as being decided by the simple fact of belonging to this group. This adherence is rather a personal matter, being related to the particular way in which the feeling of disinheritance is experienced from case to case. Those individuals, belonging to the proletariat or to other social groups, who could find a social substitute for their feeling of disinheritance, and a positive meaning for their resentment against their society formed the basic strata of the Party. The "idea" rather than the reality of the proletariat provided a strong bond between these people, and at the same time, an efficient remedy for their personal feelings of disinheritance. This shows an important trait in the individuals attracted to the party "of a new type." They had an outstanding capacity for socializing their personal resentment; the drive to form a group of their own in order to provide better conditions for the solution of their personal problems was a common trait among them. They claimed that the new type of social group resulting from their unity belonged to the working class. But, at the same time, they stressed the uniqueness of their group by distinguishing themselves from two categories of workers, who together constituted by far the majority of the working class, that is, the workers who accepted passively their proletarian condition, whom they scornfully called *Lumpenproletariat*, and the workers who deserted their class by integration with the bourgeois society, called "opportunists."

Once socialized, the resentment of the above-mentioned people grew in intensity. The fact that they formed a group of their own contributed to their complete detachment from their society, and intensified in them the belief in their aims and ideas. The ideology of the group — the Party ideology — was to them not only a body of ideas but the protective shell of their own lives; outside it, they could perceive nothing but hatred and danger.

What has been said so far suggests the idea — which can be proved by the examination of most of the Communist Parties of today — that the basis of the party "of a new type" is not made up of people who belong to the working class, or to any other class, but by people *who do not belong*. It is not the reality of belongingness, but the desire for belongingness that constitutes the driving force of the Party. It is not the industrial workers as an integrated group that prepare the ground for a totalitarian organization crystallized in the Party, but rather their desires for belongingness, unity, and social strength. In other words, it is the incapacity of modern society to integrate its members in its own structure that constitutes the first condition in the rise of contemporary totalitarian societies. Therefore the foundation of the Party is made up by those products of modern society, individuals and groups, which oversocialize their anxiety for belongingness and integration. Those who form the core of the Party are people who, because of a long period of insecurity, live under the pressure of a strong desire for a radical change in themselves and in their society. In Lenin's opinion, whoever joins the Party undergoes a process of transfiguration. One meaning of this is the following: He who is weak becomes strong, he who is alone becomes a "comrade," he who is insecure becomes ruthless and dogmatic.

The Authoritarian Personality

T. W. ADORNO, *ET AL.*

In May of 1944 when the Nazi policy of extermination of the Jews was reaching its frightful climax, the American Jewish Committee invited scholars to a conference on religious and social prejudice. As one result of this meeting, the Committee later established a Department of Scientific Research under whose auspices a number of volumes were published in a general series entitled *Studies in Prejudice.* The actual research for *The Authoritarian Personality* — one of the volumes in this series — was carried out by collaboration between the Berkeley Public Opinion Study and the Institute of Social Research. The study was not published until 1950, but much of the groundwork for it extended even further back than 1939, for one of the directors of the work was Max Horkheimer, who had headed the *Institut für Sozialforschung* in Germany. The work was intended to bring to bear the techniques of psychoanalysis and clinical psychology on complicated social and political issues. The short selection which follows is a summary of the famous F (fascist) scale intended to measure the propensity of a person to anti-democratic tendencies by identifying the characteristics of the world-view which such an individual manifests.

A. CONVENTIONALISM. Rigid adherence to conventional, middle-class values.

B. AUTHORITARIAN SUBMISSION. Submissive, uncritical attitude toward idealized moral authorities of the ingroup.

C. AUTHORITARIAN AGGRESSION. Tendency to be on the lookout for, and to condemn, reject, and punish people who violate conventional values.

D. ANTI-INTRACEPTION. Opposition to the subjective, the imaginative, the tender-minded.

E. SUPERSTITION AND STEREOTYPY. The belief in mystical determinants of the individual's fate; the disposition to think in rigid categories.

F. POWER AND "TOUGHNESS." Preoccupation with the dominance-submission, strong-weak, leader-follower dimension; identification with power figures; overemphasis upon the conventionalized attributes of the ego; exaggerated assertion of strength and toughness.

G. DESTRUCTIVENESS AND CYNICISM. Generalized hostility, vilification of the human.

H. PROJECTIVITY. The disposition to believe that wild and dangerous things go on in the world; the projection outward of unconscious emotional impulses.

J. SEX. Exaggerated concern with sexual "goings-on."

From T. W. Adorno, *et al., The Authoritarian Personality* (New York, 1950), p. 228. Reprinted by permission of Harper & Row, Publishers.

The "Authoritarian Personality" Expanded

EDWARD A. SHILS

When the study, *The Authoritarian Personality*, appeared there were various criticisms of the methods which had been used. Although the work claimed to be strictly empirical, many pointed out that it was in fact based on a series of far-reaching initial assumptions which had not been subjected to empirical tests. Thus in 1954 a new volume — *Studies in the Scope and Method of the Authoritarian Personality* — was published by another group of scholars in an attempt both to revise and to carry forward the original work. The author of one of the articles in this later volume — from which the following selection is taken — is Edward A. Shils. A sociologist at the University of Chicago, Shils has for some years devoted himself to studies of great contemporary political importance and has collaborated with Talcott Parsons in a number of highly influential works in the field of sociology, including *Theories of Society*. In criticising the earlier work on the concept of the Authoritarian Personality, Shils argues that it mostly ignored any assessment of the extreme Left in attempting to uncover the characteristics of antidemocratic behavior. He thus maintains that the character traits attributed to the fascist mind are equally attributable to the typical communist.

B<small>Y THE END</small> of the nineteenth century, it was widely believed in Continental Europe and in the United States that political institutions and activities could be described as either "radical" or "conservative." Each term had its synonyms and each admitted of variations in both directions. Radicalism moved off in one direction towards socialism, evolutionary and revolutionary, and ultimately towards anarchism, and in the other direction towards liberalism and the moderate position. On the other side, conservatism by accentuating its peculiar characteristics became reactionary, or it could modify itself in the opposite direction and move towards the "center." Radicalism was "left" and conservatism was "right." Continental and later British and American political intellectuals came to accept the validity of the dichotomy of right and left in political life even where it did not use the terminology which flourished particularly in radical and socialist circles. Every political programme could, it was

thought, be placed on this scale and be fairly judged.

The view rested, especially among socialists, on the belief that fundamentally each of the main political positions formed a coherent and indissoluble unity. Thus, for example, conservatism, according to this notion, was characterized by attachment to private property, hostility towards universal male or adult suffrage, rejection of freedom of association and assembly for working men, an acknowledgment of the rightfulness of self-enrichment by individual exertion, a repugnance for humanitarian and social welfare legislation, devotion to economic and social inequality derived from a belief in the inequality of human qualities and achievements, disapproval of state regulation of private economic activity, etc. This was called the point of view of the Right. And each element in it was thought to be peculiar and necessary to the Right Wing outlook.

In contrast to it stood the point of view

of the Left. This entailed a general deroga-
tion of private property, a preference for
political democracy including the universal
enjoyment of all civil liberties, a rejection
of pecuniary goals and standards, the es-
pousal of humanitarian goals to be achieved
through social legislation, the aspiration
towards economic and social equality based
on a sense of the fundamentally equal
dignity of all men and preference for the
collective organization or regulation of economic life. The Left also believed in progress and therefore welcomed change. It was
antagonistic towards religious institutions
and beliefs and it had great faith in science
as the liberator and benefactor of humanity.
It believed that man's individual merit and
not family connections should determine
his position in life. The Right was opposed
to the Left in all these respects and in all
others. The opposition on every point was
accentuated by the fact that the mere contention of the value of some institution or
practice by the Right made it into a target
of Leftist criticism. For example, patriotism
or loyalty to the national state found its
counterpart in the Marxist claim that the
workingman has no fatherland. The seat-
ing arrangements in legislative chambers,
ranging from extreme Left to extreme
Right, seemed to confirm the inevitable
nature of this continuum of political out-
looks.

Nor can there be any doubt that in the
decades surrounding the turn of the century in Continental political life this simplification did have a certain descriptive
truth. . . .

The Bolshevik Revolution did not
seem at first to constitute an infringement on this classification. It was obviously
the achievement of a group which stood at
the extreme left and which refused to admit that any other group could be more
left than it. Demands for more revolutionary action from within its own ranks were
labelled as "infantile leftism." More revolutionary demands emanating from outside its
ranks were derogated as petit-bourgeois romanticism or adventurism and therewith

transferred "rightward" on the continuum.
To observers among the Western intellectuals, the Bolshevik claims recommended
themselves as wholly just. The Bolsheviks
were seeming to realize the most extreme
Leftist program by equally Leftist methods.
Many liberal and socialist intellectuals in
the decade after the first world war did not
see anything fundamental to censure in the
Bolshevik regime. Even though to some of
them a few actions seemed regrettable, such
as the terror and the suppression of all opposition parties, that seemed to them to be
only a tactical necessity which an obnoxious
ancien regime and a ruthless counter-revo-
lution justified and made expedient. Bolshevism seemed to be on the road to the
realization of the classical programme of
the socialist Left and the Stalin Constitution of 1935 seemed to give veracity to this
interpretation.

The appearance of Fascism in Italy and
Germany caused little embarrassment to
those whose political *Weltanschauung*
[world view] was built within the framework of the Right-Left continuum. The
Marxist interpretation of Fascism as the
penultimate stage in the polarization of all
political life into the extreme Right and the
extreme Left prevailed almost universally
in the 1930's in many intellectual circles.
Fascism was seen as an accentuation of
bourgeois conservatism, a conservatism
driven to desperation by the inevitable crisis
of capitalism. It was devoted to private
property, opposed to political democracy
and humanitarianism, it was inegalitarian
and antiscientific and it sought to stabilize
the existing social order. The fact that it
sought to introduce fundamental changes
in the *status quo* which it was alleged to be
stabilizing was less of an embarrassment
than the fact that its elite did not consist
for the most part of big business men or
that it instituted a far reaching scheme of
regulations of private business enterprise.

This was not the first time that Marxists
were embarrassed by the insufficiency of
the Right-Left scheme. Tory Radicalism in
19th century Great Britain and the social

legislation of Bismarckian Germany had both created difficulties for the Marxist viewpoint. The former had been dismissed as an amalgam of romanticism and hypocrisy, the latter as *State* Socialism and hence fraudulent. Georges Sorel's ideas which contained elements conventionally associated with both Right and Left were written off by Marxists as Fascist.

Ingenious and erudite Marxist writers in the late 30's and early 40's sought to overcome the embarrassment for their system of thought by the argument that Nazism was the servant of German Capitalism. Through resourceful arguments they sought to demonstrate the capitalistic nature of Nazism while at the very same time rendering the interpretation insecure by the impressive body of data which they presented.

During this time, however, events in the Soviet Union, particularly the "purges," the abortion laws, the introduction of school fees, the restriction of progressive education, the persistence and growth of pronounced inequalities in income and status, the reemergence of patriotism as an official policy — these and many other backslidings from the purest ideals of Leftist extremism placed a further burden upon the now rickety structure of Right and Left as a scheme for political analysis.

What had been looked upon as a seamless unity was turning out to be a constellation of diverse elements which could be recombined in constellations which had not for many years been imagined. Hostility towards private property was now seen to be capable of combination with anti-Semitism, inequality, the repression of civil liberties, etc. Welfare legislation was seen to enter into combination with political oligarchy, the elimination of civil liberties was combined with an increase in equalitarianism. In short, what had once appeared to be a simple unidimensional scheme now turned out to be a complicated multidimensional pattern in which there were many different political positions. The attachment to private property was now perceived as compatible both with sympathy with humanitarianism and with a disapproval of welfare legislation, the respect for civil liberties could fit with either socialism or capitalism, equalitarianism could go with either democracy or oligarchy. But above all, the two poles of the continuum Right and Left which were once deemed incompatible and mutually antagonistic were discovered to overlap in many very striking respects.

Fascism and Bolshevism, only a few decades ago thought of as worlds apart, have now been recognized increasingly as sharing many very important features. Their common hostility towards civil liberties, political democracy, the common antipathy for parliamentary institutions, individualism, private enterprise, their image of the political world as a struggle between morally irreconcilable forces, their belief that all their opponents are secretly leagued against them and their own predilection for secrecy, their conviction that all forms of power are in a hostile world concentrated in a few hands and their own aspirations for concentrated and total power — all of these showed that the two extremes had much in common. . . .

The obsolete belief that all political, social and economic philosophies can be classified on the Right-Left continuum however dies very hard. A recent and very instructive instance of this steadfast adherence to the Right-Left polarity is the monumental investigation into *The Authoritarian Personality*. An examination of the manner in which political preconceptions enter into one of the most elaborate social-psychological investigations hitherto undertaken illuminates important problems of procedure in social research and offers opportunities for the further interpretation of a body of rich data. The left-right dichotomy is present not only in the general interpretive chapters written by Professor Adorno but even in the severely empirical chapters written by Professor Levinson and Dr. Sanford. The entire team of investigators proceeds as if there were an unilinear scale of political and social attitudes at the extreme right of which stands the Fascist — the product and proponent of monopoly-capitalism and at the other end what the authors call the complete democrat who — as I shall presently demonstrate — actually holds the views of the non-Stalinist Leninist.

The anti-democrat or proto-fascist — the authoritarian personality — is distinguished by anti-Semitism, ethnocentrism and political-economic conservatism. He is rigid in his beliefs — although no evidence for this is presented — he makes frequent use of stereotypes in his political perceptions and judgments, he is sympathetic with the use of violence against his enemies, he distinguishes sharply between his "ingroup" and the "outgroups" which he interprets as menacing his security. More concretely he shares the most commonplace of the vulgar clichés about Jews, foreigners, reformers, homosexuals, intellectuals, and he admires strong men, business men, successful men, manly men who have no tender side or who allow it no play in their lives.

At the other extreme is the democrat who is sympathetic with the outcasts, the underprivileged, the discriminated-against ethnic minorities, who sees through the hollowness of patriotism, who is alert to the defects of politicians and the selfishness of business men; governmental control of economic life appears to him necessary and just. He thinks wealth is not a great good, science the source of truth and progress. Indeed according to the expectations of Professor Levinson, he rejects every tenet of the anti-democrat's faith and *by implication* believes the opposite. . . .

The material gathered and the hypothesis employed by the Berkeley investigators provides a most valuable approach to the study of Bolshevism and to the re-evaluation of the idea of the political spectrum.

But the investigators accept the view that political opinions are located on a Right-Left continuum and because their political conceptions are exceedingly unsophisticated, they have described political, social and economic attitudes by sets of concrete clichés expressed in the phraseology of current usage.

Obviously a Fascist who says that the Jews have monopolized almost all the important posts in the Government is concretely different from the Bolshevik who asserts that the small circle of big business men control not only the economic life but the intellectual, political and religious life of the country. Concretely these two views are very different — one we know to be the usual paranoid anti-Semitism, — the other sounds like a somewhat crude social science proposition in which many intellectuals in the West believe. Yet looked at from another point of view, they are strikingly similar. Both aver that a small group has with doubtful legitimacy concentrated the power of the country in their hands.

The Berkeley group have emphasized, among others, the following deeper tendencies of the authoritarian of the Right:

a) Extreme hostility towards "outgroups";
b) Extreme submissiveness towards the "ingroups";
c) The establishment of sharp boundaries between the group of which one is a member and all other groups;
d) The tendency to categorize persons with respect to certain particular qualities and make "all or none" judgments;
e) A vision of the world as a realm of conflict;
f) Disdain for purely theoretical or contemplative activities;
g) A repugnance for the expression of sentiments, particularly sentiments of affection;
h) Belief that oneself and one's group are the objects of manipulative designs and that oneself and one's group can survive only by the manipulation of others;
i) The ideal of a conflictless wholly harmonious society in contrast with an environing or antecedent conflict-

ful chaos. There are other properties as well but these will serve for illustrative purposes.

Anyone well acquainted with the works of Lenin and Stalin, or with European and American Communists of recent decades, will immediately recognize that the cognitive and emotional orientations enumerated above correspond very closely to the central features of the Bolshevik *Weltanschauung*. Let us examine briefly their Bolshevik form in the order in which we have listed them:

a) The demand for complete and unqualified loyalty to the Party.
b) The insistence on the necessary conflict of interests between the working class of which the Party is the leader and all other classes and the need for unrelenting conflict against these other classes, even in times of apparent truce and cooperation.
c) The continuous application of the criteria of Party interests in judging every person and situation and the need to avoid eclecticism in doctrine and opportunism and compromise in practice.
d) The stress on the class characteristics of individuals and the interpretation of their actions in the light of their class position exclusively.

e) The belief that all history is the history of class conflict.
f) The denial of the existence of pure truth and attack on those who espouse pure science or "art for art's sake."
g) The belief that the expression of sentiment is an expression of weakness and that it interferes with the correct interpretation of reality and the choice of the right course of action.
h) The belief in the ubiquitousness of the influence of "Wall Street," the "City," the "Big Banks," "Heavy Industry," "200 families," etc. and their masked control over even the most remote spheres of life and the counter-belief in the necessity to penetrate organizations and achieve complete control over them.
i) The ideal of the classless society, without private property in the instruments of production and hence without conflict, the "realm of freedom" where man will cease his alienation and become truly human.

There are important differences between the two authoritarianisms and we shall deal with some of these below. But what is so impressive is their very far-reaching overlap.

IV. FACTORS IN THE RISE
OF TOTALITARIANISM

The Perversion of Liberal Democracy

J. L. TALMON

It is a contention common to more than one selection in this volume that totalitarianism and democracy are not simple opposites, but rather that they bear a certain relationship to each other and manifest at least some similar traits. Many have argued that certain periods of the French Revolution, for example, demonstrated totalitarian tendencies. Thus it is possible to view totalitarianism as arising from, or as the perversion of, liberal democracy. In the selection which follows J. L. Talmon, unwilling to subscribe to the views of men such as Wittfogel who stress the influence of Asian society in contributing to Russian totalitarianism, argues that totalitarianism of the Left frequently arises from the strain of political messianism which while theoretically in favor of human liberty tends to compromise that liberty in the interests of promoting the realization of the world as "it ought to be." At one time a student and associate of such outstanding English historians as Harold Laski, R. H. Tawney, and E. H. Carr, Talmon has served as Professor of Modern History at the Hebrew University of Jerusalem.

It MAY FURTHER BE maintained that whatever their original premises were, totalitarian parties and régimes of the Left have invariably tended to degenerate into soulless power machines, whose lip service to the original tenets is mere hypocrisy. Now, this is a question not only of academic interest, but of much practical importance. Even if we accept this diagnosis of the nature of Left totalitarianism when triumphant, are we to attribute its degeneration to the inevitable process of corrosion which an idea undergoes when power falls into the hands of its adherents? Or should we seek the reason for it deeper, namely in the very essence of the contradiction between ideological absolutism and individualism, inherent in modern political Messianism? When the deeds of men in power

belie their words, are they to be called hypocrites and cynics or are they victims of an intellectual delusion?

*   *   *

THE PSYCHOLOGICAL BACKGROUND

Rousseau often uses the words nature and the natural order in the same sense as his contemporaries to indicate the logical structure of the universe. He also uses nature, however, to describe the elemental as opposed to the effort and achievement of the spirit in overcoming and subduing the elemental. The historical state of nature before organized society was the reign of the elemental. The inauguration of the social state marked the triumph of the spirit.

It must be repeated that to the material-

From J. L. Talmon, *The Origins of Totalitarian Democracy* (New York, 1960), pp. 7–8, 38–43, 46–49. Reprinted by permission of Frederick A. Praeger, Inc., and Martin Secker & Warburg Limited.

ists the natural order is, so to speak, a ready-made machine to be discovered and set to work. To Rousseau, on the other hand, it is the State, when it has fulfilled its purpose. It is a categorical imperative. The materialists reached the problem of the individual versus the social order only late in their argument. Even then, supremely confident of the possibility of mutual adjustment, they failed to recognize the existence of the problem of coercion. To Rousseau the problem exists from the beginning. It is indeed the fundamental problem to him.

A motherless vagabond starved of warmth and affection, having his dream of intimacy constantly frustrated by human callousness, real or imaginary, Rousseau could never decide what he wanted, to release human nature or to moralize it by breaking it; to be alone or a part of human company. He could never make up his mind whether man was made better or worse, happier or more miserable, by people. Rousseau was one of the most ill-adjusted and egocentric natures who have left a record of their predicament. He was a bundle of contradictions, a recluse and anarchist, yearning to return to nature, given to reverie, in revolt against all social conventions, sentimental and lacrimose, abjectly self-conscious and at odds with his environment, on the one hand; and the admirer of Sparta and Rome, the preacher of discipline and the submergence of the individual in the collective entity, on the other. The secret of this dual personality was that the disciplinarian was the envious dream of the tormented paranoiac. The *Social Contract* was the sublimation of the *Discourse on the Origins of Inequality*. Rousseau speaks of his own predicament, when describing in *Émile* and elsewhere the unhappiness of man, who, after he left the state of nature, fell prey to the conflict between impulse and the duties of civilized society; always "wavering between his inclinations and his duties," neither quite man nor quite citizen, "no good to himself, nor to others," because never in accord with himself. The only salvation from this

agony, if a return to the untroubled state of nature was impossible, was either a complete self-abandonment to the elemental impulses or to "denature (*dénaturer*) man" altogether. It was in the latter case necessary to substitute a relative for an absolute existence, social consciousness for self-consciousness. Man must be made to regard himself not as a "unité numérique, l'entier absolu, qui n'a de rapport qu'à lui-même," ["numerical unity, an independently existing whole, which has no relationship excepting to itself"] but as a "unité fonctionnaire qui tient au dénominateur et dont la valeur est dans son rapport avec l'entier, qui est le corps social" ["functional unity which depends on the denominator and whose value is in his relationship with the whole, which is the social body"]. A fixed rigid and universal pattern of feeling and behaviour was to be imposed in order to create man of one piece, without contradictions, without centrifugal and anti-social urges. The task was to create citizens who would will only what the general will does, and thus be free, instead of every man being an entity in himself, torn by egotistic tensions and thus enslaved. Rousseau, the teacher of romantic spontaneity of feeling, was obsessed with the idea of man's cupidity as the root cause of moral degeneration and social evil. Hence his apotheosis of Spartan ascetic virtue and his condemnation of civilization in so far as civilization is the expression of the urge to conquer, the desire to shine and the release of human vitality, without reference to morality. He had that intense awareness of the reality of human rivalry peculiar to people who have experienced it in their souls. Either out of a sense of guilt or out of weariness, they long to be delivered from the need for external recognition and the challenge of rivalry.

Three other representatives of the totalitarian Messianic temperament to be analysed in these pages show a similar paranoiac streak. They are Robespierre, Saint-Just and Babeuf. In recent times we have had examples of the strange combination of psychological ill-adjustment and totalitarian ideology. In some cases, salvation from the impossibility of finding a balanced relationship with fellow-men is sought in the lonely superiority of dictatorial leadership. The leader identifies himself with the absolute doctrine and the refusal of others to submit comes to be regarded not as a normal difference of opinion, but as a crime. It is characteristic of the paranoiac leader that when thwarted he is quickly thrown off his precarious balance and falls victim to an orgy of self-pity, persecution mania and the suicidal urge. Leadership is the salvation of the few, but to many even mere membership of a totalitarian movement and submission to the exclusive doctrine may offer a release from ill-adjusted egotism. Periods of great stress, of mass psychosis, and intense struggle call forth marginal qualities which otherwise may have remained dormant, and bring to the top men of a peculiar neurotic mentality.

THE GENERAL WILL AND THE INDIVIDUAL

It was of vital importance to Rousseau to save the ideal of liberty, while insisting on discipline. He was very proud and had a keen sense of the heroic. Rousseau's thinking is thus dominated by a highly fruitful but dangerous ambiguity. On the one hand, the individual is said to obey nothing but his own will; on the other, he is urged to conform to some objective criterion. The contradiction is resolved by the claim that this external criterion is his better, higher, or real self, man's inner voice, as Rousseau calls it. Hence, even if constrained to obey the external standard, man cannot complain of being coerced, for in fact he is merely being made to obey his own true self. He is thus still free; indeed freer than before. For freedom is the triumph of the spirit over natural, elemental instinct. It is the acceptance of moral obligation and the disciplining of irrational and selfish urges by reason and duty. The acceptance of the obligations laid down in the Social Contract marks the birth of man's personality and his initiation into freedom. Every ex-

ercise of the general will constitutes a re-affirmation of man's freedom. . . .

Ultimately the general will is to Rousseau something like a mathematical truth or a Platonic idea. It has an objective existence of its own, whether perceived or not. It has nevertheless to be discovered by the human mind. But having discovered it, the human mind simply cannot honestly refuse to accept it. In this way the general will is at the same time outside us and within us. Man is not invited to express his personal preferences. He is not asked for his approval. He is asked whether the given proposal is or is not in conformity with the general will. "If my particular opinion had carried the day, I should have achieved the opposite of what was my will; and it is in that case that I should not have been free." For freedom is the capacity of ridding oneself of considerations, interests, preferences and prejudices, whether personal or collective, which obscure the objectively true and good, which, if I am true to my true nature, I am bound to will. What applies to the individual applies equally to the people. Man and people have to be brought to choose freedom, and if necessary to be forced to be free.

The general will becomes ultimately a question of enlightenment and morality. Although it should be the achievement of the general will to create harmony and unanimity, the whole aim of political life is really to educate and prepare men to will the general will without any sense of constraint. Human egotism must be rooted out, and human nature changed. . . .

The aim is to train men to "bear with docility the yoke of public happiness," in fact to create a new type of man, a purely political creature, without any particular private or social loyalties, any partial interests, as Rousseau would call them.

THE GENERAL WILL, POPULAR
SOVEREIGNTY, AND DICTATORSHIP

Rousseau's sovereign is the externalized general will, and, as has been said before, stands for essentially the same as the natural harmonious order. In marrying this concept with the principle of popular sovereignty, and popular self-expression, Rousseau gave rise to totalitarian democracy. The mere introduction of this latter element, coupled with the fire of Rousseau's style, lifted the eighteenth-century postulate from the plane of intellectual speculation into that of a great collective experience. It marked the birth of the modern secular religion, not merely as a system of ideas, but as a passionate faith. Rousseau's synthesis is in itself the formulation of the paradox of freedom in totalitarian democracy in terms which reveal the dilemma in the most striking form, namely, in those of will. There is such a thing as an objective general will, whether willed or not willed by anybody. To become a reality it must be willed by the people. If the people does not will it, it must be made to will it, for the general will is latent in the people's will. . . .

Rousseau demonstrates clearly the close relation between popular sovereignty taken to the extreme, and totalitarianism. The paradox calls for analysis. It is commonly held that dictatorship comes into existence and is maintained by the indifference of the people and the lack of democratic vigilance. There is nothing that Rousseau insists on more than the active and ceaseless participation of the people and of every citizen in the affairs of the State.

The State is near ruin, says Rousseau, when the citizen is too indifferent to attend a public meeting. Saturated with antiquity, Rousseau intuitively experiences the thrill of the people assembled to legislate and shape the common weal. The Republic is in a continuous state of being born. In the pre-democratic age Rousseau could not realize that the originally deliberate creation of men could become transformed into a Leviathan, which might crush its own makers. He was unaware that total and highly emotional absorption in the collective political endeavour is calculated to kill all privacy, that the excitement of the assembled crowd may exercise a most tyranni-

cal pressure, and that the extension of the scope of politics to all spheres of human interest and endeavour, without leaving any room for the process of casual and empirical activity, was the shortest way to totalitarianism. Liberty is safer in countries where politics are not considered all-important and where there are numerous levels of non-political private and collective activity, although not so much direct popular democracy, than in countries where politics take everything in their stride, and the people sit in permanent assembly.

In the latter the truth really is that, although all seem to be engaged in shaping the national will, and are doing it with a sense of elation and fulfilment, they are in fact accepting and endorsing something which is presented to them as a sole truth, while believing that it is their free choice. This is actually implied in Rousseau's image of the people willing the general will. The collective sense of elation is subject to emotional weariness. It soon gives way to apathetic and mechanical behaviour.

Rousseau is most reluctant to recognize the will of the majority, or even the will of all, as the general will. Neither does he give any indication by what signs the general will could be recognized. Its being willed by the people does not make the thing willed the expression of the general will. The blind multitude does not know what it wants, and what is its real interest. "Left to themselves, the People always desire the good, but, left to themselves, they do not always know where that good lies. The general will is always right, but the judgment guiding it is not always well informed. It must be made to see things as they are, sometimes as they ought to appear to them."

THE GENERAL WILL AS PURPOSE

The general will assumes thus the character of a purpose and as such lends itself to definition in terms of social-political ideology, a pre-ordained goal, towards which we are irresistibly driven; a solely true aim, which we will, or are bound to will, although we may not will it yet, because of our backwardness, prejudices, selfishness or ignorance.

In this case the idea of a people becomes naturally restricted to those who identify themselves with the general will and the general interest. Those outside are not really of the nation. They are aliens. This conception of the nation (or people) was soon to become a powerful political argument. Thus Sieyès claimed that the Third Estate alone constituted the nation. The Jacobins restricted the term still further, to the *sans-culottes*. To Babeuf the proletariat alone was the nation, and to Buonarroti only those who had been formally admitted to the National Community.

The very idea of an assumed preordained will, which has not yet become the actual will of the nation; the view that the nation is still therefore in its infancy, a "young nation," in the nomenclature of the *Social Contract,* gives those who claim to know and to represent the real and ultimate will of the nation — the party of the vanguard — a blank cheque to act on behalf of the people, without reference to the people's actual will. And this, as we hope later on to show it has, may express itself in two forms or rather two stages: one — the act of revolution; and the other — the effort at enthroning the general will. Those who feel themselves to be the real people rise against the system and the men in power, who are not of the people. Moreover, the very act of their insurrection, e.g. the establishment of a Revolutionary (or Insurrectionary)

Committee, abolishes *ipso facto* not only the parliamentary representative body, which is in any case, according to Rousseau, a standing attempt on the sovereignty of the people, but indeed all existing laws and institutions. For "the moment the people is legitimately assembled as a sovereign body, the jurisdiction of the government wholly lapses, the executive power is suspended, and the person of the meanest citizen is as sacred and inviolable as that of the first magistrate; for in the presence of the person represented, representatives no longer exist." The real people, or rather their leadership, once triumphant in their insurrection, become Rousseau's Legislator, who surveys clearly the whole panorama, without being swayed by partial interests and passions, and shapes the "young nation" with the help of laws derived from his superior wisdom. He prepares it to will the general will. First comes the elimination of men and influences not of the people and not identified with the general will embodied in the newly established Social Contract of the Revolution; then the re-education of the young nation to will the general will. The task of the Legislator is to create a new type of man, with a new mentality, new values, a new type of sensitiveness, free from old instincts, prejudices and bad habits. It is not enough to change the machinery of government, or even reshuffle the classes. You have to change human nature, or, in the terminology of the eighteenth century, to make man virtuous.

The Growth of Power

ALFRED COBBAN

Alfred Cobban is Professor of French History in the University of London and an editor of the journal, *History*. He has also been a visiting professor at such outstanding American universities as Harvard and the University of Chicago. Cobban has devoted most of his scholarly attention to the study of the French Revolution. But this has not prevented him from speculating on some of the more serious issues of our time, and his *Dictatorship: Its History and Theory* is a witness of the high quality of his work. The factors which Cobban mentions as responsible for the growth of power in modern society were implicit in the French Revolution and thus his contribution to the understanding of our own time is an example of the light which can be thrown on the present by a study of the past.

THE POLITICAL BASIS

THE EXPERIENCE of the French Revolution shows, then, that it is not necessary to look for a theoretical justification for the abandonment of the principle of separation of powers; indeed, one would not be very easy to find, once we have left the rule of the absolute, hereditary prince behind. The subjection of the legislative to the executive power, which is a universal characteristic of dictatorship, is a practical and not a theoretical development. Further, one is compelled to ask whether it is altogether peculiar to the dictatorial as opposed to the parliamentary state, or whether it does not represent a more general trend in the modern state. Can one not observe during the nineteenth century, even in parliamentary countries, a similar movement towards a closer connection between legislative and executive and an increasing control of the latter over the former? The key to this tendency seems to be provided by the great development everywhere of an extra-constitutional political organ, through the influence of which the activity of both legislative and executive is unified — the political party. In what way, one might reasonably ask, does the rule of a political

party in a parliamentary state, dominating legislative and executive alike, and appealing to the public through the personality of its leader, a Baldwin, say, or a Roosevelt, differ from the similar rule of a party in a dictatorial state? Only, it might be answered, through the existence in the former of alternative parties. A vital difference, admittedly, but one not particularly relevant to the principle of separation of powers. One is forced to the conclusion that the control of the legislative by the executive power represents a general trend in modern politics and therefore is not by itself a safe criterion of the totalitarian state or of dictatorial government.

Under modern conditions a more effective test is the subordination of the judicial power to the executive — appropriately enough, for it was with the proclamation of the independence of the judiciary that the theory of separation really became historically significant, in the writings of Locke and the achievements of the Glorious Revolution of 1688. The separation of executive and legislative powers is important in the history of political technique: the independence of the judiciary has something more fundamental behind it. Separation of

From Alfred Cobban, *Dictatorship: Its History and Theory* (New York, 1939), pp. 191–194, 196–197, 208–211, 226–227, 229–233, 239–240. Reprinted by permission of Jonathan Cape Limited.

powers in this connection has been described by the great jurist, Roscoe Pound, as the formula which the eighteenth century found for the attempt to avoid the over-personal administration of justice. It is more than this, it is essential to what Dicey called the Rule of Law. It is the modern version of the theory of natural law, of the belief, in the words of Gierke, that, "Law is not a common will that a thing shall be, but a common conviction that it is." The importance of this principle is so well put by the same great thinker that we cannot do better than quote him again. "I still live to-day in the conviction that our legal theory and our legal life can only thrive on one condition — that 'positivism' should somehow learn to preserve for the idea of law that original and independent title to existence which was vindicated for it by the School of Natural Law."

While the separation of legislative and executive yielded to practical political developments, the independence of the judicial power, based on the principle of natural law, was attacked by theorists. The history of the idea of natural law, from the time of the Stoics, through the *jus naturale* of the Roman lawyers and the medieval canonists, to its association with the great triumphs of the Western mind in the seventeenth and eighteenth centuries, was brought to a sudden halt by the rise of German romanticism in the early years of the nineteenth century. The romantic revolt against the rationalism of the eighteenth century swept out, along with much that was new, the law of nature, which was also the law of reason, and which was very old. The time spirit took charge of European thought with the birth of the historical age. Law was henceforth to be deemed the product of the unconscious reason of the past. Germany, and indeed all Europe more or less, was beginning to "think with its blood." Law was now conceived as the juristic formulation of history; but this still had to be the history of something. The principle of the law of nature still had a chance: it might have reasserted itself if law could

have been conceived as the reflection of a civilization or of humanity. But such Voltarian ideals were not for the age of romanticism and nationalism. The future lay with the nations, not with civilization, and law, according to the new romantic ideas, was an expression of the history of a nation. . . .

Our argument will be made clearer if we take certain specific examples of the changed attitude towards law, and consequently towards the separation of powers, in the totalitarian state. The new conception of law is to be observed first in the French Revolution, with the development of the idea of revolutionary justice, and the setting up in 1793 of a Revolutionary Tribunal to deal with counter-revolutionary charges. Six months earlier, in the September Massacres of 1792, Marat had attempted to assert popular justice in his own way. The Committee of Public Safety was more systematic, but when it declared Terror the order of the day, it meant just what Marat meant. The idea of justice as a weapon in the class struggle was beginning to emerge. Robespierre's early contributions to judicial reform show that one of his objects was the transference of judicial power from the privileged classes to the masses. That in practice the rules of law and the administration of justice in the eighteenth century, as in most or all other times, took for granted and upheld the existing class structure of society, can hardly be questioned. A revolution which attempted to alter these class relationships, it might be argued, was therefore bound to alter the judicial system, to take its administration out of the hands of the ruling classes and give it to the people.

In the French Revolution, then, is to be found a foreshadowing of the new ideas about law. A century later, the Russian Revolution brings us into the new world, juridically speaking. The belief that law and justice are merely a weapon in the hands of the ruling class is now triumphantly vindicated. The law, in the U.S.S.R., according to the official definition, is "a system of social relationships, which corresponds to the interests of the governing class and which is placed under the guarantee of the organized force of that class." Thus it is defined in terms of interests: the idealistic conception of the law of nature disappears, and law becomes no more than a scientific statement of the social and political utilities of the ruling class.

*   *   *

THE ECONOMIC BASIS

A certain historic connection between dictatorship and economic conflict is apparent at first sight, but the nature of that connection requires further examination, for evidently the economic policies of a Robespierre or a Napoleon, a Stalin or a Mussolini, are not at first sight explicable on identical grounds, while in the economic attitude of dictators such as Louis Napoleon and Hitler a certain dualism can be observed. Our first conclusion is that if we take the alternatives in modern economic policies to be socialism and capitalism, using these terms in a loose general sense, without any pretence at precise definition, then it is not self-evident that dictatorship as a political instrument is exclusively attached to either system or creed.

The totalitarian state of to-day, it must be admitted, involves an authoritarian control of the economic life of the community which is the antithesis of the *laissez-faire* individualism of nineteenth-century capitalism, but since the same tendency is to be observed in all industrial or semi-industrial states to some degree, it cannot be claimed that dictatorship must itself have been responsible for the loss of this Eden of economic purity, and equally it does not follow that its loss necessarily involves what is commonly called socialism. But before we can attempt to understand how dictatorship comes into the story and the effects of its intervention, it will be necessary to discuss very briefly the change that has come over the economic outlook of European civilization during the last half century.

There is no novelty in suggesting that capitalist society was built up in its early days on the Calvinistic virtues of the middle class. How far Calvinism was a cause, and how far a result, we need not stay to argue here. Among these virtues the greatest was thrift, which was the highest economic virtue in the nineteenth century. . . .

The end of the nineteenth century saw a change in the situation. The austerity of the captains of industry began to break down, especially when the ownership of great business undertakings passed to the second or third generation, and the real work of industrial control fell into the hands of salaried technical officers. A psychology of spending was taking the place of a psychology of saving in all classes, for at the same time the masses became aware how much wealth they were creating and how little share they had in it themselves. Their grievances were given voice and form by the various schools of socialism, latest child of the rationalist and utilitarian eighteenth century, which may be described in general terms as the conviction that economic evils — the poverty of the masses, the catastrophe that a slump is for those who cannot go much lower in their scale of existence without going under altogether — are not inevitable, and that it is the duty of the community to remedy these conditions. Just as the principle of the sovereignty of the people, or in a general sense democracy, was the conquest of the eighteenth century, so the ideal of socialism, which extended the idea of equality from the political into the economic field, was the achievement of the nineteenth century. . . .

The connection between politics and economics now began to be realized. It was discovered that the political machinery of the state formed a weight that could be thrown into the balance against the struggling industrial workers with certain effect. The conflict between the classes on the economic ground therefore tended to develop into a struggle to obtain control of the state; but in a society organized on a land-owning and capitalist basis it was found that the ordinary processes of parliamentary democracy did not easily allow real political power to be obtained by socialist parties. Hence there was a split between the section of the socialist movement that continued despite discouragement to put its faith in the ballot box, and the section that, as we have seen earlier, was prepared to sacrifice parliamentary methods and turned to the idea of physical force.

Though in theory the principles of political liberty and economic equality may necessitate one another, in practice it has not proved easy to progress towards both objects at the same time. To this difficulty can be traced the association between socialism and dictatorship, which is so evident in modern times. Wherever the school of revolutionary socialism prevailed one may say that arbitrary government was inevitable; for if the revolutionary party triumphed, then it would be necessary for it to institute a party dictatorship to crush the opposing class, and this, as the history of revolutionary France and Russia shows, turns only too easily into a personal dictatorship. If, on the other hand, it did not achieve a victory, the struggle would produce in the community that fear of the dissolution of society and of the impending collapse of law and order, from which dictatorship is most likely to result.

*   *   *

TOTALITARIANISM AND EDUCATION

. . . It was assumed, in brief, that "enlightenment" was the true progress of the human race. Such was the eighteenth-century gospel, and education, added the nineteenth-century gloss, spells enlightenment.

Now no one can deny that education has made amazing advances in the last fifty years all over the world. Yet it has not been accompanied by similar strides towards political and intellectual liberty, but by an increasing trend towards dictatorship and authoritarianism. . . .

The association of the idea of universal education with the principles of authoritarian government and of nationalism was not fortuitous or mistaken. Lacking a certain degree of education the individual was capable neither of intelligent obedience to the law, nor of sharing in any degree in the political life of the nation. Now without some such active participation of the individual, the nation in the modern sense of the term, as a conscious entity, could hardly come into existence, and nationalism would be impossible. It was believed by nineteenth-century liberals that education was necessary to the protection of the individual against the state: the idea that lack of education might be the more effective protection would have seemed to them preposterous. Yet we can see to-day that the increase in the powers of the state has gone step by step with the progress of education. Governments have discovered that a limited meaure of education is necessary to make the individual a profitable object of national propaganda and an efficient servant of the state. Experience has proved that the advocates of benevolent despotism were right when they looked to universal education to increase the authority of the government, and that the prophets of German nationalism were right when they put forward a national system of education as one of the chief springs of nationalist sentiment. . . .

But though the degree of literacy which is all that the masses have been able to obtain, even in the Western countries where education has been most widespread, may merely have been enough to make more efficient servants of the totalitarian state, it will naturally be said that the alternative is of course not less education, but more. What, then, of those whose education has been carried to a much higher level? The part that higher education has played in the past cannot be misconceived. So long as there has been an educated few, a "clerisy," as opposed to an illiterate mass, civilization has been cared for and the state has been mainly controlled by that minority. . . .

The political significance of the older education, then, was that it helped to produce a governing class, an aristocracy which was not merely one of birth. The question we are asking in this section is whether education still does this, or whether the great advance in education which is characteristic of the last few generations in most countries has been achieved at the price of a decline in political wisdom.

In answering this question we may put on one side the progress of primary education: a knowledge of reading, writing and arithmetic, although desirable, does not by itself make a statesman, even when an unnatural capacity for communicating emotion and confusing issues is added to it. As for the higher branches of education, it is evident that, as a result mainly of the great development of science during the last half-century, they have undergone a revolution, which can be observed in every civilized or semi-civilized country. An inevitable consequence of the growth of scientific education has been a concentration on the training of specialists. The scientific expert reaches his high standard by confining his attention to a specific branch of knowledge, and the accumulation of material is forcing him to concentrate on an ever narrower field. Whereas in the past knowledge was incompletely fragmented, and even the specialist had to be a person of general education, today every subject, or branch of a subject, demands a special training for itself, and it is becoming increasingly difficult to be anything but a mere expert.

It might be thought that the intensive study, even of some very restricted branch of knowledge, would at least teach an appreciation of scientific method, and provide a mental training which would enable the scientist to deal with problems in fields other than his own. But it seems to be generally agreed now that while training may develop specific abilities these are not necessarily transferable from one sphere to another. There is little evidence that scientists are more scientific in their thought outside their own particular fields than the rest of the community, nor indeed is it to be expected. The scientist is dependent on the possession of a large body of scientifically ascertained evidence: where he has not this he must either take refuge in agnosticism, or base his opinions on prejudice and guesswork. Now the mere labour that the acquiring and maintenance of his expertness in his own subject demands, by itself prohibits the specialist from devoting the time necessary to the study, either in theory or practice, of the problems of government. In the world of politics he is in fact likely to be not more but less educated than the normal educated man of past centuries.

Superficially this argument may remind one of the hackneyed criticism of the scientist as an uncultured barbarian. But this attack, if it ever had any force, is certainly worthless now, for the student of non-scientific subjects is in just the same boat. His education, too, has been becoming increasingly that of a specialist. . . .

The result is that in Western and Eastern countries alike the educated classes have been, consciously or unconsciously, throwing off their allegiance to their former intellectual and moral ideals. If we were all of us, all our time, porkers not even from the sty of Epicurus, if we could ignore ends other than that of material welfare, the loss of old principles and the absence of new ones would be of little consequence, and we might be happy, for material comfort would be all that we should need. But a spiritual void insists on being filled: a nation lacking good ends will find bad ones for itself. Prophets and teachers will not be wanting to play on the passions and exploit the ignorance of an educated class that is spiritually bankrupt, *déraciné* [uprooted or alienated]: such is what Julien Benda has called la *Trahison des Clercs* [*The Betrayal of the Intellectuals*]. Unguarded either by belief in an ancient creed, or by a rational study of the problems of social life, the expert is ready to fall a victim to any new heresy. He will seize on any gospel that has the appearance of providing a safe orthodoxy on which to base the crumbling state, so long as it is presented by demagogues sufficiently clever or by tyrants sufficiently powerful. If it can be given a pseudo-scientific veneer so much the better.

In these conditions it is not difficult to understand why the general acceptance of the principle of universal education, and the great advance of specialist studies, should have been accompanied by the rise of dictatorship and the development of the totalitarian state.

Escape from Freedom

ERICH FROMM

Born in Germany in 1900, Erich Fromm has served in a number of highly important positions in various countries throughout the world. For a time an associate of the *Institut für Sozialforschung,* he has also contributed his services to Columbia University, the New School for Social Research, Michigan State University, the National University of Mexico, and New York University. His numerous books have not only received scholarly acclaim, but also have attracted the enthusiastic attention of the educated, popular reading class. As a psychiatrist, Fromm has attempted in the selection which follows to provide an explanation of some of the less beneficial effects of modern liberty and of certain undesirable features of the modern world which have contributed, in his view, to the rise of modern totalitarianism.

EMERGENCE OF THE INDIVIDUAL

HUMAN EXISTENCE begins when the lack of fixation of action by instincts exceeds a certain point; when the adaptation to nature loses its coercive character; when the way to act is no longer fixed by hereditarily given mechanisms. In other words, *human existence and freedom are from the beginning inseparable.* Freedom is here used not in its positive sense of "freedom to" but in its negative sense of "freedom from," namely freedom from instinctual determination of his actions.

Freedom in the sense just discussed is an ambiguous gift. Man is born without the equipment for appropriate action which the animal possesses; he is dependent on his parents for a longer time than any animal, and his reactions to his surroundings are less quick and less effective than the automatically regulated instinctive actions are. He goes through all the dangers and fears which this lack of instinctive equipment implies. Yet this very helplessness of man is the basis from which human development springs; *man's biological weakness is the condition of human culture.*

From the beginning of his existence man is confronted with the choice between different courses of action. In the animal there is an uninterrupted chain of reactions starting with a stimulus, like hunger, and ending with a more or less strictly determined course of action, which does away with the tension created by the stimulus. In man that chain is interrupted. The stimulus is there but the kind of satisfaction is "open," that is, he must choose between different courses of action. Instead of a predetermined instinctive action, man has to weigh possible courses of action in his mind; he starts to think. He changes his role toward nature from that of purely passive adaptation to an active one: he produces. He invents tools and, while thus mastering nature, he separates himself from it more and more. He becomes dimly aware of himself — or rather of his group — as not being identical with nature. It dawns upon him that his is a tragic fate: to be part of nature, and yet to transcend it. He becomes aware of death as his ultimate fate even if he tries to deny it in manifold phantasies.

One particularly telling representation of the fundamental relation between man and freedom is offered in the biblical myth of man's expulsion from paradise.

The myth identifies the beginning of human history with an act of choice, but it puts all emphasis on the sinfulness of this first act of freedom and the suffering resulting from it. Man and woman live in the Garden of Eden in complete harmony with each other and with nature. There is peace and no necessity to work; there is no choice, no freedom, no thinking either. Man is forbidden to eat from the tree of knowledge of good and evil. He acts against God's command, he breaks through the state of harmony with nature of which he is a part without transcending it. From the standpoint of the Church which represented authority, this is essentially sin. From the standpoint of man, however, this is the beginning of human freedom. Acting against God's orders means freeing himself from coercion, emerging from the unconscious existence of prehuman life to the level of man. Acting against the command of authority, committing a sin, is in its positive human aspect the first act of freedom, that is, the first *human* act. In the myth the

sin in its formal aspect is the acting against God's command; in its material aspect it is the eating of the tree of knowledge. The act of disobedience as an act of freedom is the beginning of reason. The myth speaks of other consequences of the first act of freedom. The original harmony between man and nature is broken. God proclaims war between man and woman, and war between nature and man. Man has become separate from nature, he has taken the first step toward becoming human by becoming an "individual." He has committed the first act of freedom. The myth emphasizes the suffering resulting from this act. To transcend nature, to be alienated from nature and from another human being, finds man naked, ashamed. He is alone and free, yet powerless and afraid. The newly won freedom appears as a curse; he is free *from* the sweet bondage of paradise, but he is not free *to* govern himself, to realize his individuality.

"Freedom from" is not identical with positive freedom, with "freedom to." The emergence of man from nature is a long-drawn-out process; to a large extent he remains tied to the world from which he emerged; he remains part of nature — the soil he lives on, the sun and moon and stars, the trees and flowers, the animals, and the group of people with whom he is connected by the ties of blood. Primitive religions bear testimony to man's feeling of oneness with nature. Animate and inanimate nature are part of his human world or, as one may also put it, he is still part of the natural world.

These primary ties block his full human development; they stand in the way of the development of his reason and his critical capacities; they let him recognize himself and others only through the medium of his, or their, participation in a clan, a social or religious community, and not as human beings; in other words, they block his development as a free, self-determining, productive individual. But although this is one aspect, there is another one. This identity with nature, clan, religion, gives the individual security. He belongs to, he is rooted in, a structuralized whole in which he has an unquestionable place. He may suffer from hunger or suppression, but he does not suffer from the worst of all pains — complete aloneness and doubt.

We see that the process of growing human freedom has the same dialectic character that we have noticed in the process of individual growth. On the one hand it is a process of growing strength and integration, mastery of nature, growing power of human reason, and growing solidarity with other human beings. But on the other hand this growing individuation means growing isolation, insecurity, and thereby growing doubt concerning one's own role in the universe, the meaning of one's life, and with all that a growing feeling of one's own powerlessness and insignificance as an individual.

If the process of the development of mankind had been harmonious, if it had followed a certain plan, then both sides of the development — the growing strength and the growing individuation — would have been exactly balanced. As it is, the history of mankind is one of conflict and strife. Each step in the direction of growing individuation threatened people with new insecurities. Primary bonds once severed cannot be mended; once paradise is lost, man cannot return to it. There is only one possible, productive solution for the relationship of individualized man with the world: his active solidarity with all men and his spontaneous activity, love and work, which unite him again with the world, not by primary ties but as a free and independent individual.

However, if the economic, social and political conditions on which the whole process of human individuation depends, do not offer a basis for the realization of individuality in the sense just mentioned, while at the same time people have lost those ties which gave them security, this lag makes freedom an unbearable burden. It then becomes identical with doubt, with a kind of life which lacks meaning and direction.

Powerful tendencies arise to escape from this kind of freedom into submission or some kind of relationship to man and the world which promises relief from uncertainty, even if it deprives the individual of his freedom.

European and American history since the end of the Middle Ages is the history of the full emergence of the individual. It is a process which started in Italy, in the Renaissance, and which only now seems to have come to a climax. It took over four hundred years to break down the medieval world and to free people from the most apparent restraints. But while in many respects the individual has grown, has developed mentally and emotionally, and participates in cultural achievements in a degree unheard-of before, the lag between "freedom from" and "freedom to" has grown too. The result of this disproportion between freedom *from* any tie and the lack of possibilities for the positive realization of freedom and individuality has led, in Europe, to a panicky flight from freedom into new ties or at least into complete indifference.

*   *   *

FREEDOM AND DEMOCRACY

. . . Another way of paralyzing the ability to think critically is the destruction of any kind of structuralized picture of the world. Facts lose the specific quality which they can have only as parts of a structuralized whole and retain merely an abstract, quantitative meaning; each fact is just *another* fact and all that matters is whether we know more or less. Radio, moving pictures, and newspapers have a devastating effect on this score. The announcement of the bombing of a city and the death of hundreds of people is shamelessly followed or interrupted by an advertisement for soap or wine. The same speaker with the same suggestive, ingratiating, and authoritative voice, which he has just used to impress you with the seriousness of the political situation, impresses now upon his audience the merits of the particular brand of soap which pays for the news broadcast. Newsreels let pictures of torpedoed ships be followed by those of a fashion show. Newspapers tell us the trite thoughts or breakfast habits of a debutante with the same space and seriousness they use for reporting events of scientific or artistic importance. Because of all this we cease to be genuinely related to what we hear. We cease to be excited, our emotions and our critical judgment become hampered, and eventually our attitude to what is going on in the world assumes a quality of flatness and indifference. In the name of "freedom" life loses all structure; it is composed of many little pieces, each separate from the other and lacking any sense as a whole. The individual is left alone with these pieces like a child with a puzzle; the difference, however, is that the child knows what a house is and therefore can recognize the parts of the house in the little pieces he is playing with, whereas the adult does not see the meaning of the "whole," the pieces of which come into his hands. He is bewildered and afraid and just goes on gazing at his little meaningless pieces.

What has been said about the lack of "originality" in feeling and thinking holds true also of the act of *willing*. To recognize this is particularly difficult; modern man seems, if anything, to have too many wishes and his only problem seems to be that, although he knows what he wants, he cannot have it. All our energy is spent for the purpose of getting what we want, and most people never question the premise of this activity: that they know their true wants. They do not stop to think whether the aims they are pursuing are something they themselves want. In school they want to have good marks, as adults they want to be more and more successful, to make more money, to have more prestige, to buy a better car, to go places, and so on. Yet when they do stop to think in the midst of all this frantic activity, this question may come to their minds: "If I do get this new job, if I get this better car, if I can take this trip

— what then? What is the use of it all? Is it really I who wants all this? Am I not running after some goal which is supposed to make me happy and which eludes me as soon as I have reached it?" These questions, when they arise, are frightening, for they question the very basis on which man's whole activity is built, his knowledge of what he wants. People tend, therefore, to get rid as soon as possible of these disturbing thoughts. They feel that they have been bothered by these questions because they were tired or depressed — and they go on in the pursuit of the aims which they believe are their own.

Yet all this bespeaks a dim realization of the truth — the truth that modern man lives under the illusion that he knows what he wants, while he actually wants what he is *supposed* to want. In order to accept this it is necessary to realize that to know what one really wants is not comparatively easy, as most people think, but one of the most difficult problems any human being has to solve. It is a task we frantically try to avoid by accepting ready-made goals as though they were our own. Modern man is ready to take great risks when he tries to achieve the aims which are supposed to be "his"; but he is deeply afraid of taking the risk and the responsibility of giving himself his own aims. Intense activity is often mistaken for evidence of self-determined action, although we know that it may well be no more spontaneous than the behavior of an actor or a person hypnotized. When the general plot of the play is handed out, each actor can act vigorously the role he is assigned and even make up his lines and certain details of the action by himself. Yet he is only playing a role that has been handed over to him.

The particular difficulty in recognizing to what extent our wishes — and our thoughts and feelings as well — are not really our own but put into us from the outside, is closely linked up with the problem of authority and freedom. In the course of modern history the authority of the Church has been replaced by that of the

State, that of the State by that of conscience, and in our era, the latter has been
replaced by the anonymous authority of
common sense and public opinion as instruments of conformity. Because we have
freed ourselves of the older overt forms of
authority, we do not see that we have become the prey of a new kind of authority.
We have become automatons who live
under the illusion of being self-willing individuals. This illusion helps the individual
to remain unaware of his insecurity, but
this is all the help such an illusion can
give. Basically the self of the individual is
weakened, so that he feels powerless and
extremely insecure. He lives in a world to
which he has lost genuine relatedness and
in which everybody and everything has become instrumentalized, where he has become a part of the machine that his hands
have built. He thinks, feels, and wills what
he believes he is supposed to think, feel,
and will; in this very process he loses his
self upon which all genuine security of a
free individual must be built.

The loss of the self has increased the
necessity to conform, for it results in a profound doubt of one's own identity. If I am
nothing but what I believe I am supposed
to be — who am "I"? We have seen how
the doubt about one's own self started with
the breakdown of the medieval order in
which the individual had had an unquestionable place in a fixed order. The identity
of the individual has been a major problem
of modern philosophy since Descartes. Today we take for granted that we are we. Yet
the doubt about ourselves still exists, or has
even grown. In his plays Pirandello has
given expression to this feeling of modern
man. He starts with the question: Who am
I? What proof have I for my own identity
other than the continuation of my physical
self? His answer is not like Descartes' —
the affirmation of the individual self — but
its denial: I have no identity, there is no
self excepting the one which is the reflex
of what others expect me to be: I am "as
you desire me."

This loss of identity then makes it still
more imperative to conform; it means that
one can be sure of oneself only if one lives
up to the expectations of others. If we do
not live up to this picture we not only risk
disapproval and increased isolation, but we
risk losing the identity of our personality,
which means jeopardizing sanity.

By conforming with the expectations of
others, by not being different, these doubts
about one's own identity are silenced and
a certain security is gained. However, the
price paid is high. Giving up spontaneity
and individuality results in a thwarting of
life. Psychologically the automaton, while
being alive biologically, is dead emotionally
and mentally. While he goes through the
motions of living, his life runs through his
hands like sand. Behind a front of satisfaction and optimism modern man is deeply
unhappy; as a matter of fact, he is on the
verge of desperation. He desperately clings
to the notion of individuality; he wants to
be "different," and he has no greater recom-
mendation of anything than that "it is different." We are informed of the individual
name of the railroad clerk we buy our
tickets from; handbags, playing cards, and
portable radios are "personalized," by having the initials of the owner put on them.
All this indicates the hunger for "difference" and yet these are almost the last
vestiges of individuality that are left. Modern man is starved for life. But since, being an automaton, he cannot experience
life in the sense of spontaneous activity he
takes as surrogate any kind of excitement
and thrill: the thrill of drinking, of sports,
of vicariously living the excitements of fic-
titious persons on the screen.

What then is the meaning of freedom
for modern man?

He has become free from the external
bonds that would prevent him from doing
and thinking as he sees fit. He would be
free to act according to his own will, if he
knew what he wanted, thought, and felt.
But he does not know. He conforms to
anonymous authorities and adopts a self
which is not his. The more he does this,
the more powerless he feels, the more is

he forced to conform. In spite of a veneer of optimism and initiative, modern man is overcome by a profound feeling of powerlessness which makes him gaze toward approaching catastrophes as though he were paralyzed.

Looked at superficially, people appear to function well enough in economic and social life; yet it would be dangerous to overlook the deep-seated unhappiness behind that comforting veneer. If life loses its meaning because it is not lived, man becomes desperate. People do not die quietly from physical starvation; they do not die quietly from psychic starvation either. If we look only at the economic needs as far as the "normal" person is concerned, if we do not see the unconscious suffering of the average automatized person, then we fail to see the danger that threatens our culture from its human basis: the readiness to accept any ideology and any leader, if only he promises excitement and offers a political structure and symbols which allegedly give meaning and order to an individual's life. The despair of the human automaton is fertile soil for the political purposes of Fascism.

The Rise of the Masses

JOSÉ ORTEGA Y GASSET

Born in 1883, Ortega y Gasset was influential both as a political and literary figure in Spain. In addition to publishing many books, Ortega served as a member of Parliament, held the chair of metaphysics at the University of Madrid, and edited the highly respected Spanish journal, *Revista de Occidente*. Although unquestionably profound, Ortega's writings are frequently paradoxical and witty — traits which have led some critics to condemn him for frivolity. The selection which follows is taken from Ortega's *The Revolt of the Masses* which was first published in 1930. Ortega was one of the first to develop the concept of "mass man" which has significantly influenced the studies of present day historians, political scientists, and sociologists. In examining the author's point of view, however, the reader must inquire whether it has any real connection with totalitarianism, or whether, on the other hand, it amounts to nothing more than a typical "aristocratic" condemnation of the values and behavior of ordinary people.

AGGLOMERATION, fullness, was not frequent before. Why then is it now? The components of the multitudes around us have not sprung from nothing. Approximately the same number of people existed fifteen years ago. Indeed, after the war it might seem natural that their number should be less. Nevertheless, it is here we come up against the first important point.

The individuals who made up these multitudes existed, but not *qua* [strictly as] multitude. Scattered about the world in small groups, or solitary, they lived a life, to all appearances, divergent, dissociate, apart. Each individual or small group occupied a place, its own, in country, village, town, or quarter of the great city. Now, suddenly, they appear as an agglomeration, and looking in any direction our eyes meet with the multitudes. Not only in any direction, but precisely in the best places, the relatively refined creation of human culture, previously reserved to lesser groups, in a word, to minorities. The multitude has suddenly become visible, installing itself in the preferential positions in society. Before, if it existed, it passed unnoticed, occupying the background of the social stage; now it has advanced to the footlights and is the principal character. There are no longer protagonists; there is only the chorus.

The concept of the multitude is quantitative and visual. Without changing its nature, let us translate it into terms of sociology. We then meet with the notion of the "social mass." Society is always a dynamic unity of two component factors: minorities and masses. The minorities are individuals or groups of individuals which are specially qualified. The mass is the assemblage of persons not specially qualified. By masses, then, is not to be understood, solely or mainly, "the working masses." The mass is the average man. In this way what was mere quantity — the multitude — is converted into a qualitative determination: it becomes the common social quality, man as undifferentiated from other men, but as repeating in himself a generic type. What have we gained by this conversion of quantity into quality? Simply this: by means of the latter we understand the genesis of the former. It is evident to the verge of platitude that the normal formation of a multitude implies the coincidence of desires, ideas, ways of life, in the individuals who constitute it. It will be objected that this is just what happens with every social group, however select it may strive to be. This is true; but there is an essential difference. In those groups which are characterised by not being multitude and mass, the effective coincidence of its members is based on some desire, idea, or ideal, which of itself excludes the great number. To form a minority, of whatever kind, it is necessary beforehand that each member separate himself from the multi-

tude for *special,* relatively personal, reasons. Their coincidence with the others who form the minority is, then, secondary, posterior to their having each adopted an attitude of singularity, and is consequently, to a large extent, a coincidence in not coinciding. There are cases in which this singularising character of the group appears in the light of day: those English groups, which style themselves "nonconformists," where we have the grouping together of those who agree only in their disagreement in regard to the limitless multitude. This coming together of the minority precisely in order to separate themselves from the majority is a necessary ingredient in the formation of every minority. Speaking of the limited public which listened to a musician of refinement, Mallarmé wittily says that this public by its presence in small numbers stressed the absence of the multitude.

Strictly speaking, the mass, as a psychological fact, can be defined without waiting for individuals to appear in mass formation. In the presence of one individual we can decide whether he is "mass" or not. The mass is all that which sets no value on itself — good or ill — based on specific grounds, but which feels itself "just like everybody," and nevertheless is not concerned about it; is, in fact, quite happy to feel itself as one with everybody else. Imagine a humble-minded man who, having tried to estimate his own worth on specific grounds — asking himself if he has any talent for this or that, if he excels in any direction — realises that he possesses no quality of excellence. Such a man will feel that he is mediocre and commonplace, ill-gifted, but will not feel himself "mass."

When one speaks of "select minorities" it is usual for the evil-minded to twist the sense of this expression, pretending to be unaware that the select man is not the petulant person who thinks himself superior to the rest, but the man who demands more of himself than the rest, even though he may not fulfil in his person those higher exigencies. For there is no doubt that the most radical division that it is possible to make of humanity is that which splits it into two classes of creatures: those who make great demands on themselves, piling up difficulties and duties; and those who demand nothing special of themselves, but for whom to live is to be every moment what they already are, without imposing on themselves any effort towards perfection; mere buoys that float on the waves. This reminds me that orthodox Buddhism is composed of two distinct religions: one, more rigorous and difficult, the other easier and more trivial: the Mahayana — "great vehicle" or "great path" — and the Hinayana — "lesser vehicle" or "lesser path." The decisive matter is whether we attach our life to one or the other vehicle, to a maximum or a minimum of demands upon ourselves.

The division of society into masses and select minorities is, then, not a division into social classes, but into classes of men, and cannot coincide with the hierarchic separation of "upper" and "lower" classes. It is, of course, plain that in these "upper" classes, when and as long as they really are so, there is much more likelihood of finding men who adopt the "great vehicle," whereas the "lower" classes normally comprise individuals of minus quality. But, strictly speaking, within both these social classes, there are to be found mass and genuine minority. As we shall see, a characteristic of our times is the predominance, even in groups traditionally selective, of the mass and the vulgar. Thus, in the intellectual life, which of its essence requires and presupposes qualification, one can note the progressive triumph of the pseudo-intellectual, unqualified, unqualifiable, and, by their very mental texture, disqualified. Similarly, in the surviving groups of the "nobility," male and female. On the other hand, it is not rare to find to-day amongst working men, who before might be taken as the best example of what we are calling "mass," nobly disciplined minds.

There exist, then, in society, operations, activities, and functions of the most diverse order, which are of their very nature special, and which consequently cannot be properly carried out without special gifts. For example: certain pleasures of an artistic and refined character, or again the functions of government and of political judgment in public affairs. Previously these special activities were exercised by qualified minorities, or at least by those who claimed such qualification. The mass asserted no right to intervene in them; they realised that if they wished to intervene they would necessarily have to acquire those special qualities and cease being mere mass. They recognised their place in a healthy dynamic social system.

If we now revert to the facts indicated at the start, they will appear clearly as the heralds of a changed attitude in the mass. They all indicate that the mass has decided to advance to the foreground of social life, to occupy the places, to use the instruments and to enjoy the pleasures hitherto reserved to the few. It is evident, for example, that the places were never intended for the multitude, for their dimensions are too limited, and the crowd is continuously overflowing; thus manifesting to our eyes and in the clearest manner the new phenomenon: the mass, without ceasing to be mass, is supplanting the minorities.

No one, I believe, will regret that people are to-day enjoying themselves in greater measure and numbers than before, since they have now both the desire and the means of satisfying it. The evil lies in the fact that this decision taken by the masses to assume the activities proper to the minorities is not, and cannot be, manifested solely in the domain of pleasure, but that it is a general feature of our time. Thus — to anticipate what we shall see later — I believe that the political innovations of recent times signify nothing less than the political domination of the masses. The old democracy was tempered by a generous dose of liberalism and of enthusiasm for law. By serving these principles the individual bound himself to maintain a severe discipline over himself. Under the shelter of liberal principles and the rule of law, minorities could live and act. Democracy and law — life in common under the law — were synonymous. To-day we are witnessing the triumphs of a hyperdemocracy in which the mass acts directly, outside the law, imposing its aspirations and its desires by means of material pressure. It is a false interpretation of the new situation to say that the mass has grown tired of politics and handed over the exercise of it to specialised persons. Quite the contrary. That was what happened previously; that was democracy. The mass took it for granted that after all, in spite of their defects and weaknesses, the minorities understood a little more of public problems than it did itself. Now, on the other hand, the mass believes that it has the right to impose and to give force of law to notions born in the café. I doubt whether there have been other periods of history in which the multitude has come to govern more directly than in our own. That is why I speak of hyperdemocracy.

The same thing is happening in other orders, particularly in the intellectual. I may be mistaken, but the present-day writer, when he takes his pen in hand to treat a subject which he has studied deeply, has to bear in mind that the average reader, who has never concerned himself with this subject, if he reads does so with the view, not of learning something from the writer, but rather, of pronouncing judgment on him when he is not in agreement with the commonplaces that the said reader carries in his head. If the individuals who make up the mass believed themselves specially qualified, it would be a case merely of personal error, not a sociological subversion. *The characteristic of the hour is that the commonplace mind, knowing itself to be commonplace, has the assurance to proclaim the rights of the commonplace and to impose them wherever it will.* As they say in the United States: "to be different is to be indecent." The mass crushes beneath it everything that is different, everything that is excellent, individual, qualified and select. Anybody who is not like everybody, who does not think like everybody, runs the risk of being eliminated. And it is clear, of course, that this "everybody" is not "everybody." "Everybody" was normally the complex unity of the mass and the divergent, specialised minorities. Nowadays, "everybody" is the mass alone. Here we have the formidable fact of our times, described without any concealment of the brutality of its features.

V. THE FUTURE OF TOTALITARIANISM

The Coming of Planetary Totalisation

PIERRE TEILHARD DE CHARDIN

Pierre Teilhard de Chardin was surely one of the most interesting and influential thinkers of the twentieth century. Born in France in 1881, he became an ordained priest of the Catholic Church and a member of the Society of Jesus. Teilhard was a natural scientist of immense stature and he made many important contributions to his chosen field of paleontology. Much of Teilhard's thought flowed from a desire to reconcile an evolutionary picture of the world with a highly personal, but nonetheless profound, understanding of Christianity. Although he has been called the "St. Thomas Aquinas" of the twentieth century, his work has been considered questionable by many Catholic authorities, and many of his writings, while circularized among his friends, were not published until after his death. The writings of Teilhard are often difficult to understand, for, like many seminal thinkers, he often found it necessary either to invent new words or to use old ones in a new way in order to express his thought. The following selection is taken from a lecture which Teilhard delivered at the French embassy in Peking in 1945 and which was entitled: "Life and the Planets: What is Happening at This Moment on Earth?"

THIS IDEA of the planetary totalisation of human consciousness (with its unavoidable corollary, that wherever there are life-bearing planets in the Universe, they too will become encompassed, like the Earth, with some form of planetised spirit) may at first sight seem fantastic: but does it not exactly correspond to the facts, and does it not logically extend the cosmic curve of molecularisation? It may seem absurd, but in its very fantasy does it not heighten our vision of Life to the level of other and universally accepted fantasies, those of atomic physics and astronomy? However mad it may seem, the fact remains that great modern biologists, such as Julian Huxley and J. B. S. Haldane, are beginning to talk of Mankind, and to predict its future, as though they were dealing (all things being equal) with a brain of brains.

So why not?

Clearly this is a matter in which I cannot compel your assent. But I can assure you, of my own experience, that the acceptance of this organic and realistic view of the social phenomenon is both eminently satisfying to our reason and fortifying to our will.

Satisfying to the intelligence above all. For if it be true that at this moment Mankind is embarking upon what I have called its "phase of planetisation," then everything is clarified, everything in our field of vision acquires a new sharpness of outline.

The tightening network of economic and psychic bonds in which we live and from which we suffer, the growing compulsion to act, to produce, to think collectively which so disquiets us — what do they become, seen in this way, except the first por-

From Pierre Teilhard de Chardin, *The Future of Man* (New York, 1964), pp. 115–120. Reprinted by permission of Harper & Row, Publishers, and William Collins Sons & Co. Ltd.

tents of the super-organism which, woven of the threads of individual men, is preparing (theory and fact are at one on this point) not to mechanise and submerge us, but to raise us, by way of increasing complexity, to a higher awareness of our own personality?

The increasing degree, intangible, and too little noted, in which present-day thought and activity are influenced by the passion for discovery; the progressive replacement of the workshop by the laboratory, of production by research, of the desire for well-being by the desire for *more-being* — what do these things betoken if not the growth in our souls of a great impulse towards super-evolution?

The profound cleavage in every kind of social group (families, countries, professions, creeds) which during the past century has become manifest in the form of two increasingly distinct and irreconcilable human types, those who believe in progress and those who do not — what does this portend except the separation and birth of a new stratum in the biosphere?

Finally, the present war; a war which for the first time in history is as widespread as the earth itself; a conflict in which human masses as great as continents clash together; a catastrophe in which we seem to be swept off our feet as individuals — what aspect can it wear to our awakened eyes except that of a crisis of birth, almost disproportionately small in relation to the vastness of what it is destined to bring forth?

Enlightenment, therefore, for our intelligence. And, let it be added, *sustenance and necessary reassurance for our power of will*. Through the centuries life has become an increasingly heavy burden for Man the Species, just as it does for Man the Individual as the years pass. The modern world, with its prodigious growth of complexity, weighs incomparably more heavily upon the shoulders of our generation than did the ancient world upon the shoulders of our forebears. Have you never felt that this added load needs to be compensated for by an added passion, a new sense of purpose?

To my mind, this is what is "providentially" arising to sustain our courage — the hope, the belief that some immense fulfilment lies ahead of us.

If Mankind were destined to achieve its apotheosis, if Evolution were to reach its highest point, in our small, separate lives, then indeed the enormous travail of terrestrial organisation into which we are born would be no more than a tragic irrelevance. We should all be dupes. We should do better in that case to stop, to call a halt, destroy the machines, close the laboratories, and seek whatever way of escape we can find in pure pleasure or pure nirvana.

But if on the contrary Man sees a new door opening above him, a new stage for his development; if each of us can believe that he is working so that the Universe may be raised, in him and through him, to a higher level — then a new spring of energy will well forth in the heart of Earth's workers. The whole great human organism, overcoming a momentary hesitation, will draw its breath and press on with strength renewed.

Indeed, the idea, the hope of the planetisation of life is very much more than a mere matter of biological speculation. It is more of a necessity for our age than the discovery, which we so ardently pursue, of new sources of energy. It is this idea which can and must bring us the spiritual fire without which all material fires, so laboriously lighted, will presently die down on the surface of the thinking earth: the fire inspiring us with the joy of action and the love of life.

All this, you may say to me, sounds splendid: but is there not another side to the picture? You tell us that this new phase of human evolution will bring about an extension and deepening of terrestrial consciousness. But do not the facts contradict your argument? What is actually happening in the world today? Can we really detect any heightening of human consciousness even in the most highly collectivised nations? Does it not appear, on the contrary, that social totalisation leads directly to spiritual retrogression and greater materialism?

My answer is that I do not think we are yet in a position to judge recent totalitarian experiments fairly: that is to say, to decide whether, all things considered, they have produced a greater degree of enslavement or a higher level of spiritual energy. It is too early to say. But I believe this can be said, that in so far as these first attempts may seem to be tending dangerously towards the sub-human state of the ant-hill or the termitary, it is not the principle of totalisation that is at fault but the clumsy and incomplete way in which it has been applied.

We have to take into account what is required by the law of complexity if Mankind is to achieve spiritual growth through collectivisation. The first essential is that the human units involved in the process shall draw closer together, not merely under the pressure of *external* forces, or solely by the performance of material acts, but directly, centre to centre, through *internal* attraction. Not through coercion, or enslavement to a common task, but through *unanimity* in a common spirit. The construction of molecules ensues through atomic affinity. Similarly, on a higher level, it is through sympathy, and this alone, that the human elements in a personalised universe may hope to rise to the level of a higher synthesis.

It is a matter of common experience that within restricted groups (the pair, the team) unity, far from diminishing the individual, enhances, enriches and liberates him in terms of himself. True union, the union of heart and spirit, does not enslave, nor does it neutralise the individuals which it brings together. It *super-personalises* them. Let us try to picture the phenomenon on a terrestrial scale. Imagine men awakening at last, under the influence of the ever-tightening planetary embrace, to a sense of universal solidarity based on their profound community, evolutionary in its nature and purpose. The nightmares of brutalisation and mechanisation which are conjured up to terrify us and prevent our advance are at once dispelled. It is not harshness or hatred but a new kind of love, not yet experienced by man, which we must learn to look for as it is borne to us on the rising tide of planetisation.

Reflecting, even briefly, on the state of affairs which might evoke this universal love in the human heart, a love so often vainly dreamed of, but which now leaves the fields of Utopia to reveal itself as both possible and necessary, we are brought to the following conclusion: that for men upon earth, all the earth, to learn to love one another, it is not enough that they should know themselves to be members of one and the same *thing*; in "planetising" themselves they must acquire the consciousness, without losing themselves, of becoming one and the same *person*. For (and this is writ large in the Gospel) there is no total love that does not proceed from, and exist within, that which is personal.

And what does this mean except, finally, that the planetisation of Mankind, if it is to come properly into effect, presupposes, in addition to the enclosing Earth, and to the organisation and condensation of human thought, yet another factor? I mean the rise on our inward horizon of a cosmic spiritual centre, a supreme pole of consciousness, upon which all the separate consciousnesses of the world may converge and within which they may love one another: the *rise of a God*.

It is here that reason may discern, conforming to and in harmony with the law of complexity, an acceptable way of envisaging "the end of the world."

The End of Ideology?

RAYMOND ARON

During a long and successful career, Raymond Aron has served as a professor at both German and French universities and has written widely in the fields of philosophy, history, and sociology. He has been, in addition, an unusually successful journalist whose columns and articles are widely syndicated in Europe. Such distinguished accomplishments are responsible for Aron's membership in the Legion of Honor. The thesis which he puts forward in the selection which follows — that ideology no longer serves as a strong motivation for political behavior — has been argued recently by numerous sociologists on both sides of the Atlantic.

IT MAY SEEM rather paradoxical to envisage the end of the ideological age at a time when Senator McCarthy continues to play a leading role on the Washington stage, when *Les Mandarins* [a novel by the French intellectual, Simone de Beauvoir] has just won the Prix Goncourt and the flesh-and-blood "mandarins" are making the pilgrimage to Moscow and Peking. One is not, of course, so naïve as to expect peace to blossom forth in the immediate future: the idealists disillusioned or liquidated, the bureaucrats continue to reign.

The Westerners themselves may dream of political tolerance just as, three centuries ago, they tired of futile slaughter in the name of the same God for the choice of the true religion. But they have communicated to the rest of the world their faith in a radiant future. Nowhere, in Asia or in Africa, has the Welfare State spread enough benefits to stifle the impulse towards irrational and foolish hope. The nations of Europe preceded the others on the road to industrial civilisation. Now, perhaps, moved by the first glimmerings of scepticism, they are beginning to foreshadow, however prematurely, a new shape of things to come.

*   *   *

Let us look back and survey the centuries which have elapsed since the dawn of the philosophy of immanence and of modern science. Every one of the ideologies which, for a few years or for a few decades, has seized the imagination of the crowd or of thinking men, reveals, retrospectively, a simple structure with one or two guiding ideas.

The optimism of the Left was created and maintained by a strong feeling: admiration for the power of reason, certainty that the application of science to industry would revolutionise the order of human society and the condition of its individual members. The ancestral aspiration towards human brotherhood was united with faith in practical science in order to inspire either nationalism or socialism or both.

Freedom of enquiry asserted against Church orthodoxy, and the equality of fighting men established on the field of battle by the introduction of firearms, undermined the edifice of traditional hierarchies. The future would belong to free and equal citizens. After the storm which precipitated the collapse of the most grandiose edifice of aristocratic Europe, after the fall of the French monarchy, the revolutionary fervour, encouraged by flamboyant suc-

From *The Opium of the Intellectuals* by Raymond Aron, pp. 305–307, 309–312, 314, 319–324. Copyright 1957 by Raymond Aron. Reprinted by permission of Doubleday & Company, Inc., and Martin Secker & Warburg Ltd.

cesses as well as bloody defeats, split into two separate channels, nationalist and socialist.

Called upon to defend the Fatherland at the risk of their lives, the servants of the throne felt entitled to demand a State which they could call their own and rulers whose language they could understand. Historians, philosophers and novelists, stressing the individuality of ethnic or cultural groups or the right of self-determination, sensitive to the unconscious workings of the centuries or to the coherence of the cities of antiquity, elaborated the various theories of the nation. Perhaps, in justifying national passions, they merely succeeded in exacerbating them, sometimes on the level of primitive tribalism, sometimes ennobled by the dream of liberty. At all events, the sort of reasonable administration accepted by several nationalities because foreign to each of them was in the long run rendered anachronistic by the speed of primary education and conscription. . . .

National feeling remains and must remain the cement of human collectivities, but the nationalist ideology is none-the-less condemned in Western Europe. An ideology presupposes an apparently systematic formalisation of facts, interpretations, desires and predictions. The intellectual who wants to be *essentially* nationalist must interpret history as the permanent struggle of jungle states or prophesy peace between independent nations on a basis of mutual respect. The combination of revolutionary nationalism and Machiavellian diplomacy advocated by Charles Maurras could not survive the weakening of the European states.

By all means let the rulers defend tooth and nail the interests and rights of their country against the encroachments of strong and tactless allies. But how can one get excited about the temporal grandeur of a collectivity which is incapable of manufacturing its own arms? The American defence budget represents three-quarters of the total military expenditure of the Atlantic alliance. Isolation, neutrality, and the playing off of one bloc against the other, are sometimes possible and always legitimate, but they do not contribute towards an ideological transfiguration. In our century, a second-class nation-state is not an adequate framework for full human expression. . . .

Liberalism and socialism continue to inspire convictions and to provoke controversies, but it is becoming more and more difficult reasonably to transform such preferences into doctrines. Western "capitalist" society today comprises a multitude of socialist institutions. One can no longer count on collective ownership or planning to bring about a dramatic improvement in man's lot.

Technological progress lived up to men's expectations and has gone on increasing by leaps and bounds. Perhaps, some years or some decades hence, it will have overcome the limitations of material resources. But its price and its limits are now generally realised. Mechanised societies are not pacific; they deliver man from the servitudes of poverty and weakness, but they subject millions of workers to the logic of mass production, and they risk turning human beings into machines.

Neither the optimist who conjures up a vision of fraternity thanks to material plenty, nor the pessimist who visualises a consummate tyranny extended over human minds with the help of the new instruments of mass communication and torture, is quite refuted by the experience of the twentieth century. The dialogue between them, begun at the time of the first factories, is still being pursued. But it does not take the form of an ideological debate, since the opposing themes are no longer connected with a particular class or party.

The last great ideology was born of the combination of three elements: the vision of a future consistent with human aspirations, the link between this future and a particular social class, and trust in human values above and beyond the victory of the working class, thanks to planning and collective ownership. Confidence in the virtues of a socio-economic technique has begun to wane and one looks in vain for this class which is supposed to bring about the radical renewal of institutions and ideas.

The theory of the class struggle, which is still current today, is falsified by a spurious analogy: the rivalry between bourgeoisie and proletariat differs in essence from the rivalry between aristocracy and bourgeoisie. . . .

The ideologists of the proletariat are bourgeois intellectuals. The bourgeoisie, whether it derived its ideas from Montesquieu, Voltaire or Jean-Jacques Rousseau, set up its own conception of human existence and the political order in opposition to the *Ancien Régime* and the Catholic vision of the world. *The proletariat has never had a conception of the world opposed to that of the bourgeoisie; there has been an ideology of what the proletariat should be or should do, an ideology whose historical ascendancy was most powerful when the number of industrial workers was smallest.* The so-called proletarian party, in the countries where it has seized power, has had peasants rather than factory workers as its troops, and intellectuals, exasperated by the traditional hierarchy or by national humiliation, as its leaders.

The values to which the working class spontaneously subscribes differ from those of the bourgeoisie. It is not impermissible to construct antitheses between the two: the sense of solidarity against the desire for possessions, participation in the community against individualism or egoism, the generosity of the penniless against the avarice of the rich, etc. In any case there is no denying the obvious fact that the system and style of living in working-class districts are very different from those of the wealthy middle classes. So-called proletarian régimes, that is régimes governed by Communist parties, owe practically nothing to authentic working-class culture, to the parties or unions whose leaders themselves belong to the working class. . . .

It was in the hope of accomplishing fully the ambitions of the bourgeoisie — the conquest of Nature, social equality or equality of opportunity — that the ideologists handed on the torch to the proletariat. The contrast between technological progress and the misery of the workers was a crying scandal. How could one help but impute to private ownership and the anarchy of the market the survival of ancestral poverty which was in fact due to the exigencies of accumulation (capitalist or socialist), insufficient productivity and increases in population. Soft-hearted intellectuals, revolted by injustice, seized on the idea that capitalism, being in itself evil, would be destroyed by its contradictions and that its victims would eventually overthrow the privileged. Marx achieved an improbable synthesis between the Hegelian metaphysic of history, the Jacobin interpretation of the Revolution, and the pessimistic theory of the market economy developed by British authors. To maintain the continuity between the French Revolution and the Russian Revolution, it was only necessary to call Marxist ideology proletarian. But one has merely to open one's eyes to be rid of the illusion.

The market economy and total planning are rival models — which no existing economy actually reproduces — not successive stages in evolution. There is no necessary link between the phases of industrial development and the predominance of one model or the other. Backward economies approximate more to the model of the planners than do advanced economies. Mixed systems are not monsters incapable of surviving, or transitional forms on the way to the pure type; they are the normal thing. In a planned system one will find most of the categories of the market economy, more or less modified. As the standard of living rises and the Soviet consumer has more freedom of choice, the benefits and the problems of Western prosperity will appear on the other side of the Iron Curtain.

The revolutions of the twentieth century have not been proletarian revolutions; they have been thought up and carried out by intellectuals. They have overthrown the traditional power, ill-adapted to the exigencies of the technological age. The prophets imagined that capitalism would precipitate a revolution comparable to the one which convulsed France at the end of the eighteenth century. Nothing of the sort happened. On the contrary, wherever the ruling classes have been unable or unwilling to reform themselves quickly enough, the dissatisfaction of the bourgeoisie, the impatience of the intellectuals and the immemorial aspirations of the peasants have provoked an explosion. . . .

By a conspicuous paradox, the diffusion of the same technological civilisation throughout the globe gives a special character to the problems which confront each separate nation today. The political consciousness of our time is falsified by the failure to acknowledge these distinctions.

Whether liberal, socialist, conservative or Marxist, our ideologies are the legacy of a century in which Europe was aware of the plurality of civilisations but did not doubt the universality of its message. Today, factories, parliaments and schools are springing up in every latitude, the masses are in ferment, the intellectuals are taking over power. Europe, which has finished conquering and is already succumbing to its victory and the revolt of its slaves, hesitates to admit that its ideas have conquered the universe but have not kept the form they used to have in our own debates and controversies. . . .

Communism, it is said, is the first essentially European belief to have succeeded in converting millions of Asians. The first of the new catechumens were intellectuals. They had not been converted by Christianity, which ran counter to the traditional system of values and customs, whose teachings were belied by the behaviour of the invaders, and which did not accord with scientific thought, the essence of the military superiority of the imperialists. Communism attracts not because it is a Christian heresy but because it seems to be the extreme form, the definitive interpretation,

of the rationalist and optimist philosophy. It gives a coherent expression to the political hopes of the West.

Simple people are susceptible to these hopes, but indifferent to the interpretative scholasticism. In allowing themselves to be mobilised by the Party they do not become true believers in the Church. The peasants do not aspire to collective ownership but to individual ownership. The workers do not visualise in advance the building up of socialism by the *Gleichschaltung* [forced co-ordination] of the trade unions. It is the prophetism which confers on Communism a sort of spiritual substance.

What remains of this when the conquerors of the future have become the planners of the economy? "The deified militarist has been a flagrant scandal. Alexander, as the Tyrrhenian pirate told him to his face in the story as we have it from St. Augustine, would have been called not a god but a gangster if he had done what he did with a couple of accomplices instead of doing it with a whole army. And what about the deified policeman? Augustus, now, has made himself into a policeman by liquidating his fellow-gangsters, and we are grateful to him for that; but, when we are required to register our gratitude by worshipping this reformed gangster as a god, we cannot comply with much conviction or enthusiasm." What could possibly be our feeling towards Stalin when he liquidates Zinoviev and Bukharin, or towards Malenkov when he liquidates Beria? Does Communism, when it is installed in power, still contain a spiritual substance?

How long will the exaltation of the builders continue to sustain the militants? How long will national grandeur continue to testify to the mandate of the historical powers-that-be? Perhaps China will find in this mandarins' religion a durable peace. Christian Europe will not. The official orthodoxy will decline into a ritual language, or else the only authentic faith, that which no temporal good can satisfy, will revolt against the secular clericalism. Perhaps men can live without adoring a

God in spirit and in truth. They will not live long, after the "proletarian" victory, in the expectation of a paradise on this earth.

Is there, then, no alternative to faith in the proletariat but faith in Christ? Can the West offer a spiritual truth in opposition to Soviet materialism? We must be careful not to compromise religion in the struggles of temporal powers, to attribute to the system we defend virtues which it does not possess.

The liberal democracies do not represent a "Christian" civilisation. They have developed in societies whose religion was Christian, and they have been inspired to a certain extent by the absolute value which Christianity gives to the individual soul. Neither electoral and parliamentary practices nor the mechanism of the market, as such, are either Christian or contrary to the Christian spirit. Doubtless the free play of initiative, competition between buyers and sellers, would be unthinkable if human nature had not been sullied by the Fall. The individual would give of his best in the interests of others without hope of recompense, without concern for his own interests. Man being what he is, the Church, which cannot approve unbridled competition or the unlimited desire for wealth, is not obliged to condemn the economic institutions which are characteristic of industrial civilisation. The planners, too, are compelled to appeal to the appetite for money or personal glory. No régime can afford to ignore human egotism.

Communism comes into conflict with Christianity because it is atheist and totalitarian, not because it controls the economy. It arrogates to itself the sole right to educate the young. The Communist State allows religious rites to be celebrated and the sacraments to be administered; but it does not consider itself neutral, it calls religious beliefs superstitions, doomed to disappear with the progress of socialist construction. It enrols the hierarchy in political crusades; "popes," priests, bishops and Metropolitans are invited to lead the campaign in favour of peace, to denounce the conspiracies of the Vatican.

It is not for those of us who belong to no Church to recommend a choice to the believers, but it behoves us all, incorrigible liberals who tomorrow would return again to the struggle against clericalism, to fight today against this totalitarianism from which professing Christians happen to suffer as much as free-thinking scientists and artists. The tyranny we denounce is not solely directed against a faith we do not share; it is one which affects us all. The State which imposes an orthodox interpretation of day-to-day events also imposes on us an interpretation of global development and ultimately of the meaning of human existence. It seeks to subordinate all the achievements of the mind, all the activities of autonomous individuals and groups, to its pseudo-truth. In defending the freedom of religious teaching, the unbeliever defends his own freedom. . . .

The Westerners, especially the intellectuals, suffer from the fragmentation of their universe. Diffusion and obscurity in poetry, and abstraction in painting, isolate poets and artists from the big public which they affect to despise but which, in their heart of hearts, they long to serve. Physicists or mathematicians can extract energy from the atom but cannot extract freedom of movement, opinion and friendship from suspicious politicans, from a sensation-hungry Press, from anti-intellectualist demagogues or the secret police. Masters of nuclear fission but slaves of "security," the scientists, enclosed in their narrow community, feel that they lose all control over their discoveries as soon as they transmit their secrets to the generals and the politicians. The specialist has control over but a limited field of knowledge; present-day science seems to leave him as ignorant of the answers to the ultimate questions as a child awakening to consciousness. The astronomer can foretell an eclipse of the sun with faultless precision; neither the economist nor the sociologist knows whether humanity is progressing towards an atomic holocaust or Utopian peace.

That is where ideology comes in — the longing for a purpose, for communion with the people, for something controlled by an idea and a will. The feeling of belonging to the elect, the security provided by a closed system in which the whole of history as well as one's own person find their place and their meaning, the pride in joining the past to the future in present action — all this inspires and sustains the true believer, the man who is not repelled by the scholasticism, who is not disillusioned by the twists in the party line, the man who lives entirely for the cause and no longer recognises the humanity of his fellow-creatures outside the party.

Such fanaticism is not for us. We can admire the sombre grandeur of these armies of believers. We can admire their devotion, their discipline and self-sacrifice: such warrior virtues are of the kind that lead to victory. But what will remain tomorrow of the motives that led them to fight? Without a scintilla of doubt or guilt or regret, we can leave the fanatics their inevitable superiority.

* * *

Does the rejection of fanaticism encourage a reasonable faith, or merely scepticism?

One does not cease to love God when one gives up converting the pagans or the Jews and no longer reiterates: "No salvation outside the Church." Will one cease to desire a less unjust society and a less cruel lot for humanity as a whole if one refuses to subscribe to a single class, a single technique of action and a single ideological system?

True, the comparison is not unreservedly valid. Religious experience gains in authenticity as one comes to distinguish better between moral virtue and obedience to the Church. The secular religions dissolve into politico-economic opinions as soon as one abandons the dogma. Yet the man who no longer expects miraculous changes either from a revolution or an economic plan is not obliged to resign himself to the unjustifiable. It is because he likes individual human beings, participates in living communities, and respects the truth, that he refuses to surrender his soul to an abstract ideal of humanity, a tyrannical party, and an absurd scholasticism.

Perhaps it will be otherwise. Perhaps the intellectual will lose interest in politics as soon as he discovers its limitations. Let us accept joyfully this uncertain promise. Indifference will not harm us. Men, unfortunately, have not yet reached the point where they have no further occasion or motive for killing one another. If tolerance is born of doubt, let us teach everyone to doubt all the models and utopias, to challenge all the prophets of redemption and the heralds of catastrophe.

If they alone can abolish fanaticism, let us pray for the advent of the sceptics.

A Rationalist Totalitarianism?

ZBIGNIEW BRZEZINSKI

The selection which follows is taken from an article by Professor Brzezinski entitled "Totalitarianism and Rationality." The article first appeared in 1956 shortly before Soviet intervention in Hungary gave the world convincing proof that Russian Communism had not yet significantly mellowed. Professor Brzezinski's article remains one of the most coherent presentations of the view that totalitarian regimes can maintain themselves in power indefinitely although, at the same time, they may become somewhat more rational in their manipulation of power.

IT COULD BE ARGUED, and some have, that Soviet totalitarianism, the most advanced totalitarian society of our age, is now entering upon a new stage of development, the character of which will be determined by the industrialized nature of the Soviet economy. This analysis, partaking somewhat of a material determinism, stresses the incompatibilities between totalitarianism and the requirements of a modern, industrial and hence also bureaucratic order. Noting that totalitarianism in the past has seemed largely irrational, it argues that the rationalistic routines of the indispensable managers of the industrial society will necessarily transmit themselves to the totalitarian leadership and gradually effect a fundamental transformation of the system itself. This transmission will be aided by the fact that the totalitarian movement has become highly bureaucratized and therefore shares in many of the operational patterns associated with running the industrial machine. Furthermore, it is argued, the totalitarian movement itself has become increasingly staffed by the managerial-bureaucratic elements to whom party membership means no more than an important club association necessary to satisfy career ambitions. The revolutionary torch and the unending quest are accordingly displaced by the swivel chair and the punch-clock.

Totalitarianism, in the extreme form of this argument, is thus to disappear imperceptibly and unintentionally. As stability, predictability and overall rationality set in, fear, terror, and arbitrariness will fade. Mass enthusiasm and passionate unanimity will give way to disagreements on matters of expertise, and hence also on policy. Policy discussion will then become genuine arguments on alternate courses of action; selection will be made on the basis of rational (technical, objective assessments of the implications of perceived reality) considerations without violent (hence arbitrary and fear-inspiring) consequences for those whose arguments did not prevail. This, together with the growing stability of various privilege groups, will in turn lead to a form of pluralism, suggestive of the existing democratic systems. Democracy, even though likely a curtailed one, will enter by the back door.

One example of this type of reasoning is the argument advanced by I. Deutscher in his *Russia: What Next?* Deutscher stresses the point that: "the economic progress made during the Stalin era has at last brought within the reach of the people a measure of well-being which should make

From Zbigniew Brzezinski, "Totalitarianism and Rationality," The *American Political Science Review,* vol. L, no. 3 (September, 1956) pp. 751–763. Reprinted by permission of the author and The American Political Science Association.

possible an orderly winding up of Stalinism and a gradual democratic evolution." This argument leaves considerable room for dissent. Democracy involves more than what Deutscher suggests. It requires, in the view of some, a certain philosophical tradition, a basic recognition of some sort of higher law, a fundamental attitude of toleration, an absence of doctrinal fanaticism — all of which are, at most, only indirectly linked to a state of "well-being" and none of which seem to be even remotely present in the existing Soviet scene. One may also wonder what is actually meant by "a measure of well-being," especially since wants are relative. Furthermore there is little of substance in what is known today of totalitarian institutions to indicate the likelihood of such a democratic development. It is difficult to assume that the party, having such a vested interest, will be willing to resign its absolute control of the instruments of power. The argument also assumes a short-range quality to the goals of the party, and it ignores the impact of international developments on domestic policies.

Deutscher's analysis thus falls down on two counts: its highly monistic interpretation of democracy fails to see democratic development in its complex and pluralistic perspective, the economic aspects of which are merely one component part of a diversified whole; and its interpretation of Soviet totalitarianism fails to perceive the self-generating power of the system of controls and the resulting vested interests in the maintenance of these controls. Fainsod, in concluding his examination of the Soviet regime, makes this statement:

As long as the Kremlin leaders continue to see their future in terms of industrial and military might, they will probably persist in relying on totalitarian instruments to force the pace of industrialization. Those who possess absolute power do not part with it willingly. The governing formula of Soviet totalitarianism rests on a moving equilibrium of alternating phases of repression and relaxation, but its essential contours remain unchanged. The totalitarian regime does not shed its police-state characteristics; it dies when power is wrenched from its hands.

The question remains, however, whether in the long run totalitarianism is compatible with a rationalistic orientation prevailing in its extensive bureaucracy and in the managerial classes of its industrial order. To some extent, this issue, like the one discussed above, is made more complex by the general problem of the range of predictability in political science. It is doubtful that any "scientific" prediction can be made in matters not clearly connected with institutional, legal, stable processes; such as, for instance, one that presidential elections will occur in the United States in 1956 and 1960, and that, barring some drastic denouement, the contenders will be the Democratic and Republican parties. Predictability becomes more difficult, and its range much shorter, in matters involving general problems of political-social development in a system where little is known of the processes of decision-making at the top, of the motivations and considerations involved, of the nature of the various power alignments, and last, but not least, of the morale of the leaders. There are also few biographical data, beyond the barest essentials, about most of the leaders. In such cases, one must rely to a considerable degree on the projection of past experience, and estimate the future implications of current commitments of the system.

The experience of Germany with Nazi totalitarianism, albeit brief, may therefore not be irrelevant. The Nazi system was imposed with all the earmarks of revolutionary totalitarianism on a society with a highly developed industrial order, with an established and conservative managerial class, with the most efficient and routinized bureaucracy in all Europe. Yet there is no indication in all the available evidence that the fanatical, often irrational and usually brutal, Nazi leadership was in any way deterred from its purposes by the influence or orientations of the German technocrats or bureaucrats. With few exceptions, the German bureaucrats and technocrats adjusted meekly to the requirements of the totalitarian movement and were happy to reap any material benefits that Nazi successes produced. It was not until the Nazi regime began to crumble that the bureaucratic and technocratic elements, e.g., Speer, showed any initiative or purposeful action of their own. Until then, it was more a matter of the bureaucrats absorbing Nazi values, e.g., in the treatment of slave laborers, than of the Nazis absorbing a bureaucratic orientation. It seems, therefore, that a violent, arbitrary totalitarianism can, at least, arise and maintain itself in an industrially advanced area without loss of its revolutionary zeal and fanatic brutality. It did so in Germany and Italy and Czechoslovakia. The crucial factor throughout was the presence of a movement with a revolutionary morale able to wield effectively the instruments of power.

A rebuttal, however, might point to the fact that both the German and Italian systems were of brief duration, and the experience of Czechoslovakia is too recent for confident evaluation. Furthermore, the emergence of a new and imposing industrial and bureaucratic order under the totalitarian regime itself in the USSR is obviously of the greatest importance for the domestic political development of the Soviet society. It is a development not paralleled in any of the other countries mentioned, where the totalitarian movements were superimposed on already existing industrial systems.

One must acknowledge, therefore, that conceivably totalitarianism may become, because of the factors suggested and in spite of the Nazi experience, rationalistic and hence less unpredictable, arbitrary and openly terroristic. But there is no evidence to suggest that this in itself is incompatible with totalitarianism, which need not be interpreted, as H. Arendt seems inclined to do, in terms of irrational terror almost for the sake of terror. Such a rationalist system, arising in the context of one-party

domination (not to mention international pressures), could be nothing less than a rationalist dictatorship, just as total in control as its less predictable and more violent antecedent of the thirties. The institutionalized revolution which still characterizes the existing totalitarianisms will inevitably slow down in the future, but by then it will be involved in an economic commitment which also has its own political logic. The totalitarian economy, as many have observed, has been developed in the USSR over the last thirty years in keeping with plans oriented to a final (if not yet precisely defined) goal. It is thus a goal-oriented economy, the goal being communism. That this goal needs more definite formulation is, for our purposes, irrelevant. The important thing is that those in charge of the Soviet society have assumed that economic and social development in all its aspects can be purposefully steered by man in the direction of an ideal solution. This produces consequences not only economic but also political, quite different from those induced by other equally technologically advanced economic systems where, to a large extent, economic life is self-directive and ultimate goals, such as plenty and progress, are purposely vague. These goals have less bearing on current decisions than such factors as past experience, demand, prices, competition, and opportunity. In the latter case, a measure of freedom of interplay is inherent. In the former, all decisions and plans are made, or are rationalized, in terms of the ultimate goal.

Consequently it makes little *political* difference whether the range of man's alternatives is limited by uneducated revolutionaries or by scientific Ph.D.'s, once the entire economy is subjected to a process of human engineering oriented on a goal which cannot be questioned. Admittedly, operations conducted by trained bureaucrats and technocrats may be more "rational" and less directly oppressive (in so far as extreme oppression may be uneconomical, which is not entirely certain). But to be less totalitarian such operations would have to involve some degree of withdrawal on the part of those in charge from their commitment to total social and economic engineering, thus granting to those living under the system the opportunity to make important choices *not* in keeping with the goal. But such a politically meaningful development would in turn involve a further condition, which at the present appears highly unlikely, namely the decline of ideology and a basic reconsideration of the firmly instituted schemes of economic development. Barring that, the totalitarian economic system would continue to exert pressures for the maintenance of a dictatorship capable of enforcing the kind of discipline that such total plans demand. It is doubtful that as long as the party remains in power the tendency of the regime to stress unattainable goals will vanish. Indeed, it is these goals, inherent in the current ideology, which justify to the population the sacrifices which the party's domination involves. Thus, as long as the party continues to hold its successful grip on the instruments of power, we can expect it to continue stressing first the long-range goals of an ultimate utopia, and then the consequent sacrifices to achieve them, even though possibly at a diminishing rate of effort.

The rationalist tomorrow, if it ever comes, will therefore not be an introduction to a democratic form of government, but rather a stage in further totalitarian evolution, accentuating rationalist features present from the start and minimizing some of the irrational outbursts already noted. The prototypes of such a rationalist totalitarianism need not be sought only in Orwell's *1984*. They exist, in an embryonic stage, in our own industrial organizations and bureaucracies. If one could imagine the entire United States run like some executive department, with its myriad of minute, and often incomprehensible, regulations, routinized procedures, even sometimes arbitrariness of officials, one would be all the more inclined to be thankful that the rule

of law (rooted in a traditional regard for the individual) and legislative fears of administrative expansion (a democratic "irrationalist" feature) act as a check.

Totalitarianism and rationality, therefore, when viewed in a developmental perspective and not merely from a standpoint of a static definition pinpointing certain characteristics of a given epoch, are not necessarily incompatible. Rationality alone is hardly a sufficient condition for the inevitable growth of a democratic order. At different stages, totalitarianism can be characterized by a minimization of rationalist considerations (as in the thirties in the USSR), or by an increased emphasis on them. But it is as unlikely that totalitarianism can become fully rational as it is incorrect to claim that it has been essentially irrational in the past. Today, for instance, in the USSR the totalitarian system is operating in an environment where the need (as seen by the leadership) for unbridled violence, terror in its most open form, and unpredictability based on dictatorial whims seems no longer to be present or desirable. The population appears to be relatively pliant, the younger generation has absorbed a great deal of the indoctrination, resistance of an active kind is almost entirely absent. The domination of the party in the country, and of the leadership in the party, appears to be firmly established. If only the party could be satisfied with the status quo, a rationalist totalitarianism could possibly become reality.

But even then the problem of power would not disappear. Governmental rationality cannot go far beyond the realm of function and account for all human action. Basic drives for power are not likely to wane. And given the nature of the system, even if the party declines and is supplanted ultimately by the bureaucracy (or merges with it), the total control of the system over those under it will not disappear even though its exercise will become more functionally rational. In such a system it is likely that the institutional controls will be utilized to maintain the existing interests of the ruling class, and social stratification will become even more marked as position, education, and even wealth become inheritable. The abyss between those wielding power and the masses will create a real ruling caste, which itself will be highly stratified in terms of the proximity of its members to the center of power. It will create too an entire non-political stratum of those who will be given a vested interest in the *status quo* by virtue of their utility to the system, such as the specialists, artists, military scientists, etc. In many respects such a system will more nearly resemble the Nazi-Fascist dictatorship than the earlier Stalinist model. This curiously dialectical consequence might deprive Soviet totalitarianism of its revolutionary essence while maintaining its institutional forms. The lesson of history is, however, that this does not necessarily spell the end of the system.

That appears to be, however, at best only a distant prospect. The tasks that face the totalitarians today in the captive nations in Europe, among the long dormant masses of China, in the rice paddies of northern Vietnam, or in the Malayan jungles, not to speak of the virgin lands, overgrown urban centers and ever-struggling collective farms in the USSR, are very difficult and likely to command all their energies for many years to come. Indeed, the commitments currently made by the present Soviet leaders indicate that the party is not satisfied with the *status quo;* hence the abandonment of large-scale drives, which involve in turn the maintenance of discipline, does not seem imminent even in the USSR, the most developed totalitarian system. These commitments are both domestic and international. Domestically, they suggest a three-pronged attack on the following goals: an increased emphasis on party zeal, especially in terms of a reassertion of "Leninism" as defined by the present leadership; continued expansion of heavy industry with major goals set for 1960; further drives in the agricultural sector, including both reclamation projects and the diminution of private plots. On the international plane, briefly, the commitments made to China and the satellites, coupled to those now being made to the underdeveloped countries, will continue to be felt on the domestic scene through scarcities and insistence on maximum effort. At the same time, with Stalin dead and Stalinism impracticable without him, the new leadership is searching for a new basis for power both in the realm of ideological justification and practical measures. This already has meant the rejection of some of the vicious attributes of Stalinism as well as an attack on Stalin himself. This may involve in turn some unsettling consequences, as an accepted frame of reference is destroyed and old slogans and operational procedures fall by the wayside. Finally, the problem of succession, given the age bracket of the present leaders, cannot be dismissed as having been resolved entirely. From all of this, it might appear therefore that both internally and externally the likelihood of a *status quo* situation in the foreseeable future is doubtful. If so, the era of revolutionary totalitarianism may not yet be over.

Cracks in the Monolith

KARL W. DEUTSCH

Born in Prague, Karl Deutsch has taught political science at both the Massachusetts Institute of Technology and at Yale University. He has also lectured at various other universities, both in America and abroad, in the capacity of a visiting professor. The approach taken in the following selection owes a heavy debt to the development of the science of Cybernetics which, in recent years, various scholars have attempted to apply to political analysis. Essentially, Cybernetics is the science of communication and control. The most simple implication which it has for politics is that any system or regime which cannot or will not communicate — which implies that it will take seriously the views of the populace — cannot long hope to control those subject to it. More recently, Professor Deutsch has published *The Nerves of Government* in which he assesses the usefulness of such approaches as Cybernetics and Games Theory as a way of dealing with political and diplomatic problems.

Is THERE a pathology peculiar to totalitarian systems? Are there, that is to say, specific ways in which established totalitarian governments or cultures tend to be destroyed, divided, or otherwise basically changed by their own inner development?

Are there, in particular, any recurrent tendencies to stagnation or division, to schisms, heresies, or secessions — social, regional, or ideological — *which can be traced to the fundamental structure of totalitarian government,* and which could be tested, at least in principle, against available data from concrete cases? If so, what inferences for policy expectations and research programs in the free countries could be derived from them? . . .

SOME CHARACTERISTICS OF TOTALITARIANISM

Before we even approach the questions we just asked, we must first pause briefly to deal with a preliminary one. Is there a "totalitarianism" in the abstract, or as an ideal type, somewhat in Max Weber's sense, or are there only particular totalitarian systems? In this paper it will be answered tentatively that there are particular totalitarian systems which are comparable among each other to the extent to which they have certain limited performance characteristics in common.

The three most important of these characteristics are perhaps extreme *mobilization of effort, unity of command,* and effective *power of enforcement.* These three characteristics, perhaps more than any others, make totalitarian systems perform differently from other systems of social and political decision-making. Their loss is conspicuous whenever totalitarian governments succumb to stagnation or disintegration.

THE EMBARRASSMENT OF PREVIOUS COMMITMENTS

Thus the mobilization of resources required by totalitarianism presupposes that these resources have already been freed from previous commitments, both from commitments of custom and from commitments imposed by previous political systems or even by earlier stages or policies of the totalitarian regime itself. Totalitarianism thus must destroy previous custom, even

Reprinted by permission of the publishers from Carl J. Friedrich (ed.), *Totalitarianism,* Cambridge, Mass.: Harvard University Press, pp. 308–332, Copyright, 1954, by the President and Fellows of Harvard College.

where its spokesmen may profess to defend it. Its leaders must divert resources, manpower, and attention from past institutions, even where these institutions are supposed to be preserved. Finally, totalitarianism must take away resources and attention from its own past policies and past demands of consistency wherever these past policies or past commitments threaten to cut down the range of resources available to it presently for recommitment.

Changes in the previous political line, or in the old guard of decision-making personnel, are therefore not peripheral or accidental in totalitarian regimes, but seem likely to recur. As soon as the new commitments of resources mobilized by totalitarianism tend to become permanent, these resources are no longer completely available to the totalitarian regime. The more permanent and irrevocable the commitment of its resources, the less totalitarian in the long run must a regime become. Either, that is to say, its resources become frozen in commitments to an unusual strategy for an improbable goal — in which case the regime loses much of its capacity to maneuver and to learn, and thus to preserve itself, and risks stagnation or destruction — or else its resources become ever more firmly committed to patterns of activity which are quite capable of being carried on repetitively and within the limits of a self-preserving and self-maintaining society. In this event, the totalitarian regime begins to erode into an increasingly traditional society. In either case a totalitarian regime is to some extent threatened by the permanence of its own memories and of its own traditions. Either these traditions force it to persist in some ever more unrewarding strategy or pattern of behavior, or else they turn into a new network of customs and established expectations which increasingly limit the range of decisions still open to the totalitarian command.

In order to maintain the mobilization of its resources, a totalitarian regime needs therefore some machinery, formal or informal, to counteract the hardening of its own abstract traditions or professed ideologies, such as creeds, dogmas, philosophies, political doctrines, and the like, and it needs similar machinery to counteract the hardening of its own past preferences for particular geographical centers or particular groups of personnel. Traditions of doctrine, as well as preferences for geographical centers or for sociological groups of personnel, can easily become matters of heresy in totalitarian systems; but it is one of the paradoxes of totalitarianism that excessive orthodoxy in one of these three matters may have anti-totalitarian consequences and expose the die-hard orthodox partisan of the regime to some of the same penalties which threaten the heretic.

THE PROBLEM OF CONSISTENCY OF COMMANDS

The second function, unity of command and of intelligence, requires some machinery either to insure a single source of decision, or a set of arrangements or devices to insure consistency of decisions among several sources. A single source of decisions is in effect an arrangement by which all important incoming information available to the system is channeled to a point where it can be confronted with data recalled from a single integrated memory pool. The outcome of the interaction of these collected data from the outside world and the data recalled from an integrated set of memory facilities are then the current decisions of the system.

In its extreme or "ideal type" form, a totalitarian decision system would need to have five properties: (1) *transitivity*, that is, the property that each decision was either clearly superior or clearly subordinate to some other decision, and that no sequence of such hierarchically ordered decisions could be circular; (2) *rigor*, that is, uniqueness of outcome of each step at all the relevant stages of decision-making below the top; (3) *awareness of intake* and facilities for its simultaneous inspection, that is, arrangements to make sure that all important items of incoming information are confronted with each other and with data recalled from the memory facilities of the system; this involves the labeling of important items of incoming information by means of secondary symbols attached to them, and it involves the bringing together of these items for simultaneous inspection; (4) *self-awareness,* or the internal intelligence function, that is, arrangements to make sure that information about internal changes within the system itself are brought to bear on the system's current decisions; there must be symbols for the constituent sub-assemblies, organizations, resources, or personnel of the system itself, which are processed and brought to the memory facilities of the system in such a manner that the system "knows" what is going on within its own organization, and is capable of acting on this information; (5) *learning capacity,* that is, the ability to recombine items of incoming information with items recalled from memory in new patterns, so as to produce new combinations of symbols sufficient to survey, test, or devise new strategies of behavior, as well as the ability to produce new combinations of actual physical resources and manpower in such a way that the new strategies can actually be put into action; systems with this capacity will have the power to initiate new courses of behavior.

Actually existing totalitarian systems of government may well be deficient in any or all of these respects. Yet to the extent that they are so deficient, they will be less effective as totalitarian systems, and their chances for survival or expansion may be correspondingly lessened. . . .

THE LIMITED CAPACITY OE CENTRALIZED DECISION-MAKING

. . . All centralized facilities for decision-making, however, committees as well as individuals, can only give attention to a very limited number of items for decisions at the same time, and can therefore be very easily overloaded. The distributive attention of individuals is notoriously limited,

and so is the amount of business any committee can transact within a given time. Julius Caesar has been renowned for his legendary exploit of dictating seven letters at one and the same time; and chess masters who can play forty games simultaneously are objects of admiration. Major military decision systems or political decision systems, on the contrary, may easily require decisions of many hundreds of problems in substantially the same interval of time.

A simple example of the difficulties involved can be found in the problem of the plotting room of an anti-aircraft defense center in a city under air attack; by means of a number of ingenious arrangements, it may be possible there to represent at one and the same time the attack of several hundred enemy aircraft and to make decisions about how to oppose most effectively every one of them. Nevertheless, the decision-making capacity of even a very good anti-aircraft plotting center is quantitatively limited. These quantitative limitations become particularly sharp and painful when the question arises of how to defend a warship against aerial attack. Here the attacking enemy aircraft can be represented on radar screens but the number of tracks symbolizing attacking aircraft may very soon become too large for the decision-making capacity of any single individual; it is possible from this point of view to saturate not merely the physical, but rather the intellectual or cognitive defenses of the ship. Just as a massed attack of aircraft coming simultaneously from many different directions may overload the capacities of a directing center for anti-aircraft defense, so the amount of problems requiring urgent decision may overload the decision-making capacities of a government.

Moreover, the more absolute, dictatorial, or totalitarian such a government is, the more likely it is to politicize, that is, to make subject to decisions, an ever larger sphere of life, and therefore the more likely it is to be thus overloaded with decisions with which it can no longer cope, except at the price of either intolerable delays or an increasing probability of potentially critical mistakes.

The answer to this problem of the overloading of centralized decision-making facilities has been, of course, decentralization. Classes of decisions have been delegated to sub-assemblies of the system, where they are made in terms of separate pools of memories. These subordinate decision centers with their subordinate facilities for the storing of data may in turn be controlled more or less closely from some common decision-making center. Such control, however, is apt to be incomplete. Once the subordinate centers have been delegated some authority, and once they have been given their own facilities for storing memories, these subordinate centers and memory pools will in the future receive only part of their imput from the supreme government. A significant part of their future experience will be local, in terms of their own peculiar local, regional, or functional situations, or in terms of their own probabilities of internal recombinations, their own ideas, preferences, customs, or habits of behavior, as they may evolve from the internal workings of their own smaller system. The more imperfect the facilities for the pooling of experience among all the subordinate centers — and all pooling of such experience is necessarily imperfect to some extent — the faster will be this increase of the share of diversified memories and diversified experiences in each subordinate organization.

The result will be a steady drift to a peripheralization and pluralization of the centers of decision. In the long run there is thus perhaps inherent in every totalitarian system of government a tendency either toward overloading of its central facilities for the making of decisions, or toward an automatic corrosion of its original centralized structure and its disintegration into increasingly separate parts. . . .

TOTALITARIANISM AND SOME
LIMITATIONS OF TECHNOLOGY

Thus far we have listed a number of weaknesses and conflicts inherent in the working of totalitarian systems and making for their eventual stagnation, disintegration, or corrosion. But have all these tendencies not been overbalanced by the impact of new technological developments which might increase the power of dictatorial governments far beyond all precedent and all previous political and social limits?

Will not the future development of microphones and television cameras supply every totalitarian regime with cheap and ever-present spies, just as the development of tanks and airplanes has supplied them with weapons which can be concentrated in the hands of a few, and as barbed wire has supplied them with facilities for inexpensive concentration camps?

Several reasons seem to suggest that no presently indicated development of technology is likely to increase significantly the stability or cohesion of totalitarian regimes. In a world of rival powers, the concentration of effective weapons in the hands of a trusted few men is a luxury no great power can afford. Throughout all advances in military technology, governments have become more dependent, not less, on the support of millions of their citizens. Armies, navies, air forces, tank corps, civil defense and production organizations all require hundreds of thousands or millions of persons in their ranks, and the day of the quasi-aristocratic war, carried on by small groups of highly skilled professionals, seems even farther away than at the time of its early prophets in the 1920's.

To the extent, on the other hand, that decisive instruments of military power should become concentrated in the hands of a few specialists, some additional positions would be created for the power struggle within the totalitarian regime. None of the potential rivalries between the political leadership, the propagandists, the administrators, the army, the police, and any other major power group — rivalries of the kind instanced by the executions of Soviet Marshal Tukhachevsky and Soviet Police Chief Yagoda in the 1930's at the behest of the Politburo — could be wholly abolished by any technological development. The problems of mobilizing mass support for national military strength, and of insuring unity of command and cohesion among the different parts of the regime, are all essentially political in nature. They are fraught with the hopes and fears, the expectations and motives of individuals. They involve, therefore, all the difficulties of totalitarian regimes which were discussed earlier; and no increase in the gadgetry of violence will solve them.

If totalitarianism can expect no decisive aid from the technology of violence, neither can it expect such aid from any improvements in the gadgetry of supervision or persuasion. Electronic devices can be used to improve the reception and transmission of information in these processes, but they can do little or nothing to facilitate its use and thus its ultimate effectiveness. Even if supervisory television devices and microphones were to be installed in the home of every citizen, the totalitarian state would still have to find the huge numbers of officials necessary to look at and listen to the vast amounts of information thus obtained — a difficulty from which the dictatorial government in George Orwell's nightmare world of 1984 seems to have been conveniently free. Anyone who has tried to wade through several hundred pages of the transcript of a tape recording of a conference will have at least an inkling of the quantitative problem involved. Human greed cannot be listened to with understanding at very much higher speed than it can be spoken, and the talk and gossip of even one person's lifetime may well require something resembling half a lifetime's listening on the part of some luckless policeman.

The introduction of universal electronic supervision, even were it technologically feasible, would drown the totalitarian regime in an ocean of trivialities, and the addition of automatic transcription devices would merely convert their output of trivial noise into a flood of paper. Political supervision is a feedback process in which incoming information must be responded to in terms of behavior that reaches back to the citizen or subject. It thus consists in its essence in the paying of attention and the exercise of judgment and neither of these functions can be mechanized with any equipment likely to exist for the rest of this century or longer. . . .

SOME TENTATIVE PROSPECTS

. . . At this stage, any inference from our survey of the patterns of disintegration of totalitarian systems must be tentative and provisional. Thus qualified, they will be indicated here, at the risk that readers will call obvious those findings which fit in with their views, while calling unsound those which do not. Both strictures may turn out to be correct; yet perhaps it may be hoped that they will be imposed only after some careful testing. If treated thus as inferences to be tested, rather than as conclusions to be believed, the following suggestions may yet fulfill some useful function.

1. Totalitarianism is by no means immune from processes of disintegration; on the contrary, many of the dictatorial techniques which are intended to combat schism or disintegration may in fact tend to accelerate and intensify these very processes.

2. The basic processes of political integration and disintegration occur on a more fundamental level than that of mere political, military, or police techniques, or of government-run propaganda. This is even more true in the occurrence of schisms and secessions of supra-national philosophies or ideologies. Research on the probability of a future split — for instance, between the Communist regimes of Russia and China — might most profitably be aimed at these more fundamental levels.

3. Although there are significant analogies in the behavior of different totalitarian systems, the aims of particular totalitarian regimes may make a considerable difference to their ability to maintain cohesion for a longer period of time. The same seems true of the nature of the underlying social changes in the course of which a totalitarian regime may become established; and further considerable differences may be due

to the specific practices and institutions by which particular totalitarian regimes may attempt to combat their own automatic drift toward pluralization and disintegration.

4. For all these reasons, no schematic predictions can be made concerning a general probability of all totalitarian regimes to split up or disintegrate within a short period of time. In particular, a number of important performance characteristics of Russian Soviet totalitarianism, on the one hand, and of German Nazi totalitarianism on the other, differ radically from each other. What imperfect data we have surveyed seem to suggest that the Soviet dictatorship in Russia still disposes of substantial resources to stave off its own disintegration or pluralization for a considerable time.

5. These considerations apply, however, only to time scales of about twenty to fifty years. Most of the major economic and social changes in history which were violent enough to give rise to regimes with some totalitarian features were substantially completed within a period of the order of fifty years, and with the slowing down of the rate of major changes there has usually followed a period of pluralization and a dwindling of totalitarian expansiveness. If similar considerations should apply to the totalitarian regimes of Russia and China, which established themselves in consequence of revolutions which disrupted the *status quo* in these countries as early as 1911 and 1917, respectively, then we might well expect the 1970's or 1980's to bring a slowing of the expansive pressure from these two regimes, or a growing divergence of policies between them, or among some of their constituent regions, or some combination of all these changes, leading in either case to a diminution in "classic" patterns of totalitarian behavior.

SUGGESTIONS FOR ADDITIONAL READING

The task of compiling a bibliography on the subject of totalitarianism is a difficult one, and limitations of space conspire to make it even more difficult. The difficulty springs from the fact that the concept of totalitarianism is so embracing that it includes almost every question and issue of significance for the modern world. The result of this is that the citations which follow can scarcely pretend to do more than to indicate some of the major aspects of the study of totalitarianism and to note some of the more important examinations of those aspects. The books which appear in these pages form, then, only a very select list. Titles which do appear are present either because they are of fundamental importance, or because they are the most recent studies and are therefore unlikely to appear in older bibliographies.

The reader should begin by consulting some of the standard works on totalitarianism from which selections have been taken for this volume: Friedrich and Brzezinski, Arendt, Barbu, etc. The volume edited by Carl Friedrich under the title *Totalitarianism: Proceedings of a Conference Held at the American Academy of Arts and Sciences, March 1953* (Cambridge, Mass., 1954) is especially useful since it contains a large number of scholarly papers on all aspects of the subject.

The most recent study of totalitarianism is that of Barrington Moore, Jr., *Social Origins of Dictatorship and Democracy* (Boston, 1966), a work which has been highly acclaimed. It is interesting, however, to examine some of the earliest works which attempted to relate developments in Nazi Germany and Soviet Russia or to point to distinctive characteristics of a totalitarian system. In this category Ernest Frankel's *The Dual State — A Contribution to the Theory of Dictatorship* (N.Y., 1941) and Sigmund Neumann's *Permanent Revolution* (N.Y., 1942) are especially recommended. Also of note here is

the "Symposium on the Totalitarian State" contained in Vol. 82, no. 1 of the *Proceedings of the American Philosophical Society*. In addition, there are works which, while they do not embody a completely modern interpretation of totalitarianism, nonetheless deal with material which is similar in scope: as, for example, Ernst Cassirer's *The Myth of the State* (New Haven, 1946) and Bertrand de Jouvenel's *On Power* (N.Y., 1947).

It is both interesting and highly informative to approach the study of totalitarianism through works of fiction which serve to give one a "feeling" of what totalitarianism is like, even if such accounts are possibly unduly fanciful. Among the better of these works is the play *Caligula* (N.Y., 1958) by Albert Camus, in which the totalitarian is pictured as a man in search of absolute consistency. The most classic example of this literature, however, is still George Orwell's *1984* (N.Y., 1949), although his portrayal of the totalitarian society should be compared to Aldous Huxley's *Brave New World* (N.Y., 1932). Franz Kafka's *The Trial* (rev. ed., 1957) is probably the best source from which to gain an understanding of what it is like to be the subject of a totalitarian regime.

The study of totalitarianism can also be approached through studies of individual totalitarian regimes. On Russia, consult such books as the following: Merle Fainsod, *How Russia Is Ruled* (Cambridge, Mass., 1953); Wladyslaw Kulski, *The Soviet Regime* (Syracuse, 1954); and Walt Whitman Rostow, *The Dynamics of Soviet Society* (N.Y., 1954). The best of all the histories of Soviet Russia is doubtless Edward Hallett Carr's multivolumed *A History of Soviet Russia* (London, 1950–), although unfortunately the work has not proceeded far enough to be of any use for the 1930s. Donald Treadgold's *Twentieth Century Russia* (Chicago, 1954) provides an excellent and incisive summary. A recent work, Francis B. Randall's *Stalin's Russia: An Historical Reconsideration* (Glencoe, Ill., 1965), stresses the role of ideology. Abraham Brumberg (ed.), *Russia Under Khrushchev* (N.Y., 1962) contains articles on most aspects of Russian society in the period after the death of Stalin. Those anxious to come even closer to the present may consult Robert Conquest, *Russia After Khrushchev* (N.Y., 1965).

The Russian satellite system in Eastern Europe may be studied in R. Medalie, "The Stages of Totalitarian Development in Eastern Europe," *Public Policy* (Vol. VII). Standard books on the subject include Hugh Seton-Watson, *The East European Revolution* (2nd ed., N.Y., 1952) and Herbert Ripka, *Eastern Europe in the Post-War World* (N.Y., 1961). The most outstanding work on the subject is still that of Zbigniew Brzezinski, *The Soviet Bloc* (Cambridge, Mass., 1960). Roger Pethybridge, *The Development of the Communist Bloc* (Boston, 1965) contains both readings on the subject and selections from original documents. Lack of space forbids the mentioning of a large number of books devoted to individual East European regimes, but those interested in more recent developments should consult Stephen Fischer-Galati (ed.), *Eastern Europe in the Sixties* (N.Y., 1963).

With respect to Nazi Germany the reader might begin with a companion volume in the Problems in European Civilization Series entitled *The Nazi Revolution* (Boston, 1959) and edited by John Snell. Hannah Vogt's *The Burden of Guilt* (N.Y., 1964) is an excellent summary of German history in the twentieth century. It should also be noted that the eminent historian of Germany, Hajo Holborn, is currently in the process of completing a three volume study of the history of modern Germany and that Volume III, when it appears, will doubtless be a valuable contribution to the literature on the Nazi period. Maurice Baumont, *et al.*, *The Third Reich* (N.Y., 1955) contains several

articles, all written by highly qualified scholars, on various aspects of the Nazi regime. An earlier account, and still a classic despite its Marxist bias, is that of Franz Neumann, *Behemoth* (N.Y., 1942). A still earlier study by Hermann Rauschning, *The Revolution of Nihilism* (N.Y., 1939), was written on the basis of personal interviews with Hitler. Despite its shortcomings, which are especially evident when the author attempts to account for the origins of Nazism, William Shirer's *Rise and Fall of the Third Reich* (N.Y., 1960) is an interesting and informative narrative. A more microscopic study of the Nazi phenomenon is contained in William S. Allen, *The Nazi Seizure of Power: The Experience of a Single German Town, 1930–1935* (Chicago, 1965). George Mosse, currently one of the most outstanding of the students of National Socialism, has recently published a book of selected documents highly illustrative of the Nazi "style" under the title *Nazi Culture: Intellectual, Cultural and Social Life in the Third Reich* (N.Y., 1966).

The place of Fascist Italy within the ranks of totalitarian systems is, of course, highly disputable, but the reader may wish to consult one of the following works: Herman Finer, *Mussolini's Italy* (N.Y., 1935); Gaetano Salvemini, *Under the Axe of Fascism* (N.Y., 1936); Giuseppe A. Borgese, *Goliath — The March of Fascism* (N.Y., 1937); and Denis Mack Smith, *Italy, A Modern History* (Ann Arbor, 1959).

Of late, great attention has been devoted to the study of Fascism as a European phenomenon. In this category, at least three works should be mentioned. Ernst Nolte's *Three Faces of Fascism* (N.Y., 1966) has been widely acclaimed as a brilliant analysis which no scholar interested in the subject would dare to ignore. The reader should also consult Hans Rogger and Eugen Weber (eds.), *The European Right* (Berkeley, 1966), and Vol. I, no. 1 of the *Journal of Contemporary History* which is devoted to an examination of "International Fascism (1920–1945)." It should be pointed out that among scholars currently involved in the study of Fascism there is sometimes an implicit, and occasionally an explicit, belief that too much attention has been paid to the debate over totalitarianism and to the attempt to subsume Fascist and Communist regimes under a common concept. (Interestingly, Nolte, who expresses grave reservations about the concept of totalitarianism, is willing to entertain the possibility that Russia passed through a Fascist stage under Stalin.) The issue here, however, is not purely semantic for it is possible to point to some regimes or movements which were clearly Fascist, but not totalitarian if one accepts the more recent formulations of that term. Moreover, it is probably true that the widespread study of totalitarianism played a part in holding back a needed investigation of Fascism. At this juncture it would be difficult to say whether recent studies of Fascism will lead to a decline in the use of the term "totalitarian" or whether they will merely enrich the understanding of the term.

Lack of space prevents any attempt to list works dealing with Communist China except to mention the quite recent study of Franz Schurmann, *Ideology and Organization in Communist China* (Berkeley, 1966).

The student of totalitarianism may also continue his investigation of the subject by more thoroughly examining various aspects of the general concept. Among studies of the leadership and the elite of totalitarian movements several works should be mentioned. Isaac Deutscher's *Stalin: A Political Biography* (N.Y., 1949) is still the standard work on the subject, but the shorter portrait in George Kennan's *Russia and the West under Lenin and Stalin* (N.Y., 1960) is highly interesting. Leonard Schapiro, *The Communist Party of the Soviet Union* (N.Y., 1959) is excellent history. Also consult John A. Armstrong, *The Soviet Bureaucratic Elite* (N.Y., 1959), and the very recent study of Abdurakhman Avtorkhanov, *The Communist Party Apparatus*

(Chicago, 1966). On the Nazi aspect of this question, the literature is far more extensive and few Nazis of importance have escaped the grasp of biographers. Alan Bullock's *Hitler: A Study in Tyranny* (London, 1953) is still the most satisfying and complete account of the German dictator. But the portraits drawn by Konrad Heiden and Ernst Nolte, in works already mentioned in this volume, are also of great value. Daniel Lerner's *The Nazi Elite* (Stanford, 1957) approaches the subject from a sociological point of view and G. M. Gilbert's *Psychology of Dictatorship* (Washington, D.C., 1955) contains observations drawn from the study of Nazi leaders held prisoner at Nuremberg. A highly acclaimed study of the Nazi leadership, which stresses the role of alienation — Joachim C. Fest, *Das Geschichte des Dritten Reiches: Profile einer Totalitarian Herrschaft* (Munich, 1963) — has unfortunately not yet been translated into English. For a highly interesting account of the relationship between two modern dictators see Frederick Deakin, *The Brutal Friendship: Mussolini, Hitler and the Fall of Italian Fascism* (N.Y., 1962).

It is necessary to distinguish several different questions involved in the examination of totalitarian ideologies. With respect to the basic tenets of such ideologies, the selections contained in *Communism, Fascism and Democracy* (N.Y., 1961), edited by Carl Cohen, are most helpful. For an understanding of the fundamental ideas of Nazism it is essential to read Hitler's *Mein Kampf* (numerous editions) although it is, for the most part, a trite and dull book. The reader will also find much helpful information on this matter in the abovementioned works by Mosse and Nolte. On Russian communism one should consult Nathan Leites, *A Study of Bolshevism* (Glencoe, Ill., 1953). The best account of all aspects of Soviet thought is still to be found in Gustav Wetter's *Dialectical Materialism* (N.Y., 1958). One should also consult Bertram Wolfe's recent study, *Marxism: One Hundred Years in the Life of a Doctrine* (N.Y., 1965). There are numerous accounts which trace the intellectual backgrounds of these ideologies. For Russia see, among many works in the field, Avrahm Yarmolinsky's *Road to Revolution: A Century of Russian Radicalism* (N.Y., 1962). For the German side of the question two works are especially important: *The Politics of Cultural Despair* (Berkeley, 1961), by Fritz Stern, and George Mosse's even more recent account, *The Crisis of German Ideology: Intellectual Origins of the Third Reich* (N.Y., 1964). For a discussion of the nature and consequences of ideological commitment Albert Camus' *The Rebel* (N.Y., 1956) is unsurpassed, although Eric Hoffer's *The True Believer* (N.Y., 1951) is highly interesting. The reader would also be well advised to acquaint himself with the different ways in which the term "ideology" has been used. Here, he might most profitably consult the appropriate article in *A Dictionary of the Social Sciences* (Glencoe, Ill., 1965). On the more recent arguments concerning the decline of ideology see, aside from Aron, the following: Edward Shils, "The End of Ideology?" in the November, 1955 issue of *Encounter,* and Daniel Bell's *The End of Ideology* (Glencoe, Ill., 1960), which also contains a criticism of the concept of mass society.

If the concept of ideology is a many-sided one, the situation with respect to the twin concepts of mass society and alienation is equally difficult. Here, too, the proper articles in the above-mentioned *Dictionary of the Social Sciences* are most useful. On mass society, see especially William Kornhauser, *The Politics of Mass Society* (Glencoe, Ill., 1959) which distinguishes between "aristocratic" and "democratic" uses of the term. For typical statements on the state of modern man see *Man in the Modern Age* (Garden City, N.Y., 1957) by the eminent German philosopher, Karl Jaspers, and the more recent work of Hannah Arendt, *The Human Condition* (Chicago, 1958). David Riesman's classic study, *The Lonely Crowd* (New Haven,

1950), is essential reading. For particular, but nonetheless crucial, aspects of mass society consult Eric Larrabee and Rolf Meyersohn, *Mass Leisure* (Glencoe, Ill., 1958); Bernard Rosenberg and David White, *Mass Culture* (Glencoe, Ill., 1957); and the Spring, 1960 issue of *Daedalus* devoted to "Mass Culture and Mass Media."

With respect to alienation, a much-needed clarification of the various meanings of the term can be found in Harold Rosenberg's review of the Sykes Collection of Essays on Alienation which appeared in the Book Review Section of the *New York Times* of December 20, 1964. Also consult Fritz Pappenheim, *The Alienation of Modern Man* (N.Y., 1959) and Eric and Mary Josephson (eds.), *Man Alone: Alienation in Modern Society* (N.Y., 1962).

It would also be well to examine various aspects of the nature of totalitarian propaganda. In this regard the study by Alex Inkeles, *Public Opinion in Soviet Russia* (Cambridge, Mass., 1950) is the best in the field. With respect to Nazi propaganda two recent works may be mentioned, although there are numerous older studies: Z. A. B. Zeman, *Nazi Propaganda* (N.Y., 1964) and Ernest Bramsted, *Goebbels and National Socialist Propaganda, 1925–1945* (Lansing, Mich., 1965).

Several books, from which selections in this volume have been taken, are essential reading on the subject of totalitarian terror. The views of Hannah Arendt and several of the articles in the work edited by Carl Friedrich are especially important. On the Russian purges, as an example of such terror, the two best works are Nathan Leites and Elas Bernaud, *The Ritual of Liquidation* (Glencoe, Ill., 1954) and Zbigniew Brzezinski's *Permanent Purge — Politics in Soviet Totalitarianism* (Cambridge, Mass., 1955). For purposes of comparison, however, Henry Kamen's article on "The Spanish Inquisition," which appeared in the Autumn, 1965 issue of *Horizon,* is worth reading. There is, of course, an extensive literature on the concentration camps, both Russian and German. For the former see David Dallin and Boris Nikolaevsky, *Forced Labor in Soviet Russia* (New Haven, 1947) and the more recent study by Roger Baldwin (ed.), *A New Slavery — Forced Labor: The Communist Betrayal of Human Rights* (N.Y., 1953). On the German camps, aside from the account of Kogon, the reader should see David Rousset, *The Other Kingdom* (N.Y., 1947). In this connection, two recent books on Eichmann are also of great value: Hannah Arendt, *Eichmann in Jerusalem: A Report on the Banality of Evil* (N.Y., 1963) and the book by Eichmann's chief Israeli prosecutor, Gideon Hausner, *Justice in Jerusalem* (N.Y., 1966). With respect to the much disputed point of the effects of the concentration camps on human personality, the reader should consult Elie Aron Cohen's *Human Behavior in the Concentration Camp* (N.Y., 1953).

A final point of great importance for those who argue the distinction between modern totalitarianism and traditional dictatorships has to do with the relation between the regime and subsidiary organizations within the state. Here, various questions should be studied such as the position of the churches, on which there is an abundant literature. The question may more easily be examined, however, by consulting two books on the position of the armed forces under totalitarian regimes: Zbigniew Brzezinski (ed.), *Political Controls in the Soviet Army* (N.Y., 1954) and John Wheeler-Bennett, *The Nemesis of Power: The German Army in Politics, 1918–1945* (London, 1953).